m·

Popular Politics,
Riot and Labour

LIVERPOOL HISTORICAL STUDIES
published for the
Department of History, University of Liverpool

JOHN BELCHEM (ed.)

Popular Politics, Riot and Labour

ESSAYS IN
LIVERPOOL HISTORY 1790–1940

Published for the
Department of History
University of Liverpool

LIVERPOOL UNIVERSITY PRESS

1992

Front cover illustration: An arrest during the Liverpool riot of 1911 (Carbonora Collection)

Liverpool Historical Studies, no. 8
General Editors: C. H. Clough and P. E. H. Hair

First published 1992
by the Liverpool University Press
Senate House, PO Box 147, Liverpool, L69 3BX

British Library Cataloguing in Publication Data
A British Library CIP record is available
ISBN 0 85323 427 2

Printed and bound in the European Community by
Redwood Press Limited, Melksham, England

Preface

This project has grown considerably in scope since it was first discussed by a small group of researchers - Anne Bryson, Kevin Moore and myself - working on Liverpool in the first half of the nineteenth century. The chronology has been extended to enable a broader understanding of popular politics, riot and labour. Suggestions for further reading can be found in the footnotes accompanying each contribution: in these references, London is the place of publication unless otherwise stated.

In editing this collection, I have incurred many debts, none greater than that I owe to Anne Bryson. Without her remarkable technical and word-processing skills, it would not have been possible to produce this book with such speed and proficiency - and in such good humour. In undertaking her arduous task, Anne was helped by the facilities and advice generously made available by Lawrie Schonfelder, Director of the Computer Laboratory at the University of Liverpool. I would also like to thank the general editors of the Liverpool Historical Studies series, together with Robin Bloxsidge of Liverpool University Press, for encouragement and assistance throughout the preparation of this volume. Mary Belchem provided help, inspiration and sustenance.

John Belchem
Liverpool, December 1991

Contents

Figures

Tables

Maps

The Contributors

John Belchem is Senior Lecturer in History and Director of Combined Honours in Arts at the University of Liverpool. His main publications include *'Orator' Hunt: Henry Hunt and English Working-Class Radicalism*; *Industrialization and the Working Class: The English Experience 1750-1900*; and *Class, Party and the Political System in Britain 1867-1914*.

John Bohstedt teaches British history at the University of Tennessee, Knoxville. He is author of *Riot and Community Politics in England and Wales, 1790-1910,* and articles on women in riots.

Anne Bryson has recently been awarded an M.Phil by the Open University for her thesis on 'Riot and its Control in Liverpool, 1815-1860'. For a 'day-job', she works as a clerical officer in the Computer Laboratory, University of Liverpool.

Sam Davies is Senior Lecturer in History in the School of Social Science, Liverpool Polytechnic. He is a co-author of *Genuinely Seeking Work: Mass Unemployment on Merseyside in the 1930s*, which will be published in early 1992.

Alan Little has just completed a doctoral thesis at Manchester University on the demise and aftermath of Chartism in Leicestershire. Appropriately for somebody interested in ex-Chartists, he now works for an insurance company, as a computing Project Leader.

Kevin Moore is Museum Officer, St Helens Museum. He has published widely both in museum studies, a subject he embraced after completing his thesis on popular politics in early nineteenth century Liverpool, and on Merseyside history, through his involvement in the Docklands History Project.

Norman H. Murdoch has been a member of the History Department at the University of Cincinnati since 1968. He has published a number of articles and books, most of which reflect his interest in Salvation Army history.

Michael Power is in the Department of Economic and Social History at the University of Liverpool. He has published work on seventeeth-century London, and is a past editor of the *Transactions of the Historic Society of Lancashire and Cheshire.*

Eric Taplin was Head of the Department of Social Studies at Liverpool Polytechnic from 1974 to 1984. He is now a Fellow of the University of Liverpool in the Department of Economic and Social History. A specialist in British labour history, he is particularly interested in industrial relations in nineteenth-century Liverpool. He was a founder member of the North West Labour History Group and is its chairperson.

1: Introduction: The Peculiarities of Liverpool

John Belchem

The 'shock city' of post-industrial Britain, Liverpool is now identified by a self-defeating image, condemned to failure by a micro-culture of truculent defiance, collective solidarity and fatalist humour. At odds with the dominant enterprise culture, these anachronistic 'scouse' characteristics prohibit successful regeneration in 'opportunity Britain'. Much of the image, however, is media myth, lacking in historical resonance beyond the city's recent economic decline. In contrast to its current projection, Liverpool's past is not well-known. Failing to conform to the main narratives of modern British history, the city has attracted little attention other than as the exception which proved the rule.[1] In exploring the contrast between contemporary image and historical experience, the following essays seek to reconstruct a distinctive identity in a manner which belies media distortion or historiographical condescension. Covering a variety of topics concerned with popular collective and associational behaviour, they critically address the 'peculiarities' of Liverpool, the traditional distinctive features of its labour history. By offering a positive reassessment of such factors as casualism and the absence of large scale manufacturing, sectarianism and ethnicity, and the continuing propensity to riot, the essays illuminate the complex social history of Liverpool popular politics.

In its economic structure, in the absence of mills, factories and 'machinofacture', Liverpool was by no means exceptional. Viewed through the revisionist perspective of the 'myth' of the industrial revolution, it is not Liverpool, but its industrial hinterland - the cotton factory district - which appears atypical.[2] Economic growth in the first industrial nation was

---

[1] 'Liverpool says much that is unrepeatable ... (it) stands as warning to anyone wishing to paint a national picture by enlarging local tints', Michael Bentley, *The Climax of Liberal Politics* (1987), 30.

[2] M.Fores, 'The myth of a British industrial revolution', *History*, lxvi (1981), 181-98. See also J.B. Sharpless, 'The economic structure of port cities in the mid-nineteenth century: Boston and Liverpool, 1840-1860', *Journal of Historical Geography*, 2 (1976), 131-43.

1

sustained by a complex process of 'combined and uneven development' in which over 75 per cent of manufacturing remained in unmodernized industries in the 1840s, small in scale, little affected by the use of steam power and characterized neither by high productivity nor comparative advantage.[3] Liverpool epitomized the process. The dock system was vast, modern and complex, a triumph of civic enterprise and civil engineering: 'in magnitude, cost and durability, the docks of Liverpool', Herman Melville recorded, 'surpass all others in the world'.[4] Dock development squeezed out the old waterfront craft industries, an early instance of de-industrialization, but throughout the town work continued in the small-scale unmechanized units of the 'age of manufactures'. Liverpool, as Kevin Moore's occupational analysis of the 1841 census suggests, was in several respects a typical manufacturing town with a significant artisan sector and new port-based processing and refining plants.[5] In projecting an identity, however, Liverpool chose to disregard such manufacturing and industrial activity.

From the construction of its innovatory wet-docks system in the early eighteenth century, Liverpool identified its prosperity with commerce, not with manufacture. In the process, as Michael Power shows, Liverpool was to become the great seaport and second city of industrial Britain.[6] Having overhauled Bristol, nineteenth-century Liverpool sought to rival London in its commercial infrastructure, to establish itself as a 'self-dependent financial centre'.[7] Guidebooks welcomed the absence of industry, noting with relief that the curse of the factory system stopped short of Liverpool and its independent workers.[8] The 'great emporium of British commerce', Liverpool took exaggerated pride in its commercial image, aspiring to the status of 'the modern Tyre'.[9] Picton's civic improvement proposals encouraged its citizens to 'render the external appearance of their town worthy the exalted rank she

---

[3]R. Samuel, 'The workshop of the world: steam power and hand technology in mid-Victorian Britain', *History Workshop Journal*, 3 (1977), 6 - 72. N. Crafts, *British Economic Growth during the Industrial Revolution* (Oxford, 1985), 68-9 and *passim*.

[4]Herman Melville, *Redburn* (1849: Penguin edn, 1987), 230.

[5]See below ch 3.

[6]See below ch 2.

[7]*Chamber of Commerce. Report of the Special Committee appointed to consider what steps can be taken for the purpose of constituting Liverpool a self-dependent financial centre* (Liverpool, 1863).

[8]*The Stranger in Liverpool; or, An historical and descriptive view of the town of Liverpool and its environs* (Liverpool, 1846), 108-9.

[9]*Morning Chronicle*, 20 May 1850, 'Labour and the Poor: Liverpool', the first of 20 weekly letters. *Nation*, 24 Sept 1872, reprinted in H. Heinrick, *A Survey of the Irish in England (1872)*, Alan O'Day (ed.) (1990), 87.

seems destined to fill in the commerce of the world'.[10] Subscription societies attended to the promotion of literature and the arts, supplemented by a number of voluntary associations specifically geared to the education and recreation of young clerks, 'Liverpool gentlemen' - not 'Manchester men' - in the making.[11] Through the hasty invention of tradition, Liverpool acquired a number of 'old families' to attest to the nobility of commerce.[12] The ethos was to endure, preventing a wider (and much-needed) industrial diversification. Eschewing the 'second industrial revolution', Liverpool entered the twentieth century with a distinct (and distorted) economic structure. In the 1920s, when only 37 per cent of Liverpool workers were engaged in production compared with the national average of 67 per cent, the Corporation still expressed satisfaction in the absence of manufacturing and industrial blight.[13]

In its early industrial history, Liverpool seems to have conformed to the national norm. Modest economic growth was achieved through the intensification of labour and its greater exploitation. Although engaged in distinctive labour markets, Liverpool workers experienced familiar and common problems, the kind of tensions and pressures which drew workers elsewhere into class-based political action in the age of the Chartists. Some workers were fortunate, immune from adverse changes in the labour process. A small number of craft workers in the luxury trades continued to work in customary and respected manner, catering for a local market second only to London - Liverpool produced more millionaires (mostly from the 'old families') than any other city.[14] Building and construction workers, trades dominated by native Liverpudlians and Welsh immigrants, enjoyed 'boom town' conditions as Liverpool displayed its 'superabundant wealth' in impressive buildings. At the lower end of the market, however, work practices were under threat. Liverpool was in the forefront in 1833-4 when the Operative Builders united to defend traditional standards and practices against capitalist 'general contracting' and 'jerry-building', a term coined on Merseyside.[15]

There was similar 'scamping' in the artisan trades - yet to be replaced by factory production or regional specialization - which supplied basic needs and requirements. Employers and middlemen undercut each other in

---

[10]J.A. Picton, *Liverpool Improvements, and how to accomplish them* (Liverpool, 1853), 24.

[11]For a useful survey of societies and institutes, see *Roscoe Magazine*, March 1849.

[12]Tony Lane, *Liverpool: Gateway of Empire* (1987), ch 2.

[13]P.J. Waller, *Democracy and Sectarianism. A political and social history of Liverpool 1868-1939* (Liverpool, 1981), 330.

[14]Lane, 54-5.

[15]*Morning Chronicle,* 20 May and 16 Sept 1850, letters 1 and 18. William Hamling, *A Short History of the Liverpool Trades' Council 1848-1948* (Liverpool, 1948), 11-12.

competition for a huge local market swollen by sailors and emigrants, easy victims of the notorious waterfront 'sharps'.[16] Liverpool tailors, shoemakers, furniture-makers and the like, seem to have descended into 'dishonourable' status more quickly than their London counterparts, unable to stem the influx of cheap labour, either female or immigrant Irish. Beneath this sweated sector was the 'secondary economy' of the streets, the domain of hawkers and costermongers (trades in which the Irish excelled), common lodging-house keepers, bookies, pawnbrokers and prostitutes. Kept at a distance from respectable areas, this boisterous arena catered for the needs of the city's poorest inhabitants and least wary visitors - sailors and emigrants were compelled to risk their fortune ashore by regulations prohibiting fire and light in the docks at night.[17] In the absence of a significant Spencean presence, however, Liverpool seems to have lacked a tavern-based 'radical' culture linking the ultra-radical underground with the 'criminal' underworld.[18] Here, as my essay suggests, pub-based secret networks were ethnic and nationalist, the preserve of the Ribbonmen.[19]

Chartism recruited reasonably well among the town's 'insecure' craft workers (see Alan Little's Appendix on subscribers to the National Land Company), but remained disappointingly weak without the support of waterfront artisan trades. The absence of shipwrights and allied trades points to the weakness of Chartist ideology, its inability to transcend economic and party divisions.[20] As freeman voters, shipwrights were Tories, an allegiance which suggests 'the autonomy of the political', behaviour determined less by socio-economic factors than by political structures, by the inherited pattern of rights and endowments.[21] Under the old unreformed system shipwrights had relied on their bartering power at the polls to secure measures to regulate the

---

[16]*Morning Chronicle,* 24 June and 1 July, letters 6 and 7. 'Of all sea-ports in the world', Melville recorded, 'Liverpool, perhaps, most abounds in all the variety of land-sharks, land-rats and other vermin, which make the hapless mariner their prey', *Redburn,* 202. One emigrant, wise by experience, wrote that 'if a man had 7 senses, it would take 500 senses largely developed to counteract the sharpers of Liverpool', Thomas Reilly to Kelly, 19 June 1848, National Library of Ireland Mss 10,511 (2).

[17]M. Brogden, *The Police: Autonomy and Consent* (1982), 43-73. *Morning Chronicle,* 3 June 1850, letter 3.

[18]Iain McCalman, *Radical Underworld: Prophets, revolutionaries and pornographers in London, 1795-1840* (Cambridge, 1988).

[19]See below ch 4.

[20]John Belchem, 'Beyond *Chartist Studies*: class, community and party in early Victorian populist politics' in D. Fraser (ed), *Cities, Class and Communication: Essays in honour of Asa Briggs* (1990), 113-21.

[21]M.Savage, *The Dynamics of Working-Class Politics: The Labour Movement in Preston, 1880-1940* (Cambridge, 1987), 7-12.

trade from the elected Tory authorities.[22] After 1832, at a time of increasing under-employment in the trade, they struggled to retain their franchise and other vestigial perquisites in alliance with the Tories, popular defenders of traditional liberties. Once shipbuilding was lost to Birkenhead, the Liverpool shipwrights were left to concentrate on the more erratic ship-repair business - in this respect they were in the somewhat anomalous position of a skilled trade with an employment pattern similar to that of the casualism of the docks. Furthermore, their livelihood depended on protection, on the continuance of the Navigation Act, since foreign ships made minimal use of local repair facilities.[23] Economic logic continued to underpin their traditional Tory allegiance.

Liverpool was unable to develop a strong Chartist movement because of the conflict of interest between waterfront artisans, freemen who looked to the Tories to defend their rights and uphold protection against foreign competition, and 'Liberal' dock workers, the stevedores and porters for whom free trade meant more trade through the port. Protectionist but not Tory, radical but not Liberal, Chartism failed to establish a coherent identity outside partisan discourse. Thus, it was not casualism and sectarianism that hindered class mobilization in Liverpool, Kevin Moore concludes, but the popularity and purchase of party politics. The attempted 'new unionism' of the 1870s, the subject of Eric Taplin's essay, displayed similar traits.[24] Although sectional, the organization of semi-skilled and unskilled workers was an important advance, but it was not maintained. In the absence of an independent working-class tradition, the new unions turned for leadership and guidance to an eccentric 'Tory' philanthropist with pronounced anti-union views and an advanced Liberal employer, whose enthusiasm for 'new model' unionism was of little relevance to striking unskilled workers.

The deference and servility displayed during the disputes of the 1870s were later to be replaced by more familiar attitudes among Liverpool's casual and unskilled workers, militancy and defiant independence. When the organized labour movement eventually established itself in maritime, dockland and casual labour markets, it (necessarily?) took the form of big bureaucratic unions, a structure which quickly provoked a militant 'rank and file'

---

[22]Kevin Moore, 'Liverpool in the "Heroic Age" of Popular Radicalism, 1815 to 1820', *Transactions of the Historic Society of Lancashire and Cheshire*, 138 (1989), 148-54.

[23]*Shipbuilding in Liverpool. Evidence taken before the Committee appointed by the Town Council to consider the present state of the Shipbuilding Trade in Liverpool, and the best means which can be adopted for encouraging it* (Liverpool, 1850), 134-5, 150-7, 159. *Morning Chronicle*, 9 Sept 1850, letter 17.

[24]See below ch 6.

reaction.[25] Casual labourers lacked the guaranteed time, relevant experience or financial resources for regular involvement and subscription. Full-time officials perforce dominated their unions, bureaucrats who sought union incorporation in national agreements with employers, to which end they were prepared both to discipline and decasualize the membership. In so doing, they offended against the independence and pride of the Liverpool labourer. For all its ills, casualism was a cherished symbol of independence, the best guarantee of freedom from irksome work-discipline, from the tyranny of the factory bell. In protesting against decasualization, the workers were championed by Syndicalist advocates of direct action,[26] but the incidence of subsequent rank and file militancy seems to have been determined less by theory and praxis than by specific grievances and traditional attitudes. Liverpool workers continued to protest against impositions and innovations - national agreements, bureaucratic structures and new work practices - which denied their residual independence and democratic local autonomy. This assertive local pride was to persist long after the decline of the docks, shipping and casualism. Workers in the new industrial plants of the Merseyside Development Area gained a reputation for antipathy to factory discipline and managerial prerogatives, prompting some observers to trace a cultural continuity back to the old traditions of waterside casualism and seafaring independence, the legacy of dockers who offered themselves for employment when they wished and of seamen who were able to pick and choose their ships.[27]

Viewed from the workers' perspective, casualism was not a curse, but a culture to be defended. Hence the strong opposition back in the 1840s to the permanent labour schemes - manned by 'ring-droppers brought from London' - introduced at the new Albert Dock. Ironically, the Albert Dock is now the show-piece of 'heritage' Liverpool: in its own brief day, it was distinctly untypical and much opposed, 'the sole dock in the port, constructed upon the model of those in London - surrounded by its own warehouses, worked by its own porters, and denying access within its gate to ragged children, beggars, thieves, and all who can give no account of their business'. Confronted by the new development, warehouse owners joined porters and carters in defence of the old, dispersed, unenclosed system, their best safeguard against monopoly and dictation by the Dock Trustees. Casualism

---

[25]Rank and filism is the subject of much controversy in labour history, see the articles by Zeitlin, Price, Cronin and Hyman in *International Review of Social History*, 34 (1989).

[26]Bob Holton, 'Syndicalism and Labour on Merseyside, 1906-1914' in H.R. Hikins (ed), *Building the Union: studies on the growth of the workers' movement, Merseyside, 1756-1967* (Liverpool, 1973), 121-50.

[27]R. Bean and P. Stoney, 'Strikes on Merseyside: a regional analysis', *Industrial Relations Journal*, 17 (1986), 9-23.

continued, but customary wages and differentials were steadily eroded as middlemen - lumpers, master porters and warehousemen - underbid each other by exploiting the new arrivals, 'the green hands - the "Grecians" - unskilled porters that are always coming over on the chance of work'. The porters protested, advising the 'merchants and brokers' of the false economy of the middlemen's unrestricted recruitment policy: 'The Master Porters will employ any Men who will work very hard, altogether regardless of the waste and injury the Goods of the merchant sustain by this hurried and careless way of doing work'.[28] It was a valid point. Although casual, dock labour was neither undifferentiated nor unskilled. In both stevedorage and porterage, there was a premium on proficiency and specialist know-how, useful adjuncts to stamina and strength. Wind and tide permitting, those with the 'knack' were the first to find employment.[29]

Specialist ability was at least as important as sectarian allegiance in the dock labour market, particularly when steam replaced sail, intensifying the demand for a quick turn round in port. Thus, the sharp labour division between the two ends of the docks cannot be explained simply in terms of the sectarian geography of a Catholic north and a Protestant south: account must be taken of other factors, of the different types of job specialism, docks, vessels and employers. Religious differences, Eric Taplin has observed, were less divisive than historians have assumed: 'There was undoubtedly an undercurrent of petty argument and recrimination that weakened unified action but in the event of a major conflict the labourers acted together and religious differences were subsumed for the more important immediate issue at stake'.[30] Sectarianism was a decisive factor in certain occupations - the carters, for example, were almost exclusively Protestant - and at certain hiring stands, but it was by no means an irrefragable force throughout the wider labour market and industrial relations. Its strength and appeal, John Bohstedt suggests, lay outside work, in the provision of positive and attractive forms of political and associational culture.[31]

At the workplace, the unbridgeable division was not sectarian, but sexual. Casual labour on the docks was a male preserve, a symbol of tough masculinity. In the absence of textile factories, female employment was

---

[28]*Morning Chronicle*, 27 May, 10 and 17 June 1850, letters 2,4 and 5. T.J. Hutton, *Hope for the Warehouse-Owners and Freedom to Commerce, showing the evil of building warehouses round the docks for the benefit of the Dock Estate, in opposition to private warehouse property* (Liverpool, 1848). 'To the Merchants and Brokers of Liverpool, 9 March 1848', posting-bill in Public Record Office: Home Office Papers 45/2410B. *Liverpool Mercury*, 10 and 14 Mar, 14 Apr, and 26 Dec 1848.
[29]E.L. Taplin, *Liverpool Dockers and Seamen 1870-1890* (Hull, 1974), 7-10.
[30]*Ibid*, 11.
[31]See below ch 8.

restricted to domestic service - which was to remain the largest single female occupation into the twentieth century - and to a small number of 'sweated' trades. Here, too, the Liverpool version of the male-breadwinner ethic prevailed:

> The needlewomen of Liverpool are very often the wives of sailors. If they get their husbands' monthly money pretty regularly they do not care for needlework, but if there is any falling off in that they apply for slop-work ... Some of them are the wives of porters and dock-labourers, who take to slop-work when their husbands are out of employ, and leave it off as soon as the husbands get a few jobs to keep them going.[32]

At times of protracted distress, women and children were compelled to undertake a variety of tasks to boost the family income, from corn-stealing and other transit crime to degrading occupations servicing the street economy such as the chip, grit and oakum 'trades'.[33]

Despite the limited prospects for female and family earnings, the Liverpool casual labour market attracted vast numbers of impoverished Irish migrants. Sectarian reaction to their presence was held in check by two factors: the comparatively self-contained nature of Irish immigration; and the solidarity ethos of most work gangs. It was Welsh migrants, not the Irish, who constituted the economic threat to resident artisans and tradesmen. Confined to the bottom of the labour market, the Irish found a 'niche' in the kind of labouring jobs which native workers wished not to do themselves, whether in the docks or in waterfront industry:

> At the chemical manufactories nearly all the dirty work is done by the Irish, under an overseer, who is not generally Irish. In soaperies and sugar-houses the common dirty work is usually done by them. All the low departments of industry are filled by the Irish.[34]

As the influx continued, wage rates and employment levels were reduced, but only among the Irish themselves in the worst and lowest paid jobs. Their swelling numbers, however, may have exercised a 'crowding-out' effect,

---

[32]*Morning Chronicle*, 24 June 1850, letter 6.
[33]*Morning Chronicle*, 17 June 1850, letter 5.
[34]Parliamentary Papers, 1836 (40) XXXIV: Royal Commission on the Condition of the Poorer Classes in Ireland. Appendix G, The State of the Irish Poor in Great Britain, 28, evidence of Samuel Holme.

limiting the extent of in-migration by poor labourers in agricultural areas adjacent to Liverpool.[35]

Although restricted in this way, the Irish were by no means segregated from other workers. They often worked directly alongside skilled craftsmen and others within a 'work gang', performing the physical and menial tasks. Here there were grounds for conflict over the rhythm and pace of work. In an attempt to boost their immediate earnings to send remittances home, newly-arrived migrants were prepared to work hard and fast - as the porters rued - to shun the traditional codes and practices by which native workers defended their residual control of the labour process. Most new arrivals, however, were quickly acculturated: work gangs tended to produce a sense of labour solidarity - a community of work - strong enough to override divisions of skill, ethnicity and religion, if not gender. Furthermore, the Irish were able to contribute 'organizational' experience derived from their secret 'Ribbon' societies. In the building strike of 1833, Samuel Holme observed, Irish labourers were to the fore:

> The late turn-out of mechanics and labourers has been almost entirely organized by Irish: they are all bound together by secret oaths, which were probably suggested by the Irish; and, although the Irish were the poorest mechanics, they took the lead in this turn-out. The English submitted in the most singular manner to be led by the nose.[36]

Labour solidarity, however, did not extend into class-based political mobilization. Sectarian allegiance was the crucial determinant in the political arena, accentuating the traditional partisan divisions in this 'Whig and Tory-Ridden Town'.[37] The reforms of the 1830s challenged the smooth operation of the time-honoured ways and means by which Tories and freemen trades negotiated within a framework of mutual advantage: political support was exchanged for economic protection, for judicious intervention in trade matters and disputes. Briefly ejected from office, the Tories, seeking a wider popular base beyond the diminishing freeman vote, added a sectarian inflexion to their protectionist rhetoric. Their success in this regard was aided by two distinctive features of Irish immigration to the city.

---

[35]J. G. Williamson, 'The impact of the Irish on British labor markets during the industrial revolution', *Journal of Economic History*, xlvi (1986), 717.

[36]*Ibid*, 28.

[37]Kevin Moore, '"This Whig and Tory Ridden Town": Popular Politics in Liverpool, 1815-1850', unpublished M.Phil thesis, University of Liverpool, 1988.

First, Liverpool attracted significant numbers of migrants, both Catholic and Protestant, from Ulster and adjoining counties, 'these silly people retaining here', Cornewall Lewis reported, 'the absurd enmities which disgraced and degraded them at home'.[38] Ulster Protestants, it seems, were the necessary catalyst which activated the latent anti-catholicism of the native workforce - without their presence, Orangeism failed to develop among native workers in other areas of Irish immigration. Even in Liverpool, the Orange lodges were initially restricted to Ulster ranks. Sectarian violence began as an internal Irish 'private battle' - to use Anne Bryson's useful terminology - one expression of the various regional and factional tensions within the immigrant community. At first, indeed, it was not sectarianism, but the arrival of seasonal harvest migrants from the west which provoked the most violent intra-Irish incidents. 'I am unable to hire a Connaught man', Samuel Holme reported, 'he is always spoken of in terms of contempt by the others; he is discovered immediately, and they will persecute him till he quits'.[39] Sectarian violence came to the fore, however, when Orangeism was appropriated and amplified by the local establishment. Incorporated into the Tory narrative of religious and constitutional freedom, Orangeism became the primary expression of allegiance, the symbol of inclusive national identity, for all Protestants, native and immigrant alike.[40]

Here the second distinctive feature of the Liverpool Irish ensured the effectiveness of sectarian politics. While other 'exiles of Erin' distributed (and integrated) themselves throughout the host society,[41] those who remained in Liverpool were for the most part a class apart, unable, unsuited or unwilling to take advantage of opportunities elsewhere in Britain or the new world. Lacking the capacity to progress, they congregated at the bottom of the local occupational, social and residential hierarchy, easy targets of sectarian abuse.

Sectarianism entered Tory politics through the demagogic oratory of the Rev. Hugh McNeile, one of Liverpool's 'Irish brigade' of immigrant Ulster pastors. A staunch anti-reformer, McNeile, a Protestant and protectionist, combined biblical scholarship with populist political rhetoric. In exposing the

---

[38]The State of the Irish Poor in Britain, 21.

[39]*Ibid*, 29. Anne Bryson, 'Riot and its control in Liverpool, 1815-1860', unpublished M.Phil thesis, Open University, 1990. Frank Neal, *Sectarian Violence: the Liverpool experience, 1819 to 1914* (Manchester, 1988), chs 1 and 2. See also Tom Gallagher, 'A Tale of Two Cities: communal strife in Glasgow and Liverpool before 1914' in R. Swift and S. Gilley (eds), *The Irish in the Victorian City* (1985), 106-29.

[40]Joan Smith, 'Class, skill and sectarianism in Glasgow and Liverpool, 1880-1914' in R.J. Morris (ed), *Class, power and social structure in British nineteenth-century towns* (Leicester, 1986), 158-215.

[41]See the essays by David Fitzpatrick, Colin Pooley and Graham Davis in R. Swift and S. Gilley (eds), *The Irish in Britain* (1989).

threat to freedom - to the liberty and property of the Anglican establishment in church and state - he condemned tyrannical Catholicism *and* its misguided ally, radical Dissent, with its dangerous manifesto of 'liberal' reform and free trade. His Operative Protestant Association was quickly incorporated within the panoply of local Tory organizations alongside the Operative Conservative Association and other militant Protestant voluntary groups, the rejuvenated Orange Order included.[42] Much like the 'pillarization' prevalent in the Netherlands, this interlocking associational network - party, popular and sectarian - facilitated ready interaction between the classes.[43] Local notables continued to monopolize political positions - there was no working-class Conservative councillor before 1914 - but as need arose, they were able to mingle at ease within the network, displaying the common touch which soon became a distinguishing (and essential) characteristic of local Tory leadership, a style perfected in Archibald Salvidge's electoral machine, perhaps the most remarkable example of British 'boss politics'.[44]

This is not to suggest that the Protestant working class were passive instruments in this political construction, manipulated at will by the Tory caucus. Sectarian ideology derived its resonance from its 'practical adequacy', from its ability to make discursive - and common - sense of the world.[45] Religious enthusiasms and antagonisms, John Bohstedt notes, were interwoven with positive social and political values.[46] Seen from below, 'No Popery' served to protect the 'marginal privilege' of the Protestant worker, an advantage which Tories could neither neglect nor infringe without serious electoral consequences. Thus, local Tory bosses were frequently compelled to adopt policies and practices at odds with the orthodox political economy of mainstream middle-class conservatism. Forwood was drawn beyond the rhetoric of 'Tory democracy' into local collectivism, a Tory version of municipal socialism.[47] Recognizing the continuing popular appeal of protectionism, Salvidge, his successor, defied local 'business conservatism' to uphold Tariff Reform, championing local working-class interests against the

---

[42]Barbara Whittingham-Jones, *The Pedigree of Liverpool Politics: White, Orange and Green* (Liverpool, 1936), 34-40.

[43]Marlou Schrover, 'Labour Relations in the Dutch Margarine Industry 1870-1954', *History Workshop Journal*, 30 (1990), 58.

[44]Waller, *passim*. Joan Smith, 'Labour Tradition in Glasgow and Liverpool', *History Workshop Journal*, 17 (1984), 32-56.

[45]E.W. McFarland, *Protestants First. Orangeism in Nineteenth-Century Scotland* (Edinburgh, 1990), 19-21.

[46]See below ch 8.

[47]B.D. White, *A History of the Corporation of Liverpool 1835-1914* (Liverpool, 1951), ch 13. See also Joan Smith, 'Commonsense thought and working class consciousness: some aspects of the Glasgow and Liverpool labour movements in the early years of the twentieth century', unpublished Ph.D thesis, University of Edinburgh, 1980, 277-87.

'lower-middle-class fraud, called Liberalism or "Free Trade"'.[48] Other slogans, however, passed out of Salvidge's control. 'No Popery' acquired a libertarian anti-establishment tenor, a populist inflexion altogether different from McNeile's original formulation. Introduced to defend the Tory-Anglican establishment, it was appropriated by militant Dissent, by Protestants prepared to take to the streets to condemn the 'Romish' ritualism of the Established Church.[49] In this respect, riot was a symptom of temporary breakdown and dysfunction within the city's sectarian formations.

Liberalism lacked an alternative framework of popular organization and associational culture. Here Liverpool differed from other towns and cities. Elsewhere, Liberalism thrived - as Chartism receded - by incorporating the 'new-model' associations of the mid-Victorian labour aristocracy. In Liverpool, as Joan Smith has stressed, this Lib-Lab political formation failed to emerge.[50] Without a substantial craft elite, the new agencies of collective self-help struggled to survive, dependent for the most part on the uniformed working class, on postmen and railwaymen who enjoyed permanent employment if not skilled status. Among casual labourers, collective mutuality was perforce restricted to 'tontines', short-term dividing societies usually constructed along religious and ethnic lines. The local Liberals did nothing to alleviate these actuarial difficulties, preferring to preserve their distance from the crude conviviality of working-class associational culture.

An exclusive elite of progressive (usually unitarian) merchants, mainly in the American as opposed to West Indian and African trade, Liverpool Liberals kept aloof from popular involvement, safeguarding the integrity of reform from contaminating contact with drink, ignorance and vulgar prejudice. These elitist attitudes harked back to their exclusion from corrupt freeman politics, benighted times in which they had defied prejudice and power to espouse abolition of the slave trade, Catholic emancipation and other unpopular causes.[51] After gaining the suffrage in the 1830s, they remained 'advanced' in their views, but such rational radicalism allowed no role for popular involvement or mass agitation. Significantly, the 'celebrations' to mark the passing of the Reform Bill were restricted to an exclusive dinner for 350 'nobs':

Other towns celebrated the great national redemption with processions, illuminations, and meetings, with dinners for all

---

[48]Waller, 210-13.

[49]Whittingham-Jones, 47-8.

[50]Joan Smith's challenging work, with its emphasis on theory, is essential reading for all students of Liverpool labour history.

[51]Moore, 'Liverpool in the "Heroic Age"', 140-2.

classes, poor as well as rich. Liverpool had no meeting ... no procession, no illumination, no dinners for the poor, as well as the rich; but one solitary large dinner to a small number, at fifteen shillings a head.[52]

In their brief exercise of power, the Liberal elite purged the carnival and corruption of traditional electoral politics without offering an alternative forum for popular participation, leaving the field free for Tory (and Orange) organizational initiatives. George Melly, 'a Liberal of the most advanced principles of social science', was characteristically incredulous of the subsequent electoral consequences, bemoaning the hegemony of Tory protectionism in 'the largest commercial port in the world - and commerce is another word for free trade - commerce is another word for radicalism - commerce is another word for free and enlightened opinion'.[53]

The absence of a Liberal network of political patronage and economic protection left the non-Protestant working class - the Catholic Irish - reliant upon their own 'ethnic' resources, upon a network of voluntary associations based on nationality and creed, not on class. In the Chartist period, as my paper demonstrates, ethnicity and class were in apparent competition: paradoxically, the genuine 'physical force' politicians of 1848 were middle-class Irish nationalists to whom Chartist 'class politics' were anathema.[54] Ethnicity, however, is best understood, as several contributors suggest, as an alternative, not an obstacle, to class identity.

In Irish-Liverpool, ethnic consciousness was fostered first in the pub, later by the parish. Liverpool was notorious for its numerous pubs: Hume's survey noted nearly 1500 in the borough in 1858.[55] Competition for custom was intense, particularly in Irish areas where publicans encouraged various forms of convivial and bibulous associational culture, extending from legally approved Hibernian burial and friendly societies to secret Ribbon branches linked to networks across the Irish Sea. Not to be outdone, the Catholic church, having failed to eradicate Ribbonism by proscription, decided to develop a rival, parish-based framework of associational culture, offering cradle to grave sustenance and support for Irish immigrants, male and female. Thereafter national and religious identity were to flourish in a symbiotic relationship which 'made Irish, Catholic, and Catholic, Irish'.[56] This Catholic

---

[52]*Liverpool Examiner*, 2 Dec 1832.

[53]*Northern Daily Times*, 28 Oct 1857, newspaper cutting in Danson Archive, National Museums and Galleries on Merseyside.

[54]See below ch 4.

[55]Abraham Hume, *Condition of Liverpool, religious and social, including notices of the state of education, morals, pauperism and crime* (Liverpool, 1858), 28.

[56]See below ch 4.

infrastructure soon facilitated a new nationalist mobilization, home rule, a popular programme which caught the distant Liberals unawares. With the emergence of the Irish Nationalists, the traditional Liberal alignment of the Catholic wards was finally ruptured. Once the Irish National Party passed into the hands of second-generation (i.e. Liverpool-born) Irish, however, it displayed less interest in the fate of Ireland than in the immediate needs of the local Catholic community in housing and employment.[57] Here the leaders developed a distinctive political style, exploiting the system for short-term ends. Perfected by the Harford brothers and T.P. O'Connor, M.P. for the Scotland division, this form of community politics depended first on a large network of confidants able to produce the goods, particularly within the council, and second on the continued estrangement of the Liverpool-Irish from other (class-based) political formations.[58] After Irish independence, the Irish National Party was briefly replaced by a Catholic party before Labour finally gained control of the working-class Catholic wards, inheriting their political style:

> Labour absorbed councillors who had been instruments of the church and it inherited organizations that knew more about clientism, autocracy and priestly patronage than about beliefs in democratic and constitutional procedures which were the hallmarks of the Labour Party and the "respectable" working class. Although the Labour Party was now formally much larger, it was in practice two parties and the Catholic section, organised as a caucus, was dominant.[59]

Somewhat later than the Tories, then, Liverpool Labour developed its own form of 'boss politics'. However, the system failed to deliver the benefits and gains derived from Irish domination of the Democratic Party in north American cities. For working-class women, as Sam Davies shows, the religious complexion of the Liverpool Labour machine from the mid 1920s hindered the discussion and promotion of crucial issues.[60]

---

[57]Bernard O'Connell, 'Irish Nationalism in Liverpool, 1873-1923', *Éire-Ireland*, 10 (1975), 24-37.

[58]A. Shallice, 'Orange and Green and militancy: Sectarianism and working-class politics in Liverpool, 1900-1914', *Bulletin of the North-West Labour History Society*, 6 (1979-80), 15-32. See also L.W. Brady, *T.P. O'Connor and the Liverpool Irish* (1983).

[59]Lane, 138.

[60]See below ch 9. See also A. Shallice, 'Liverpool Labourism and Irish Nationalism in the 1920s and 1930s', *Bulletin of the North-West Labour History Society*, 8 (1981-2), 19-28.

Sectarianism, it is suggested here, was political in construction and positive in function, offering identity, pride and protection to workers often without access to exclusive or institutionalized forms of organized labour. Its negative aspects have much to do with social geography, with fierce border disputes over contested territory. Residential concentration, however, was not a requirement for sectarian or other loyalties. Welsh migrants, for example, were relatively dispersed across the city, but displayed a strong sense of 'community', bonded together by strong cultural and linguistic ties: families travelled long distances to worship together in Welsh-speaking Calvinist chapels; Welsh newspapers circulated in the city; and the National Eisteddfod was held there on several occasions.[61] The Catholic Irish were more concentrated, but census analysis has revealed significant numbers of Irish migrants in skilled and white-collar occupations spread across the residential structure, found mainly in localities associated with middle-class residents.[62] Ethnicity, however, did not diminish with spatial distance. 'Successful' migrants moved out - at least to the fringes of the slums - but many stood forward as 'Irish' leaders, mobilizing and assisting their less fortunate compatriots. In praising the upwardly mobile in its 1872 survey, the *Nation* sought to marshal the electoral influence of the top Liverpool-Irish, the 'one-fifth to one sixth above the ranks of ordinary toil - a proportion which most strikingly exemplifies the intelligence, industry and good conduct of those who have risen, when we consider that all, or nearly all, had to force their way from the lowest ranks and against the most adverse odds'.[63]

Most of the Liverpool-Irish, however, remained restricted in their residential options, unable to benefit from developments in transport and by-law housing. Dependent on the casual labour market, they continued to crowd together alongside other dock labourers in low standard housing with high rates of multiple occupancy in areas adjacent to the docks and hiring stands: the 'instant slum' of the north with its purpose-built court housing; and the failed middle-class suburb of the south end, hastily 'made down' into overcrowded and cellared street housing.[64] According to recent calculations,

---

[61]Richard Dennis, *English Industrial Cities of the Nineteenth Century: A Social Geography* (Cambridge, 1984), 228-30. C.G. Pooley, 'The residential segregation of migrant communities in mid-Victorian Liverpool', *Transactions of the Institute of British Geographers*, ii (1977), 364-72.

[62]C.G. Pooley, 'Segregation or integration? The residential experience of the Irish in mid-Victorian Britain' in Swift and Gilley, (eds), *The Irish in Britain*, 74-80.

[63]*Nation*, 24 Sept 1872, reprinted in O'Day (ed), 90-1.

[64]I.C. Taylor, '"Black Spot on the Mersey". A study of environment and society in eighteenth and nineteenth century Liverpool', unpublished Ph.D thesis, University of Liverpool, 1976. See also J.D. Papworth, 'The Irish in Liverpool 1835-71: Segregation and Dispersal', unpublished Ph.D thesis, University of Liverpool, 1982.

77 per cent of dock workers in the 1870s lived within one mile of the nearest dock, less than fifteen minutes walk from home to work.[65] Skilled workers in the port-based manufacturing sector of iron-founding, ship-repairing and marine engineering, a labour market which drew workers from Scotland, Wales and the Black Country, chose to travel further, avoiding the low-status, mainly Irish central areas in favour of the intermediate suburbs, such as Kirkdale and western Everton. Across the 'collar gap', workers in the clerical sector travelled further still to indulge their higher aspirations: blessed with regular income and less need to be close to the workplace, they moved out to the new decent terraces of suburban Everton and West Derby.[66]

Stratification, a process which began with the physical and cultural segregation noted by Michael Power,[67] was a complex phenomenon in the Liverpool urban mosaic, an amalgam of socio-economic, ethnic and sectarian variables. The north end soon emerged as a distinctively Irish - and Catholic - community, as new churches, the centre of associational life, encouraged the tendency to residential propinquity. Cultural provision was less cohesive in the south end, an area of more mixed social and ethnic composition, including a significant Ulster Protestant presence.[68] By the late nineteenth century, Great Homer Street was the acknowledged boundary between Catholic and Protestant Liverpool with the most partisan Orange district running north of Netherfield Road.[69] Other borders were less clearly defined: they were to witness considerable sectarian violence, a form of ritualized territorial skirmishing. Direct invasions into 'enemy' territory, into well-defined enclaves, were comparatively rare and generally ill-advised, as was the case with the Salvation Army incursion into the Catholic heartland studied by Norman Murdoch.[70]

Sectarian disorder was much influenced by the attitude of the authorities, particularly when it occurred - as in the annual set-piece clashes - in the public ceremonial space of the city centre. Important changes in policy and perception, in the maintenance and definition of public order, are highlighted in Anne Bryson's comprehensive typology of street disturbance,

---

[65]R. Lawton and C.G. Pooley, 'The Social Geography of Merseyside in the Nineteenth Century', Final report to the SSRC, July 1976 (Dept of Geography, University of Liverpool), 60.

[66]*Ibid*, 61-3. See also G. Anderson, 'Inequalities in the workplace: The gap between manual and white-collar workers in the port of Liverpool from the 1850s to the 1930s', *Labour History Review*, 56 (1991), 36-48.

[67]See below ch 2.

[68]Papworth, 183-90.

[69]Neal, 196.

[70]See below ch 7.

a study from above.[71] The Liverpool authorities were experienced and competent in crowd control: the funeral of Huskisson in 1830, for example, was carefully organized with the provision of crash barriers to hold back the crowds. Elections apart, most crowd activity in early-nineteenth century Liverpool, whether riotous or recreational, occurred in non-work time. The prevalence of casualism notwithstanding, Liverpool seems to have conformed to a defined and institutionalized pattern of 'mass phenomena'.[72] By the mid-Victorian period, the attention of the police and other coercive agencies was concentrated on the residuum, on a separate and discrete 'brutish and criminal' minority outside the main body of the working people. Working-class communities, Protestant and Catholic, were left to discipline themselves and defend their sectarian borders. The authorities remained on the alert, however, in fear of riot and disorder in the city centre.

In the absence of 'modernization', riot remained the characteristic form of protest in Liverpool, preserving the spirit of rebellious direct action implanted by seamen in the eighteenth century.[73] There were bread riots in the city as late as 1855.[74] The potential for disorder remained strong, aggravated by a political culture which encouraged sectarian rivalry, and by conflict 'on the Mersey beat'[75] as the police sought to contain and conceal the 'secondary economy' of the streets. It was not until the near-anarchy (and fragile class unity) of the great transport strike of 1911, however, that the authorities took decisive steps to eradicate street disturbance, finally removing any 'official' sanction for sectarian mobilization. But rioting continued in other forms: the anti-German riots which followed the sinking of the 'Lusitania' (with many Liverpool crew on board) were more ferocious than was the case elsewhere; in 1919, amid the dislocation of the transition to peace, the city experienced its first major race riots, shortly followed by looting and rioting when the police went on strike.[76]

Although banished from city centre streets, sectarianism remained a powerful force until inter-war slum clearance undermined its cultural and

---

[71]See below ch 5.

[72]Mark Harrison, *Crowds and History. Mass Phenomena in English Towns 1790-1835* (Cambridge, 1988), 99, 131-6, 202.

[73]Marcus Rediker, *Between the Devil and the Deep Blue Sea. Merchant seamen, pirates and the Anglo-American maritime world, 1700-1750* (Cambridge, 1987), 249-51. See below ch 2 for the 1775 riots.

[74]R.M. Jones,'The Liverpool Bread Riots, 1855', *Bulletin of the North-West Labour History Society*, 6 (1979-80), 33-42.

[75]M. Brogden, *On the Mersey beat: policing in Liverpool between the wars* (Oxford, 1991).

[76]Smith, thesis, chs 8 and 9. Roy May and Robin Cohen, 'The Interaction between race and colonialism; a case study of the Liverpool race riots of 1919', University of Birmingham, Faculty of Commerce and Social Science Discussion Paper, Series E, 1974.

community infrastructure. Some 140,000 people - 15 per cent of the total population - were rehoused, many in distant suburban estates without shops, schools, pubs or churches. There was little improvement over time as the housing committee operated a ban on second-generation houses, forcing the children of the new suburbanites to vacate the neighbourhood on marriage. Without kinship groups or adequate facilities, the new estates lacked the character, culture and welfare networks of the old slums.[77] Although much lamented, the 'community' mentality of the slums had co-existed with a wider culture, a seafaring cosmopolitanism which made Liverpool particularly receptive to foreign ideas (not least Syndicalism) and to American popular music. Perhaps this accounts for the distinctive 'expressionist' nature of working-class fiction in inter-war Liverpool. While writers elsewhere reconstructed the enclosed world of the slum, the Liverpool school addressed issues of dislocation, rootlessness and alienation.[78]

Devoid of sectarian structures, suburban estates became solid Labour territory. It was not until 1955, however, that Labour gained control of the municipal council, a generation later than equivalent triumphs in other major conurbations.[79]

Liverpool, then, took a backward role in the forward march of Labour. The city, indeed, lacks a militant political past. Throughout the decades of labour's 'turning-point', socialist and syndicalist activists either kowtowed to sectarian prejudice or failed to acknowledge its force, an important contrast to developments in Glasgow as Joan Smith's comparative analysis has shown.[80] After mass trade union reconstruction and the decline of casualism, Liverpool politics still remained in the hands of Tory Democracy, the Irish Nationalists and right-wing labour organizers. How then has Liverpool acquired its current reputation? Militancy, it would seem, is a symptom of decay and collapse, of the belated and abortive attempt at structural change.

Having prided itself on its commercial superiority, Liverpool was compelled to widen its industrial base by the depression of the 1930s, throughout which the local unemployment rate remained resolutely above 18 per cent, double the national average. The pace of diversification quickened after the second world war when Merseyside was declared a Development Area, bringing new opportunities for women, particularly in the food

---

[77]Madeline McKenna, 'The suburbanization of the working-class population of Liverpool between the wars', *Social History*, 16 (1991), 173-89.

[78]K. Worpole, *Dockers and Detectives: Popular Reading: Popular Writing* (1983), ch.4. Through oral history and other means, historians are now attempting to reconstruct the old community ethos, see the publications of the Docklands History Project.

[79]R.S.W. Davies, 'The Liverpool Labour Party and the Liverpool Working Class, 1900-39', *Bulletin of the North-West Labour History Society*, 6 (1979-80), 2-14.

[80]Smith, 'Labour Tradition'.

processing industry. The unemployment rate, however, remained disproportionately high, often 2½ times the national average, accentuated by the propensity of industrial combines to close their new Merseyside plants once development aid and other short-term advantages were exhausted. Here, of course, Merseyside militancy - a myth in the making - helped to justify a board-room decision taken far away from Liverpool.[81]

There was some reality behind the militant image. The local workforce, accustomed to the independence of casual and maritime labour, found it difficult to adjust to factory discipline and managerial prerogatives, a 'culture clash' considerably exacerbated by the large size of new plant on Merseyside and the high level of external ownership and control. Furthermore, there was an unusual predominance of 'strike-prone' industries throughout the sub-region: docks, shipbuilding, and more recently, electrical engineering and motor vehicle-building. The high level of strikes has always been concentrated in these prominent and 'visible' areas, often leading to lay-offs elsewhere. Within these industries, disputes have arisen less over wages than over two main sets of issues: discipline and dismissal; and redundancy, manning and work allocation.[82] From the start, the new car factories of the 1960s were the site of industrial relations upheaval as increased competition in the industry led to conflicts of workplace control and authority. At the same time, workers on the dwindling docks struggled to retain residual control of the labour process as the port adjusted to the end of Empire, entry into the EEC and containerization. Redundancy disputes were soon to follow in the nascent industrial sector, provoked by successive waves of factory closures, particularly in electrical engineering, as a number of corporations closed a Merseyside plant before others elsewhere.

External disinvestment diminished the local resource base, but public service employment continued as the one area of growth until cuts in central government support placed the city financially 'on the brink'.[83] Through its budgetary defiance, its local resistance to central state policy, Liverpool - the city that 'dared to fight'[84] - acquired a reputation for political recalcitrance to match its 'strike-prone' industrial image.

Such political militancy was quite out of character. Unable to gain control of the council until 1955, Labour subsequently shared power with the Conservatives until the local Liberal revival led to the confused coalition

---

[81]Waller, 330, 350-1. Pat Ayers and Jan Lambertz, 'Marriage relations, money and domestic violence in working-class Liverpool, 1919-39' in Jane Lewis (ed), *Labour and Love: women's experience of home and family 1850-1940* (Oxford, 1986), 200. Merseyside Socialist Research Group, *Merseyside in Crisis* (n.p., 1980), *passim*.

[82]Bean and Stoney, *passim*.

[83]Michael Parkinson, *Liverpool on the Brink* (1985).

[84]P. Taafe and T. Mulhearn, *Liverpool: A City that Dared to Fight* (1988).

politics of 1974-83, the 'lost decade'. In the absence of any overall party majority, the Liberals controlled the city through minority and coalition administrations, hoping to enlarge their electoral base by restricting expenditure and holding down the rates. Such frugality went unacknowledged when the Conservative government introduced its controversial grant system, an ideologically-charged initiative to roll back the frontiers of the state and curb public expenditure. Having previously limited its expenditure, Liverpool considered itself unfairly treated: its targets were more stringent than those of profligate Labour authorities who had developed large base budgets during the 1970s. Furthermore, the block grant system failed to take account of the city's economic deprivation and population loss, fundamental problems which had defied solution in the absence of any coherent strategy during the 'lost decade'. This was the context in which 'Militant' came to power. Having already captured the moribund party machine, reduced to an empty shell by slum clearance of the old inner-city Catholic wards, Militant activists gained support among leaders of white and blue collar public sector unions. Under this pressure, the Liverpool Labour party abandoned its traditional right of centre position. To preserve jobs and the city, there seemed no alternative to confrontation, to the 'blackmail and bankruptcy' strategy of the Militant Tendency.[85]

Having gained control, Militant chose to operate municipal politics as a tightly-controlled centralized state, denying any role to collective self-help and working-class voluntarism, ignoring the associational endeavours of ethnic, gender, special interest and minority groups. By excluding new forms of associational culture and participatory democracy - different in composition from the old Irish and sectarian formations - Militant failed both to restructure Labour and to relieve the frustration of inner-city citizens who had taken to the streets in 1981 to protest against their marginalized status.[86] Militant has been (partially?) purged, but Liverpool, the most working-class city in Britain, still lacks an inclusive Labour identity. Liverpool has yet to transform its distinct and defiant culture of decline into an active agenda for change.

---

[85]Michael Parkinson, 'Liverpool's fiscal crisis: an anatomy of failure' in M.Parkinson, B. Foley and D. Judd (eds), *Regenerating the cities: the UK crisis and the US experience* (Manchester, 1988), 110-27.

[86]Gideon Ben-Tovim, 'Race, politics and urban regeneration: lessons from Liverpool' in *ibid*, 141-55. Paul Cooper, 'Competing explanations of the Merseyside Riots of 1981', *British Journal of Criminology*, 25 (1985), 60-8.

2: The Growth of Liverpool

M.J. Power

Modern Liverpool is a city whose problems are extreme. This is at least in part due to its history, moulded by the powerful forces of international trade, mass immigration and appalling public health. The Victorian city in which these operated grew out of an eighteenth-century town which itself was remarkable. The very speed with which it grew created opportunities and problems which could not but be intense. It was the fulcrum between England and Ireland, and, increasingly, between industrializing Britain and the world. Aptly described in 1796 as a 'nautical vortex', it experienced pressures which made it a town of extremes, even before the nineteenth century.[1] To understand the intensity of modern Liverpool's experience the historian needs to take account of the peculiarities of its early development as a major port. It is this task which this essay will attempt.

A perception of the town's unique character from an early date may be gained by reflecting on the reactions the town provoked among observers. As early as 1698 it appeared to Celia Fiennes as 'London in miniature', an encomium confirming Defoe's impression of 'a large handsome, well built and increasing a thriving town'.[2] A century later the analogy was to a fabled Italian entrepot: 'That immense place which stands like another Venice upon the waters ... intersected by those numerous docks ... where there are riches overflowing ... This quondam village which is now fit to be a proud capital for any empire in the world, has started up like an enchanted palace, even in the memory of living men'.[3]

All did not share so positive a reaction. Samuel Curwen, visiting from North America in 1780, voiced his disappointment: 'the whole complexion of the place was nautical and so infinitely below all our expectations that nought but the thought of the few hours we had to pass here rendered it tolerable'.[4]

---

[1] J.A. Picton, *Memorials of Liverpool, historical and topographical* (1875), I, 254.

[2] D.J. Pope, Shipping and trade in the port of Liverpool, 1783-1793, unpublished Ph.D. thesis, University of Liverpool, 2 vols, 1970, ii, 8-9.

[3] Lord Erskine in 1792, quoted in Pope, ii, 481-2.

[4] F. Vigier, *Change and apathy: Liverpool and Manchester during the Industrial Revolution* (1970), 52.

Even to a native inhabitant, Richard Brooke's father, remembering the town of his youth in the late-eighteenth century, it was 'a seaport town of very moderate pretensions'.[5]

Enthusiastic or not, most commentators seemed to agree on its nautical bias and its rapid growth, to the extent that it was claimed as 'the first town in the kingdom in point of size and commercial importance, the Metropolis excepted' by the end of the century.[6] It is the rapidity with which an insignificant mid-seventeenth fishing town on the Mersey was transformed into what could be claimed to be Britain's second city which makes Liverpool remarkable, and goes some way to explaining its peculiar urban character.

Economic Growth

In Jan de Vries' typology of European towns eighteenth-century Liverpool enjoyed the signal advantages of being situated in north-west Europe and having an economy based on Atlantic trade.[7] The result was a considerable early-eighteenth century growth: from about 7,000 inhabitants in 1708 the town increased to over 34,000 by 1773. The period of industrialization which followed saw more remarkable growth still: by 1801 it had grown to over 77,000, and by 1841 stood at 223,000, or more if outlying suburbs are included.[8] A fivefold increase in the seventy years before industrialization was followed by a sevenfold increase in the seventy years during industrialization. The demographic components of the growth have been described by Langton and Laxton. It was partly due to natural increase, Liverpool registering more births than deaths throughout the eighteenth century, but more important was in-migration. Between 1773 and 1801, for example, 80 per cent of the population increase was due to in-migration and only 20 per cent to natural increase.[9] Much of this migration was from the adjoining counties of Lancashire and Cheshire but Welsh, Scottish and Irish migrants were increasing in numbers, and the Celtic component of nineteenth-century Liverpool society was first introduced well before the massive Irish famine migration of the 1840s.[10]

---

[5]R. Brooke, *Liverpool as it was during the last quarter of the eighteenth century, 1775 to 1800* (Liverpool, 1853), 37.

[6]W. Moss, *The Liverpool Guide; including a sketch of the environs: with a map of the town* (Liverpool, 1796), 1.

[7]J.de Vries, *European Urbanisation* (1984), 138-42, 158-72.

[8]R. Lawton, 'The genesis of population' in W. Smith, F. J. Monkhouse and H. R. Wilkinson (eds), *A Scientific Survey of Merseyside* (1953), 121-2.

[9]J. Langton and P. Laxton, 'Parish registers and urban structure: the example of eighteenth-century Liverpool', *Urban History Yearbook* (1978), 76.

[10]Lawton, 122-7.

Population moves to economic opportunity, and in the case of Liverpool this was trade. The town took over from Chester as the major north-west port of England in the late-seventeenth century. In 1709 it handled 14,600 tons of shipping; by 1751 this had doubled to 29,200 tons; by 1800 it had increased fifteen times, to 450,000 tons; and by 1855 it grew nine times more, to 4 million tons.[11] The early staple trade was to Ireland, imports of food and linen, exports of salt and men, and so important did this Irish Sea trade remain that even in the late 1780s it accounted for 'more than the Africa, North America and West Indies trades combined'.[12] The eighteenth century saw oceanic trade take off; exports of manufactures to West Africa, of slaves from Africa to the West Indies and North America, and imports of sugar and tobacco back to Liverpool made up the infamous triangular trade.[13] Industrialization and the reaction against the slave trade towards the end of the century induced major adaptation; West Africa became less important as a trading partner, Northern Europe and North America more important. Major imports were added to sugar and tobacco: raw cotton to feed Lancashire mills, timber, corn and fruit. And exports grew spectacularly, cotton and woollen cloth from Lancashire and Yorkshire, metal goods from Sheffield and Birmingham, and ceramics from Staffordshire.[14]

The slave trade is notoriously associated with Liverpool but recent work has modified our perception of its importance and profitability.[15] By the 1740s Liverpool had overtaken Bristol and London as the nation's most important slave trade port but, in the context of the town's overall trade, slaves were only one element in a complex trading pattern. As significant were tobacco and sugar: imports of tobacco grew from 600 tons in 1704 to 8,400 tons by 1810; sugar imports increased from 760 tons to 46,000 tons over the same period. Even these considerable increases were overshadowed by raw cotton imports which grew from 2,000 tons in 1785, to 64,000 tons in 1810, to 360,000 tons in 1850, and United States wheat imports which leapt from 8,000 tons in 1810 to 75,000 tons in 1850.[16]

---

[11]S. Marriner, *The economic and social development of Merseyside* (1982), 31.

[12]J. Langton, 'Liverpool and its hinterland in the late-eighteenth century', in *Commerce industry and transport: studies in economic change on Merseyside,* B.L. Anderson and P.J.M. Stoney, (eds), (1983), 2.

[13] See F. Hyde, B. Parkinson, S. Marriner, 'The nature and profitability of the Liverpool slave trade', *Economic History Review,* 2nd series, 5 (1952-3).

[14]Pope, ii, 476-7.

[15]F.E. Hyde, *Liverpool and the Mersey: the development of a port 1700-1970* (1971), 31-4; see also essays in R. Anstey and P. Hair (eds), *Liverpool, the slave trade and abolition* (Historic Society of Lancashire and Cheshire, 1976).

[16]F.E. Hyde, *Liverpool and the Mersey: the development of a port 1700-1970* (Newton Abbot, 1971), 26-41.

A plethora of trade figures can confuse. What emerges most clearly from the Liverpool statistics is the exponential growth in trade during industrialization which eclipsed even the considerable eighteenth-century growth, despite the disruption of the wars with France (1793-1815) and the United States (1812-13), and trade crises in 1793, 1797 and 1813. Equally obvious during this period was the diversification of exports, a range of manufactures being added to the traditional staple commodities of coal and salt. By 1857 the annual value of exports reached £55 million, and Liverpool accounted for about half the exports of the entire nation.[17]

Much of this trade boom was caused by economic forces outside Liverpool, the growth of Lancashire, Yorkshire, Staffordshire and Warwickshire industry, the relaxation of the navigation laws in 1787 which opened South American trade, and the loss of the East India Company monopoly in 1813 which opened up eastern trade to Liverpool.[18] But as important was the remarkable and sustained effort made by the port to foster trade. Within the town this meant the creation of a large dock system, pioneering enclosed wet docks where ships could lie out of the fierce tide of the Mersey. It began with the Old Dock created from the Liver Pool, an inlet from the Mersey, in 1715; the Salthouse Dock followed in 1738, George's Dock in 1762, Duke's Dock in 1773, King's and Queen's Docks in 1788 and 1796, Union or Coburg Dock in 1811, and Prince's Dock in 1821. The dock engineers, successively Thomas Steers and Henry Berry, provided some 72 acres of docks before Jesse Hartley created the grandest dock architecture in Britain in Victoria's reign.[19] Ramsey Muir's enthusiastic comparison of the docks with the Egyptian pyramids is overstated no doubt, but one can see his point.[20]

The dock system was the key to the expansion of Liverpool's world-wide trade. Almost as important were internal transport improvements. Much has been made of an internal triangular trade between south-west Lancashire coal mines, mid-Cheshire salt mines, and Liverpool, which enabled salt to be moved, refined and exported in quantity to Ireland and Northern Europe.[21] The tonnage of coal carried to Liverpool and exported rose from 8,500 in 1770 to a quarter of a million tons in 1852, and salt increased from 14,000 in 1752 to 186,000 tons in 1820.[22] A commentator in the 1790s described

---

[17]*Ibid*, 36, 41.

[18]*Ibid*, 41-2.

[19]Marriner, 30-2; the best guide to the surviving docks is N. Ritchie Noakes, *Liverpool's Historic Waterfront* (1984).

[20]R. Muir, *History of Liverpool* (1907), 301.

[21]T.C. Barker, 'Lancashire coal, Cheshire salt and the rise of Liverpool', *Transactions of the Historic Society of Lancashire and Cheshire*, 103 (1951), 83-101.

[22]Hyde, 30, 41.

the salt trade as 'the nursing mother' of the port.[23] The way to shift such material was by water, and successive improvements to rivers (the Weaver navigation into Cheshire, 1721), and the building of canals (Sankey Brook to Haydock and Parr collieries, 1757-61; the Bridgewater Canal to Worsley colliery, 1759-61; the Leeds-Liverpool Canal through the Wigan coalfield, 1770-1816) were early signs of the significant investment in transport infrastructure that was to be so important a part of industrialization.[24] From being the worst connected port in the country, Liverpool, as Langton's authoritative survey shows, was by 1800 the best connected. The flow of goods along the waterways confirms the character of Liverpool's overseas trade; inland was carried raw materials for manufacture; towards Liverpool manufactures for export.[25]

Such improvements were the achievement of Liverpool entrepreneurs usually acting together as a town corporation. The town government of Liverpool was, from the renewal of its charter in 1695, extremely narrowly based. About forty councillors controlled the town and exercised the power of electing their successors. At the time of the reform of municipal corporations in 1835 Liverpool was recognized to be one of the least democratic of town governments. What it lacked in accountability Liverpool made up in its single-minded devotion to furthering commerce. Merchants made up some 80 per cent of the town council in the late-eighteenth century.[26] It was the corporation, spurred on by Thomas Johnson, M.P. for the town, which obtained the act of 1709 to build the first dock, put up the capital to carry out the scheme, and employed a succession of great dock engineers throughout the eighteenth and early-nineteenth centuries. Likewise, it was the corporation which initiated the survey of Sankey Brook in 1754, employing its engineer, Henry Berry, to do it. And, again, the town was involved in having the Leeds-Liverpool Canal re-directed through the Wigan coalfield in the 1770s.[27] Perhaps the clearest evidence of its commercial purpose was displayed in the depressed trading conditions in the wars from 1793 to 1815. When confidence evaporated in 1793 and banks were in danger of foundering, the corporation obtained a unique act of parliament empowering it to mint £300,000 to restore confidence. In the period that followed it pushed ahead with planning new docks and warehouses, building a new Exchange, and lobbying against the 1807 Orders in Council which

---

[23]Barker, 83.
[24]Marriner, 18-25.
[25]Langton, 7, 11-12.
[26]Muir, 166-74, 263-8; for an analysis of the council see Pope, ii, 451.
[27]Mariner, 31-1, 19-21.

prohibited trade with the French empire.[28] This was a corporation of merchants which acted with an almost aggressive commercial optimism. Moreover it invested in the commercial infrastructure of the port to the exclusion of almost every other need, as we shall see.

Who, then, made up this commercial elite, the Liverpool bourgeoisie? Our knowledge of them is disappointingly patchy. We lack even an idea of their numbers. One contemporary identified 150 Liverpool notables between 1775 and 1800, among whom there were 70 merchants, 5 bankers, 4 lawyers, 7 doctors, 5 clergy, 32 town officials, 1 manufacturer and 1 landowner (25 more were not described).[29] But this is hardly a reliable figure. Thomas Baines, a nineteenth-century historian of Liverpool, asserts that some 220 merchant enterprises were concerned in the commercial crisis of 1793, which is perhaps nearer the mark.[30] David Pope's thesis on shipping and trade in Liverpool 1783-93 is the most systematic analysis of Liverpool overseas trade that we have. Though he concentrates on commodities rather than the merchants who carried them some tentative generalizations can be deduced from his work. Some Liverpool merchants were indigenous; more were in-migrants, most from Lancashire and Cheshire. Many came from non-merchant families, from service at sea, or from craft or trade families, or from yeoman or clerical stock, and were apprenticed to Liverpool merchant houses to make good by luck or judgement. Some founded dynasties, the most notable being the Rathbones. Sawyers from Macclesfield, they migrated to Liverpool before 1730 to become timber merchants, shipbuilders and shipowners. By 1868 four generations had traded and contributed to the Liverpool community.[31]

Most notable about Liverpool merchants was their flexibility. They formed and broke partnerships as they saw commercial advantage. Though many specialized in certain commodities (salt, corn, timber, slaves), or places (the Baltic, West Africa), most found whatever trade they could, hawking their ships around the Atlantic, particularly in the early development of the transatlantic trade. Moreover, many developed other entrepreneurial interests: in industrial extraction or production (Nicholas Ashton, John Blackburne in salt); or in broking (Samuel McDowall); or in banking (William Clarke, Arthur Heywood). The occasional foreigner added an exotic flavour: Henry Wilckens

---

[28]F. Vigier, 75-6.
[29]R. Brooke, 464-85.
[30]T. Baines, *History of Liverpool* (1852), 494-5.
[31]Pope, ii, 425-33; E.A. Rathbone, *Records of the Rathbone Family* (Edinburgh, 1913), passim.

from Bremen settled as a dealer in salt, and achieved the distinction of becoming mayor of the town.[32]

It is not easy to generalize about the attitudes of such a varied group of people. Checkland describes the typical Liverpool merchant as a 'mercantilist, a materialist and an empiricist'. As the beneficiaries of the English Navigation Acts they clearly approved of government protection but opposed regulation which interfered with their trade, as in the abolition of the slave trade. They were men of action, adept at speculating and adapting, not men of theory or principle. Henry Wilckens said 'theoretical Adam Smiths bury practice'; and their following commercial advantage at the expense of principle is perhaps most clearly shown in the later years of the slave trade, and their continuing to trade directly between Ireland and the English colonies after this had been forbidden by statute.[33] Not surprizingly some proved skilled at privateering.[34]

Liverpool's success was, then, based on specializing in trade of many kinds, and serving as a conduit for imports of European and colonial raw materials and exports of cotton, woollen, metal and ceramic manufactures. As William Moss put it in 1796: 'the long established manufactories of adjoining neighbourhoods have rendered anything similar unnecessary here; and the minds of the inhabitants are more turned to the exportation than the manufacture of the different articles of commerce'.[35] But to see eighteenth-century Liverpool as only a port would be wrong. Manufactures associated with raw material imports flourished: sugar refining and tobacco manufacturing were important for example. To provide ships for the port there were said to be 3,000 shipwrights and associated businesses, such as roperies. Some 40 breweries were active.[36] Salt refining took place by Salthouse Dock. Pottery was an important craft with some 20 manufactories, the most famous being the Herculaneum, established in 1796. Metal manufactures were represented too: a copper and four ironfoundries were active. Three glassworks operated. Watchmaking was a renowned specialism. There were even four cotton mills in business, as well as a dyeworks, a stocking manufactory and a vitriol works.[37]

Quantitative support for this industrial activity is provided by an analysis of occupational ascriptions in the parish registers of Liverpool by

---

[32]Pope, ii, 433-46.
[33]S. Checkland, 'Business attitudes in Liverpool 1793-1807', *Economic History Review,* 2nd series, 5 (1952-3), 58; Pope, ii, 447-50.
[34]Baines, 493-4.
[35]*The Liverpool Guide* (Liverpool, 1796), 93-4.
[36]Moss, 93-4.
[37]Marriner, 47-57; Moss, 93-4; Langton, 15-17.

Langton and Laxton which proves the importance of industry in the town. Mariners, to be sure, were very numerous, accounting for about 25 per cent of the workforce. But craftsmen of all kinds outnumbered them, making up almost 50 per cent, and in the 1760s their number seemed to be increasing proportionately.[38] There was something of a manufacturing surge in late-eighteenth century Liverpool, largely explained by the influx of cheap raw materials, especially coal and salt, by way of the new waterway network. The town became a 'cornucopia of industrial resources'.[39] A great proportion of the raw materials was shipped out, but sufficient was retained to allow Liverpool to begin to emerge as an industrial town as well as a commercial entrepot.

As England industrialized, however, Liverpool de-industrialized. Investment was concentrated on trade and the port rather than manufacturing after 1800. Shipbuilding moved across the Mersey to Birkenhead; potteries closed down; salt refining moved upriver to Garston, and later to Widnes (and with it the nascent chemical industry); the cotton mills failed. By 1840 the occupation structure had changed dramatically; skilled craftsmen were few, and the Liverpool workforce had adapted to its nineteenth-century port-orientated pattern, dominated by commerce, and serviced by an army of mariners and unskilled and semi-skilled workers. Whereas in 1760 labourers accounted for a little over 10 per cent of the workforce by 1840 they had grown to almost 20 per cent.[40]

A detailed study of this de-industrialization has yet to be attempted. The most persuasive brief analysis of the reasons for the fundamental transformation is provided by Langton who argues that specialized centres of manufacture in north-west England achieved economies of scale which gave them an advantage over a port which had spawned a range of disparate industries but concentrated on none. The cheap and abundant coal, on which Liverpool's industrial surge had been mounted, was increasingly diverted elsewhere, resulting in a sharp increase in its price in Liverpool. Moreover, the supply of skilled manpower was diverted from Liverpool to other Lancashire manufacturing centres, and the resultant shortage resulted in a sharp rise in wages in Liverpool.[41] Such factors nipped manufacturing in the bud and created a port-centred economy in Liverpool in the early decades of the nineteenth century. The monopolization of investment and physical space by

---

[38]Langton and Laxton, 80.

[39]Langton, 15.

[40]P. Laxton, 'Observations on reconstructing the population dynamics of English cities c1750-1850: Liverpool as a case study', typescript paper delivered to seminar on Urbanisation and Population Dynamics in History at Keio University, Japan, January 1986.

[41]Langton, 17-20.

dock building, the hostility in Liverpool to the noise and dirt of manufacture, the effect of mass in-migration of unskilled Irish labour, destined, as it were, to provide low-cost casual labour for the needs of a growing port, must also have played their part. Already by 1800 commentators were aware of the increasingly commercial orientation of the town. 'Arts and sciences are inimical to the spot; absorbed in the nautical vortex the only pursuit of the inhabitants is commerce'.[42]

Social Consequences

Many of the demographic and economic developments outlined above, the rapid increase in eighteenth-century population, the high rate of in-migration, the wealth created by trade, the problems caused by de-industrialization, must have had an impact of Liverpool society, though too little research has been done to be at all specific about the social consequences of rapid growth. To begin with an obvious generalization, a small town of 7,000 people, as was Liverpool around 1700, will necessarily have a different feeling of community than one of 77,000, the size of Liverpool by 1801. Late-seventeenth century Liverpool was a physically small town, still situated within its medieval streets. Many inhabitants, certainly the heads of households, were expected to attend the port moot court, a communal assembly. And though there were governors and governed, rich and poor, the proceedings of the courts suggest that all were subject to rules of clearing ditches, keeping up fences, pasturing cattle and keeping markets which pre-suppose a rough communality in the society.[43]

This impression is confirmed by what we know about the geographical structure of the pre-industrial town. Sjoberg's well known model sets the elite at the centre of a town, and poorer groups clustering around the periphery. But with only five main streets, Old Hall, Tithebarn, Juggler, Dale and Castle, it is debatable whether centre and periphery would have been distinguishable in Liverpool. The governors lived among the governed. Merchants, craftsmen, fishermen, agriculturalists lived close together on rising ground above the Mersey and the Pool, their trades conducted from and in their houses in the town, in the traditional pre-industrial pattern.[44] This is not to argue that the

---

[42]Picton, 254.

[43]See, for example, G. Chandler and E.K. Wilson, *Liverpool under Charles I* (Liverpool, 1965), which contains Wilson's excellent transcription of the town books to 1649. After that date the manuscript town books are kept in the Liverpool Record Office, 352 MIN/COU 1/3-16.

[44]G. Sjoberg, *The pre-industrial city* (1960), 97-100, 118-23.

community worked smoothly, for there is much evidence of tension, but simply that its members lived and squabbled together in close proximity.

It is as a town increases in population and physical size that its society must fragment, whether this happens by different occupation groups establishing distinct quarters, a characteristic of large medieval towns, or by higher wealth or status groups separating themselves from the commoners, and distancing themselves from the congested, work-dominated, antiquated streets of the old town, as in modern towns.[45] In the case of Liverpool such social differentiation becomes obvious by the late-eighteenth century. On gently rising land east of the Old Dock, ceded by Lord Molyneux to the Corporation in 1777, Lord Street, Church Street, Hanover Street and Duke Street were built. They formed the core of a late-eighteenth-century 'new town' into which moved the merchants, brokers, lawyers and doctors who were at the apex of an increasingly complex Liverpool society; and the development of squares, such as Clayton Square and Williamson Square, and the siting of a theatre and library in the area underlined the social tone. Duke Street was described as the first attempt to provide an airy retreat from the busy parts of the town, its housing neat and elegant. Great George and Rodney Streets were to continue the process, and the survival today of their Georgian elegance demonstrates the success of this late-eighteenth century bourgeois enterprise.[46]

In sharp contrast were the suburbs which spread by the river, south of the Old Dock, a district called Harrington, and north of the old town, around Vauxhall Road. Here, in the 1770s, cheap slum housing was built to house the poorer classes. These were houses usually arranged around a 10 foot wide court or passageway, with windows facing inwards. Water supply was inadequate, sanitation grossly so, with, commonly, one midden for every six houses. The density of settlement was extreme, reaching 260 houses per acre. They were built on corporation land, leased and developed by the same entrepreneurs who mounted the trade of the eighteenth-century port. William Crosbie, a mayor in 1772 for example, leased land on which sub-lessees built Crosbie Street.[47]

There are signs, then, of a growing physical separation of classes in Liverpool. The old town, a place of trade and residence in the seventeenth century, with a heterogeneous mixture of merchants, craftsmen, labourers,

---

[45]J.E. Vance, 'Land assignment in pre-capitalist, capitalist and post-capitalist cities', *Economic Geography*, xlvii (1971), 101-20.

[46]Moss, 18-19.

[47]I. Taylor, 'Court and cellar dwellings: the eighteenth-century origin of the Liverpool slum', *Transactions of the Historic Society of Lancashire and Cheshire*, 122 (1970), 76-86.

agriculturalists and mariners, remained central, but lost its gentility and began the process of becoming a place to trade rather than a place to live. Old Hall Street and White Cross, 'once the most genteel part of town', was by 1796 regarded as narrow and dirty.[48] The bourgeoisie escaped to live in a new genteel quarter; the poor colonized new but low-rent and squalid suburbs near the docks. Not only did these suffer from the commercial clatter of docks and shipbuilding yards, but were also affected by industry: in Harrington was an iron foundry, a salt works and an oil house, and, near Vauxhall Road, iron mills, white lead works, an ash manufactory and the coal wharves at the head o⁕ the Leeds-Liverpool Canal.[49]

A further stage in the separation of middle from working class occurred when the wealthiest merchants sought 'green' residences in the villages around Liverpool. Everton, situated on a hill overlooking the port, was one such, colonized by the villas of the wealthy from 1757 when George Campbell built 'St Domingo'. Thomas Leyland moved north to Walton Hall in 1802, John Gladstone to Litherland in 1813. John Blackburne moved east to Wavertree hall. Nicholas Ashton moved south to Woolton Hall in 1772, Peter Baker to Carnatic Hall, and William Greenbank to Greenbank Hall in 1787, both in Mossley Hill. These are only some examples of dozens of Liverpool merchants who moved out of the urban area in search of clean air, peace and nature.[50]

Physical separation was one sign of a fragmenting urban society. Cultural differences are a second indicator. There is some evidence of distinct bourgeois and proletarian cultures evolving in late-eighteenth century Liverpool. Contemporary writers distinguish what men and women of substance wore and what they did for amusement: dresscoats, buckled shoes, heels, hoops and fans were for the fashionable. Merchants frequented coffee houses, in the churchyard of St Nicholas, the parish church, or on Paradise Street, where newspapers and intelligence of ships' movements were available. Balls took place in the Exchange assembly room. Clubs, such as the Unanimous Club, founded in 1753, provided Saturday evening entertainment. A theatre was established in Drury Lane in the early-eighteenth century, moving to Williamson Square in 1772, and a library was set up in 1756 in St Paul's Square, moving to permanent premises in the Lyceum in Bold Street in 1803. Walks were established in Ranelagh Gardens, Duke Street, Mount Pleasant and Everton Terrace.[51]

Such facilities were not for the exclusive use of the bourgeoisie, but their location and frequent expense suggest they were not aimed at the

---

[48]Moss, 60.
[49]Moss, 17, 24-5, 57-9.
[50]Pope, ii, 461-70.
[51]Brooke, 257-60, 164-5, 262, 290-8, 85-6, 89-92, 160-1.

proletariat who developed alternative amusements: the 917 public houses in 1797 (a reduction from the 1,500 a few years earlier);[52] cock fighting along Lime Street on Shrove Tuesday; Folly Fair along London Road at Eastertime, with the custom of lifting passers-by off their feet till a forfeit was paid; dog fighting and bull-baiting.[53] There is, of course, a value judgement in assigning coffee houses, clubs, theatres and libraries to the middle class, and pubs, cock fighting, and bull-baiting to the working class when the historian lacks direct evidence of the people who actually enjoyed each kind of amusement. But in justification such a division between the classes is upheld by the late-eighteenth century writers who described the Liverpool they knew. They were, of course, writing from within the bourgeois camp.

The vision such writers had of themselves and their class can add something to our perception of the hard-headed merchants on whose enterprise the trading fortune of Liverpool was made:

> Though few of the merchants have more education than befits a counting house, they are genteel in their address. They are hospitable, very friendly to strangers, even those of whom they have the least knowledge. Their tables are plenteously furnished, and their viands well served up; their rum is excellent of which they consume large quantities in punch when the West India fleet comes in, mostly with lime.[54]

How genteel they were we might have doubts of when reading the rules of the Unanimous Club, which seem designed to improve what might be described as gross behaviour, swearing, drunkenness and so on. And though a late-eighteenth century writer claimed that 'Commerce induces general harmony and sociability', untarnished by distinctions found in polished life, and produced 'that medium or quality so rational, grateful and desirable in society', we should take this encomium with a grain of salt. From what we know of the growing distinction between 'polite' and 'proletarian' Liverpool, equality was not a feature of the town. And such praise was meted out to the promoters of the slave trade and the builders of slums.[55] It is clear that the Liverpool bourgeoisie lived well and had a talent for getting on with others. Salesmen

---

[52]F.M. Eden, *The state of the poor* (1797), under 'Liverpool'.
[53]Brooke, 266-9, 113, 299-300.
[54]Letter of Samuel Derrick, 1760, in Baines, 475.
[55]Moss, 117.

usually do. But equally they were self-interested, philistine in their culture, and hostile to others with views opposed to them.

Among these was Dr James Currie, a Scot who settled in Liverpool in 1780 to practise medicine and found his views on the slave trade sharply opposed to the trading majority. He illustrates a division in polite society as the town continued to grow in the late-eighteenth century, coming as he did from the professional rather than the commercial middle class. With the opening of the Infirmary in 1749 and the Dispensary in 1778 there was an increasing medical presence in Liverpool made up of men with an outlook which did not always coincide with the merchants of the town.[56] Among the doctors Currie was exceptional in bringing from his education in Edinburgh a lively interest in philosophy and political economy as well as in medicine. But he met like-minded 'rationalist intellectuals' at the Philosophical and Literary Society, men such as William Roscoe, the art collector and historian of Florence, and Edward Rushton, the poet.[57]

Such men were isolated from the main stream of commercial endeavour. In Liverpool a man not engaged in business was said by William Shepherd, minister at Gateacre chapel, to be 'held in very light estimation in the public opinion'. Currie felt himself in a strange environment, 'shut up in this angle between the Mersey and the Irish Sea'. 'It is impossible not to rust here even if one had talents of a better kind' he wrote to a friend in 1800.[58] The fact that many professionals and intellectuals were dissenters or unitarians cut them off further from the prevailing anglican temper of the town. They worshipped at chapels at Benn's Garden, Rushton Street or Paradise Street, rather than in the anglican parish churches of St Nicholas, St Peter or St Thomas. Their difference was underlined by allegiance to whig principles rather than the dominant tory allegiance of the commercial majority. The issue of slavery was what marked them out as most distinct. When Roscoe stood as an abolitionist candidate for parliamant in 1806, the gulf between commerce and the professional-intellectual group in Liverpool had never seemed wider.[59]

The division in the middle class was not, of course, clear cut. Some merchants, William Rathbone prominent among them, were unitarian and whig. And the two groups did co-exist, tension only surfacing at election time. Dr Currie felt able to defend those in the opposing camp even in the battle

---

[56]On the medical history of the town see T.H. Bickerton, *A medical history of Liverpool from the earliest days to the year 1920* (1936).

[57]Checkland, 66-72.

[58]Checkland, 61, 72-3.

[59]Checkland, 63-6; for a study of elections in Liverpool at this time see E. Menzies, 'The freeman voter in Liverpool, 1802 - 1835', *Transactions of the Historic Society of Lancashire and Cheshire*, 124 (1972).

over abolition. He wrote to William Wilberforce: 'Of those of my acquaintance who are and have been Guinea men [ie. slavers] a great majority are men of general fair character - that some of them are men of considerable improvement of mind - and ... amongst them more than one ... of uncommon integrity and kindness of heart'.[60] This was, perhaps, special pleading from a man who had chosen to settle in Liverpool, but it does soften generalizations about the aggressive commercial nature of the Liverpool bourgeoisie.

Our knowledge of the working class is more sketchy. We can infer that it was divided between a maritime and a land sector (some 6,000 seamen were estimated in the 1801 census), between the small number of craftsmen who were freemen of the town with the vote, and the unfree majority, and, increasingly after 1800, between Englishmen and migrant Welsh and Irish workers bringing different languages, religions and customs.[61] All, however, lived close to the margin in a port where trade depression and war could create unemployment and distress. In the war with the colonies, 1775-83, some 10,000 people were estimated to have become dependent on relief. And during and immediately after the war with France similar crises occurred in 1809, 1812 and 1816.[62] The situation of the unemployed can only have been made worse as the industrial boom of the 1790s came to an end, and workshops and factories closed down.

Reaction to the resultant distress was surprizingly spasmodic. The most dramatic resentment flared in late-August 1775, when the potential instability of a large seafaring population suddenly became real. After seamen's wages had been reduced by a third in the depressed conditions of trade at the beginning of the war with the colonies, mariners on Captain Yates' ship, the Derby, being fitted for a Guinea voyage, unrigged the ship. A riot, involving between 2,000 and 3,000 seamen, spread into the town. The Exchange was besieged, and after several rioters has been killed by gunshot, the building was bombarded with a cannon, and several merchants had their houses ransacked: Thomas Ratcliffe in Whitechapel, William James in Rainford Gardens, Thomas Yates in Cleveland Square, and John Simmons in St Paul's Square. Order was restored by dragoons brought in from Manchester on 31 August.[63]

The few other riots in this period suggest that grievances other than wages and employment were more likely to provoke violence: the pressing of men in war in the 1770s; an increase in the price of tickets at the Theatre

---

[60]W.W. Currie, *Memoir of the Life, Writings, and Correspondence of James Currie, M.D., F.R.S., of Liverpool* (1831), 115-6.

[61]Baines, 507; for a discussion of free and unfree see Muir, 171-3; for Irish migration see F. Neal, *Sectarian Violence: the Liverpool experience 1819-1914* (Manchester, 1988), 7-15.

[62]Baines, 448-9, 538, 547; Picton, 334.

[63]Brooke, 326-47.

Royal in 1811; and, most ominously, an election riot in Castle Street against William Roscoe's support for catholic toleration in 1807 which resulted in the death of one of his supporters.[64] The rousing of religious passions so early in the century was perhaps an omen of the sectarian struggle soon to be brought about by Irish immigration. The first Orange riot occurred in 1819.[65]

Maintaining Community

It seems from the above that in spite of rapid growth, the growing gulf between middle and working classes and the insecurities of life in a major port tension seldom broke into open conflict during this period. This might be explained by the efforts made by the increasingly wealthy elite to provide for the poor and disadvantaged, and to create a decent urban environment. Philanthropy was, according to William Moss, a dominant feature of the town.[66] What can be deduced from efforts to span the divide between rich and poor, and create a Liverpool community?

What is obvious is that limited public effort was put into this. Liverpool Corporation defined its responsibility to the community in the late-eighteenth and early-nineteenth century narrowly. It saw its role as keeping order, fostering trade, and, to an extent, advancing the anglican religion by building new churches as the population increased. Some seven new churches were added to the town during the eighteenth century. Other objectives, which might be considered in the common interest, were considered a private affair. The water supply was left to private enterprise; refuse collection was contracted out; street lighting the corporation would install, but only if residents took over the cost of running it. No responsibility was admitted for regulating building and sewerage on the corporation estate.[67] The concept of a community responsibility for public health hardly existed, and in any case most late-eighteenth century writers thought Liverpool a healthy place.[68]

This restricted attitude to the public good, and belief in private effort extended to education and individual health care. Liverpool had a grammar school dating from the sixteenth century. It was allowed to die in 1802. Sunday schools were begun in 1786 but only in response to individual initiative in the parishes. A day school in Moorfields was established in 1790, and a free school built by Stephen Waterworth, a sugar refiner, in Hunter

---

[64]Baines, 453; Picton, 293, 278-9.
[65]Picton, 354; Neal, 40.
[66]Moss, 118-9.
[67]Vigier, 54-5.
[68]Moss, 105, 111, 115.

Street in 1792.[69] For a town approaching 70,000 people the lack of educational provision was a disgrace, and even William Moss, whose Guide of 1796 is so proud of the town, admitted that 'the lack of a public academy was always the cause of an unfavourable reflection on the town'.[70]

Health care was better provided but only through voluntary effort. An Infirmary was established in 1745-9 on land donated by the corporation, and a Dispensary in 1778.[71] But the costs of these institutions were borne by private subscription or by grants from the parish vestry. The same was true of orphanages, such as the Blue Coat School, established by Bryan Blundell in 1709, a private charity; so too were three almshouses for sailors' widows.[72]

The one exception to this voluntary philosophy was the provision for the poor, but only because of a statutory duty laid on parishes by the Old Poor Law. Outdoor relief was given to 2,700 paupers in 1797, and the workhouse accommodated 1,200 more.[73] The massive size of the workhouse is one indication of the scale of Liverpool's poverty problem, and as elsewhere in England in the war years, the burden of poverty seemed to grow appreciably worse. Successive attempts were made from 1786 to 1813 to raise a poor rate on shipping or from dock revenues, rather than from domestic ratepayers, but without success. By 1816 the cost of poor relief had got out of control and a determined period of expenditure control was begun, including a policy of returning Irish vagrant paupers to their own country. Some 7,000 were returned in 1827.[74]

We have, then, a town in which the public good was equated with commerce. Money was willingly put into dock construction to this end. But other needs, utilities, building and sewerage regulation, education, health and culture were regarded as private domain. And though voluntary effort was significant it always lagged well behind need, and the quality of life in the Liverpool community suffered. Only poor relief was regarded as a necessity that had to be met. The period we are describing is, of course, of some significance. The eighteenth century was not a time when the concept of government responsibility for the public good was readily accepted. Occasionally a crisis would jolt an anticipatory consciousness of the need for a concerted public policy. In 1802 an epidemic led the corporation, prodded

---

[69]Vigier, 58; Brooke, 379-82, 394-5, 403.
[70]Moss, 95-7.
[71]Vigier, 58.
[72]Brooke, 64-6.
[73]F.M. Eden, under Liverpool.
[74]W.L. Blease, 'The poor law in Liverpool 1681-1834', *Transactions of the Historic Society of Lancashire and Cheshire*, 61 (1909), 138-65.

by Dr Currie, to apply for a Liverpool Improvement Act to regulate housing, but it was not passed, and public control of the environment had to wait for the Health of the Towns Act of 1842, and the mid-nineteenth century era of urban reform.[75]

The opportunity lost proved disastrous for Liverpool. In the last decades of the eighteenth century, with a population rising to 77,000, the illusion of a healthy town, with its fresh sea breezes and the largely outdoor character of many of its workers, could just be maintained. But with the vicissitudes of war between 1793 and 1815, the de-skilling and consequent decline in the early decades of the nineteenth century, the increasing in-migration of poor Irish, and the legacy of an unplanned and neglected urban environment, the city of a quarter of a million people which Dr Duncan, the first Medical Officer of Health, took responsibility for the in 1840s was, by then in a state of almost pathological distress.[76]

---

[75]Taylor, 87-90.
[76]Vigier, 173-5, 181-4.

3: 'This Whig and Tory Ridden Town': Popular Politics in Liverpool in the Chartist Era

Kevin Moore

Has Liverpool always been a political enigma? The city has often had a major influence on national political developments, and yet rarely has its own politics mirrored the wider national picture. The Chartist period appears to have been no exception. The working people of Liverpool appear to have played only a very minor role in Chartism, judging by the general accounts of the movement's historians, despite the major impact of the movement on the country in these years.[1] And yet an understanding of working-class politics in Liverpool in the Chartist era is crucial to an understanding of Chartism as a whole, given the sheer size and economic significance of the city. From the 1820s Liverpool became the largest provincial town in mainland Britain, overtaking Edinburgh. The growth of its population between 1801 and 1851 was extraordinary, from 82,000 to 376,000, a rise of 360 per cent. In this period Liverpool also became firmly established as the second largest port after London. Despite this, there has been no systematic study of the role of the working people of Liverpool in either the trade union struggles of this period or the radical political movements which reached their highest peak in Chartism. Hence it is impossible to assess whether the impression that they were largely uninvolved is an accurate one. A lack of working-class politics of any kind has tended to be assumed by those writing about other aspects of Liverpool's history in this period, with the inference that it was a product of the peculiarities of the city's occupational structure, combined with the implications of the city having an unparalleled proportion of Irish-born people in its population.[2]

This paper will suggest that there was a stronger Chartist movement

---

[1]This is as true of the most recent as the earliest accounts; see in particular R. G. Gammage, *History of the Chartist Movement, 1837 - 1854* (1854, reprinted 1969); Dorothy Thompson, *The Chartists, Popular Politics in the Industrial Revolution* (1984).

[2]See, for example, Iain C. Taylor, 'Black Spot on the Mersey. A study of environment and society in eighteenth and nineteenth century Liverpool', unpublished PhD thesis, University of Liverpool, 1976, 7 - 11; Francois Vigier, *Change and Apathy. Liverpool and Manchester during the Industrial Revolution* (1970), 67 - 9.

in Liverpool than has hitherto been recognized, but that it was still comparatively weakly supported. It will be argued that the explanations posited in terms of occupational structure and Irish ethnicity do have some validity, but not to the extent hitherto assumed, or indeed, in the manner imagined. Other factors, not previously considered, play a much fuller part in the explanation of the comparative failure of Liverpool Chartism. Its weakness was not so much a reflection of a general lack of involvement in politics by the working class, as that it faced strong competition from other political forces for their support. There were other flourishing forms of working-class politics - partisan and nationalist - as significant locally as the Chartist movement itself. The key to an understanding of the weakness of Liverpool Chartism lies in an appreciation of the strength and appeal of these alternative working-class political tendencies, in what the Liverpool Chartists themselves called a 'Whig and Tory ridden town'.

The Liverpool Chartists

How strongly did Chartism develop in Liverpool? In January 1838 a Liverpool Working Men's Association (Liverpool WMA) was formed, modelled on the London association. The first Liverpool Chartist meeting to come to the notice of the press was in May of that year, when Feargus O'Connor lectured in the Queen's Theatre, 'to advocate Universal Suffrage', the *Northern Star* putting the attendance at 4 - 5,000. O'Connor returned to speak at a meeting in the Old Infirmary Grounds, Lime Street, in September, the first outdoor Chartist demonstration in Liverpool. The *Northern Star* claimed that 'from 5 - 7,000 hardy working men' attended, the *Liverpool Mercury* just 2,000 - 2,500, but the latter had to admit that the weather was 'exceedingly unfavourable'. While the Liverpool WMA continued to hold regular meetings, the next major demonstration was on May 20th 1839, in Queen's Square, coinciding with meetings throughout the country, as the Chartist Convention sought to test its support and determine its strategy. The by now hostile *Mercury* had to admit that there were 8 - 10,000 people in the Square, but claimed that only about a thousand were bona fide Chartists. The *Northern Star* put the figure at 12 - 15,000, but had to concede that some in the crowd had come to oppose.[3]

The numbers present at these main meetings of 1838 and 1839 were small for a city of Liverpool's size, when compared with other major cities. For example, the figures suggested by Read as being most likely for the

---

[3]*Address, with the Objects and Rules of the Liverpool Working Men's Association, established January 1838* (Liverpool, 1838); *Northern Star*, 19 May and 29 Sept 1838, and 25 May 1839; *Liverpool Mercury*, 28 Sept 1838 and 24 May 1839.

Manchester meetings of September 1838 and May 1839 are 50,000 and 30,000 respectively.[4] At these Manchester meetings - as also in such places as Leeds and Newcastle - Chartists flocked in from the many surrounding towns, whereas there were no equivalent nearby towns or out-townships to bolster Liverpool demonstrations. Even so, it is clear that Liverpool Chartism was considerably weaker than in the manufacturing districts in particular. Robert Lowery, who came to speak at the meeting in September 1838, felt that in Liverpool 'the population did not appear to be imbued with the ideas, and the meeting was not as large as we had expected'.[5]

Chartism began to develop much more strongly in Liverpool after the Newport Rising. This led to a sustained campaign to raise money for the defence of Frost, Williams and Jones, regular meetings being held throughout the first half of 1840. The Liverpool Chartists earned the thanks of the *Star* for the aid they gave to those Chartists who were tried at the Liverpool Assizes in April: 'They opened both their houses and their pockets to their brethren, and manfully sustained them through their many difficulties'. Although the trials were probably held in Liverpool because it was not a Chartist stronghold, the movement continued to develop in the city throughout 1840 and 1841. At a weekly meeting of the Liverpool WMA in September, the report of the Committee of management for the previous quarter showed that 'the position which the Chartists of Liverpool occupy is by far superior to any in which they have ever stood in that town'. The meeting voted that the Liverpool WMA would be dissolved, and henceforth they would be a locality of the National Charter Association (NCA). In December, the *Northern Star* reported that the Liverpool Chartists were now in a much more favourable position than even six months previously. They had a public room for their weekly meetings, which could hold 600 people, 'which on every Wednesday evening is crammed to suffocation'. Indeed, so much so, that other premises were to be sought in the south of the town.[6] In January and February 1841, a series of lectures by William Bairstow of Manchester, in the Owenite Hall of Science, drew audiences of up to 1,500 people. However, the report of the Liverpool Chartists to the *Star* demonstrates just how far the town was seen as lagging behind the movement as a whole:

> The cause is progressing here with more rapidity than can be
> imagined, considering the powerful influence we have to

[4]D. Read, 'Chartism in Manchester', in Asa Briggs (ed), *Chartist Studies* (1959), 44, 47.

[5]Quoted in Brian Harrison and Pat Hollis (eds), *Robert Lowery, Radical and Chartist* (1979), 110.

[6]*Northern Star*, 11 Apr, 22 Aug, 19 Sept and 5 Dec 1840.

contend with. Mr Bairstow's lectures converted some who have since joined us ... We are determined to redeem the character of this town and no longer to be a drag chain on the movement.[7]

The regular weekly meetings continued to be well supported throughout 1841, besides a number of larger meetings and other activities. In April, Peter McDouall spoke in the Association Room in Preston Street to between 850 and 900 people, hundreds being turned away due to lack of space; apparently, he 'created a powerful impression even in this sink of corruption'. A discussion class was formed in May, and met every Sunday evening. As elsewhere in the country, a local committee was formed in July to raise money to purchase a press for Bronterre O'Brien. In August, Lawrence Pitkethly reported to the *Star* on the Liverpool Committee which organized the despatch and distribution of that newspaper and other Chartist literature to Ireland. A lecture by Christopher Doyle, on 3 September, was 'by far the most numerous meeting we have had in this town'. At the end of the month, the Queen's Theatre was filled for a soirée in honour of O'Connor and O'Brien, though the former was unable to attend. Over 500 persons of both sexes partook of the tea. The object was to raise funds for the O'Brien press committee, which, when it was wound up in November, had raised £17. At the end of October it was announced that the Chartists had changed rooms from Preston Street, as this was now too small, due to increasing attendances, even though it could apparently hold nearly one thousand.[8]

The movement appears to have lost much of its momentum in Liverpool in 1842. The regular weekly meetings continued to draw reasonable attendances, but it proved increasingly difficult to draw the uncommitted to larger public meetings. This may have been a reflection of the severe economic distress of that year. When R. K. Philp came to speak in the Queen's Theatre in June Bernard McCartney, a leading local Chartist, alluded to 'the thinness of the meeting, which he attributed to the depressed position of the great bulk of the working population'. By the beginning of August even the regular meetings were switched back to the smaller room in Preston Street. The strikes in the manufacturing districts in August drew larger numbers to a couple of meetings, but did not signal a revival in fortunes.[9]

The period 1843 to 1847 marked a steady decline in the Chartist

---

[7]*Ibid*, 30 Jan 1841.

[8]*Ibid*, 1 May, 29 May, 24 July, 7 Aug, 18 Sept, 13 and 30 Nov 1841.

[9]*Northern Star*, 1 Jan, 22 Jan, 19 Feb, 5 Mar, 30 Apr, 30 July, 24 Sept 1842; *Liverpool Mercury*, 10 June, 19 and 26 Aug, and 2 Sept 1842; *Liverpool Mail*, 20 Aug 1842; and in general see K. C. Moore '"This Whig and Tory Ridden Town": Popular Politics in Liverpool, 1815 - 1850', unpublished MPhil thesis, University of Liverpool, 1987, 274 - 277.

movement in Liverpool, as elsewhere in the country. The weekly meetings were gradually reduced to a small hard core of supporters, and the only major stimuli were the visits of O'Connor. When he lectured on Irish Repeal in December 1843, the *Star* claimed that many people had to be turned away, but its report shows just how far the movement had lost support, while noting that 542 new members had been enrolled:

> ...our good old cause is now fairly afloat again. We took £12 10s (£12.50) at the door, which will get us out of our difficulties; and Mr. O'Connor has promised us another visit, when our numbers number 1,000, which will be very shortly'.[10]

O'Connor returned to speak in July 1844, which suggests that membership may perhaps have reached 1,000. The meeting in the Nelson Assembly Rooms was 'overcrowded' according to the *Mercury*, and over £12 was taken in admissions at the door. However, a meeting in April to elect a delegate to the National Convention in Manchester was 'thinly attended', and a 'Chartist camp meeting' in June on the sands at Waterloo attracted only about 60 people. Two lectures by Bronterre O'Brien in the week following O'Connor's visit were badly attended, so much so that the speaker observed 'that he never was in such an infernal hole'. 'About 40 individuals' attended the second, and O'Brien 'administered some severe reproofs to his brother Chartists for their non-attendance'. A meeting on Frost, Williams and Jones in November was attended, according to the *Mercury*, by not more than 50 people. The speaker, after complaining of the 'thin attendance', spoke of 'the apathy existing in Liverpool in the cause of Chartism'. In May, a branch of the Chartist Land Association was formed, but this does not appear to have been particularly successful. By June 1846, the position was such that it was felt necessary to have the following message inserted in the *Northern Star*: 'The Council sincerely hope that the members of the Liverpool locality will bestir themselves, and do something worthy of the first commercial town in the country'. A meeting in September concluded that the only way numbers could be increased would be to get O'Connor to lecture. But O'Connor did not return to Liverpool after his visit in 1844.[11] Liverpool Chartism enjoyed only a minor revival in 1848, overshadowed by the potentially insurrectionary activities of the Liverpool Irish rebels.[12]

---

[10]*Liverpool Mercury*, 8 Dec 1843; *Northern Star*, 9 Dec 1843.
[11]*Liverpool Mercury*, 5 Apr, 21 June, 12 and 19 July 1844, and 13 Feb 1846; *Northern Star*, 13 July and 15 Nov 1844, 17 May 1845, and 27 June and 12 Sept 1846.
[12]See ch 4, below; see also Moore, ch 6.

Liverpool Chartism: The Impact of Occupational Structure, Gender and Ethnicity

Liverpool thus had a stronger Chartist movement than has hitherto been acknowledged. Yet it was clearly considerably weaker than in the nearby manufacturing districts. We are able to appreciate the frustrations of the Liverpool Chartists in their inability to attract significant support, but they have left us little or no indication as to why the town was a 'drag chain on the movement'. Explanations by historians of the weakness of radical politics in Liverpool in this era have focused on the occupational structure, characterizing the city as almost totally dependent on its role as a port, and thus not a manufacturing centre of any consequence. Thus, it is argued, most of the workers in the town were unskilled, whether involved in the loading and unloading of ships, or in the construction of the docks. The few industries which actually expanded with the port, such as soap-boiling and sugar-refining, are also pictured as requiring largely unskilled labour. Industries with skilled workers which had flourished in the eighteenth century, such as shipbuilding and pottery, were in decline after 1800. Such a workforce, it is generally agreed, could have little connection with trade unionism or working-class radicalism at this time. Indeed, it has been argued that the disappearance of the traditional craft industries like shipbuilding and pottery 'meant the extinction of embryonic working men's organizations that had been able to evolve within the fairly restricted confines of the apprenticed trades ... With their disappearance, the workforce was unorganized and powerless'.[13] The 'casual' nature of a workforce largely engaged in the loading and unloading of ships is seen as important as its 'unskilled' quality. Eric Midwinter, commenting that Liverpool was 'strangely quiet' during the 'Chartist uprisings', has considered that 'possibly the very crudity of Liverpool's labour mart, with its haphazard drifting character, prevented considerable mass action'.[14] Such views probably owe much to contemporary accounts of the nature of Liverpool's economy, which tended to sharply contrast its 'unskilled' and 'casual' labour market with the need for skilled manufacturing workers in the Manchester area.[15]

---

[13]Taylor 'Black Spot on the Mersey', 8, and in general 7 - 11; see also M. Brogden, *The Police: Autonomy and Consent* (1982), 43 - 7.

[14]Eric Midwinter, 'The Inauguration of the Liverpool Police Force', in his *Old Liverpool*, (1971) 57.

[15]See, for example, the comments of William Cooke Taylor, quoted in *Northern Star*, 26 Sept 1840.

It can be demonstrated, however, that the traditional impression of the occupational structure is rather misleading. Contemporary commentators like W. Cooke Taylor highlighted what set Liverpool apart, but in the process over-emphasized the importance of dock labour. A study of the 1841 census figures of occupation does much to challenge the accepted view of an overwhelmingly unskilled and casual workforce. The structure of the adult male workforce will be examined first, because the generally accepted view of the occupational structure is based on the nature of male waged labour. Table 3.1 provides an overall picture of the occupational structure of the adult male workforce in 1841, and also provides a comparison with the figures produced by Robert Sykes for Manchester and Salford, using the same methodology.[16] Comparison is fortuitously aided by the close similarity of the aggregate totals. The figures show that 42.6 per cent of those enumerated in Liverpool were employed in 'manufacture', including building. Throughout this period, Liverpool remained a major centre of manufacturing, for the same reasons that, as Prothero has shown, London remained the country's principal centre of production.[17] Manufacturing remained largely on a 'handicraft' basis: small-scale, unmechanised and labour intensive, based both in small workshops and still to a large extent in the home. The demand for such everyday items as clothes, shoes and furniture in Liverpool, as in other towns, was still largely met by local workers. With no changes in technology in these trades, the rapid growth in demand led to a large increase in the number of shoemakers, tailors, cabinet-makers, etc. The building industry was also extremely significant, given the particularly marked growth of the city and the docks. Furthermore, account must be taken of the continued importance of several industries in which the town had long specialized, particularly watchmaking and the food, drink and tobacco trades. Shipbuilding did not actually decline, though it did not grow, yet ship repair required an increasingly large labour force, as the trade of the port grew so rapidly. The engineering and metal-working trades employed as many men in Liverpool as the Manchester/Salford conurbation, largely because the city had important steam-engine and iron- and steamship construction industries in this period.[18]

Liverpool was thus an important manufacturing centre in this era. The status of the men employed in its industries was predominantly artisan. The experience of these artisan trades in Liverpool was largely akin to that of their

---

[16]R. Sykes, 'Popular Politics and Trade Unionism in South-East Lancashire, 1829 - 1842', unpublished PhD thesis, University of Manchester, 1982, Table 1.7, appendix 1. For a detailed explanation of the derivation of the Liverpool figures, see Moore, app 1.

[17]I. Prothero, *Artisans and Politics in Early Nineteenth Century London. John Gast and his Times* (1979), 4.

[18]For a fuller analysis, see Moore, thesis, 12 - 35.

Table 3.1

Occupational Analysis of Males Aged 20 and Over, 1841

	Liverpool		Manchester and Salford	
	Number	%	Number	%
Textile manufacturing	436	0.6	14,412	19.8
Textile finishing	110	0.2	3,855	5.3
Building	7,419	10.3	5,873	8.1
Engineering and metal work	5,444	7.5	5,675	7.8
Clothing	6,447	8.9	5,819	8.0
Upper craft	2,463	3.4	1,781	2.5
Food, etc, manufacture	1,753	2.4	1,208	1.7
Shipbuilding and allied trades	3,261	4.5	-	-
Miscellaneous manufacture	3,292	4.6	3,410	4.7
Domestic service	1,840	2.5	1,893	2.6
Seamen	4,288	5.9	-	-
Other transport	4,161	5.8	5,563	7.7
General labouring	14,581	20.2	6,729	9.3
Mining and agriculture	1,649	2.3	1,466	2.0
Others	15,192	21.0	14,852	20.5
Total	72,336		72,536	

counterparts in the Chartist strongholds. The rise of both the factory system and the related spread of 'slop' or 'sweated' working practices threatened to erode or even end their customary craft status. Most of the Liverpool trades faced such challenges, not just the likes of the tailors and shoemakers, but also the building workers, and the shipbuilding, ship repair and allied trades. It is also clear that most trades had a strong tradition of unions to protect their interests.[19] Iorwerth Prothero has argued that trades with earnings over 30 shillings a week were likely to remain aloof from the wider trade union movement and political radicalism. These labour 'aristocrats' made up only a very small proportion of the Liverpool artisans, as can be seen from Table 3.1. Though the figure is larger than that for Manchester/Salford, the 'upper craft' category for Liverpool includes the one thousand clock and watchmakers, who in fact lost their high status and wages in the 1840s, and thus played a significant part in the local Chartist movement.[20]

All this suggests that on the basis of the occupational structure and the status and experience of the trades, one might have expected the development of a significant working-class radical movement. It was likely to be weaker than in Manchester, the figure of 42.6 per cent in manufacturing in Liverpool comparing with 57.4 per cent in Manchester and 67.8 per cent in Oldham, but both Manchester and Oldham were particularly strong centres of radical politics.[21] Clearly, then, other factors must be considered in order to account for the comparative weakness of Liverpool Chartism.

What light can an occupational analysis of Liverpool Chartism throw onto this question? Who were the Liverpool Chartists? One of the few sources available is the committee list sent in by branches of the NCA and recorded in the *Northern Star*. This, unfortunately, only gives us the occupations of 26 committee members (all male) for the Liverpool and Toxteth Park branches, namely 8 tailors, 4 shoemakers, 3 painters, 2 blockmakers, 2 watchmakers, 2 blacksmiths, a joiner, a bricklayer, a brass turner, a stonemason and a porter.[22] The only other available source is the (incomplete) list of members of the Chartist Land Company, which gives 171 names and their occupations for Liverpool.[23] There are problems of representativeness with both sources, but taking them together, they provide a rough outline of the local occupational structure of the movement.

Trades which were prominent in Chartism nationally dominated the

---

[19]*Ibid*, 12 - 35, 294 - 317.

[20]I. Prothero, 'London Chartism and the Trades', *Economic History Review*, Second Series, xxiv, (1971); Moore, thesis, 298 - 9.

[21]The Oldham figure is from Sykes, Table 1.7.

[22]*Northern Star*, 10 Apr 1841, 30 Apr, 1 Oct and 24 Dec 1842.

[23]For a detailed study of these figures, see A. Little's Appendix: 'Liverpool Chartists - Subscribers to the National Land Company, 1847 - 8', in this volume.

movement locally, particularly tailors, shoemakers, blacksmiths and building-trade artisans. These trades all faced the same threat to their craft status locally as was the case across the country. However, Liverpool Chartism was seriously weakened by the fact that the riverside artisan trades were almost entirely absent from the movement. Only two blockmakers appear in the NCA list, and two coopers and four sawyers in the Land Company lists, but these last two trades were not necessarily directly connected with shipping. Riverside trades were not absent because they were 'upper trades', aloof and 'aristocratic'. The dependence of the Liverpool shipwrights on repair rather than building meant that this key group lacked regular 'aristocratic' earnings. Only the sailmakers might be placed in the 'upper' trade category; however, they gradually lost their aristocratic 'status'. As a whole, riverside artisan trades endured very similar problems to those trades that were heavily represented in the Chartist movement.[24] Hence their absence from Liverpool Chartism requires further explanation.

Unskilled workers appear to have played little role in Chartism across the country. It would thus seem to be a crucial source of weakness to the prospects of the movement in Liverpool that about 25 per cent of the male workforce were unskilled, whether labourers or seamen. This compared with a figure of only about 10 per cent for the unskilled in Manchester/Salford (see Table 3.1). Yet if the general labourers in most large towns were too poor, too uneducated, and too disorganized to be involved in Chartism, it has to be considered whether the same conclusions can be reached about those employed in the particular kinds of unskilled work found in a port such as Liverpool. It can be argued that the label 'unskilled' has been misapplied to at least some among both the dock labour force and those who worked at sea, and there is some evidence of organization among both dockers and seamen in this period.[25] There was at least some involvement in radicalism and Chartism by the unskilled, a porter appearing among the NCA committee members, and 20 labourers and one mariner among the Land Company members. Indeed, a significant number of the unskilled in Liverpool were, as we shall see, involved in politics in the Chartist era - but in the Irish Repeal movement.

If the nature of the male occupational structure in itself cannot explain the comparative weakness of Liverpool Chartism, an analysis of the female labour market strongly suggests that the nature of women's work is an important contributory explanatory factor. When compared to Manchester or even London, there was a particularly marked lack of employment

---

[24]Moore, thesis, 308 - 16.
[25]*Ibid*, 320 - 2, 325 - 9.

opportunities in Liverpool for women.[26] There is no evidence of any trade union organization among women in Liverpool, despite developments elsewhere. As there were very few jobs outside the home, they remained largely isolated from each other and unable to combine, despite sharing similar employment. Domestic service, the main employment outside the home, actually left the women concerned even more isolated, separated even from their own families. Fewer Liverpool women shared the work experience of their husbands than in other towns, as relatively few male artisans worked in the home, the major exceptions being a fair proportion of the tailors and shoemakers. This is significant because Chartism was strongest where women were involved, and was thus a movement of the whole working-class community. Women's involvement seems to have been greatest in areas where either a high proportion of women worked outside the home, which gave them independence, confidence and the strength of numbers to organize; or where many women shared the work experience of the men in the home. The Lancashire textile towns were an example of the former, Nottingham of the latter, two of the strongest areas of the radical movement.[27] Women's participation in radicalism and Chartism in Liverpool appears to have been proportionately even weaker than that of men. While a seamstress and a housekeeper appear in the Land Company Lists, and women were involved in the local Chartist movement, there was never a women's organization, nor even a women's meeting. The relative lack of women's involvement in Liverpool was thus an important contributory factor to the overall weakness of the movement.

A further factor which militated against the involvement of Liverpool women in Chartism was the comparative absence of an anti-poor law movement in the city. The 1834 Poor Law Reform had little impact in Liverpool, as poor relief had been run on the harsh lines of the act since 1821.[28] The unimportance of both the poor law issue and factory reform also helps to explain why Chartism was as slow to develop in Liverpool as in London, only reaching its peak in 1840-1 - after the Newport Rising - rather than in 1838-9. However, Chartism developed in places where neither the poor law nor factory reform were significant issues, so their absence in

---

[26]For this analysis in detail, see *Ibid*, 49 - 63.

[27]For the importance of women in the Chartist movement in these areas, see Thompson, 120 - 151, and J. Epstein, 'Some Organizational and Cultural Aspects of the Chartist Movement in Nottingham', in J. Epstein and D. Thompson (eds), *The Chartist Experience: Studies in Working-Class Radicalism and Culture, 1830 - 1860*, (1982), 221 - 68.

[28]S. Kelly, 'The Select Vestry of Liverpool and the Administration of the Poor Law, 1821 - 1871', unpublished MA thesis, University of Liverpool, 1971; E. Midwinter, 'Liverpool and the New Poor Law', in his *Old Liverpool*, (1971).

Liverpool does not in itself explain the relative weakness of Chartism in the city.

The massive influx of Irish immigrants into Liverpool in the Chartist era has also been used to explain the weakness of Chartism in the town, since the Liverpool Irish are shown as having a powerful and independent political movement from the mid 1830s.[29] Of the population in 1851, 22.3 per cent were Irish-born, the highest percentage for any English town.[30] It has been argued that Irish migrants had little to do with native working-class radicals until 1848. Any moves towards links between Irish Repealers and Chartists were successfully crushed by the joint intervention of Daniel O'Connell and the Catholic Church. Dorothy Thompson, however, has provided a great deal of evidence of overlap between the two movements, even in terms of dual membership, particularly in the manufacturing districts.[31] What were the relative strengths of the two movements in Liverpool, and what links were there between them?

The Irish repeal movement was a significant rival to the Chartist movement in Liverpool - indeed, it can be argued that it drew more support. A branch of the Precursors, formed in November 1838, had 2,500 members by April 1839. When O'Connell spoke in the Queen's Theatre in August 1840, 'the capacious building was crammed in every part, and in the streets there were thousands unable to gain admission'. By this time O'Connell had wound up the Precursor societies and was urging his supporters to unite with the Liberals. The *Mercury* claimed that 10,000 people attended a Liverpool meeting on Lord Morpeth's Registration Bill in February 1841, at which the chief speakers were leading Liberals, and leading Irish reformers, such as Thomas McEnteer. But from January 1841 a Repeal movement developed, and a 'Repealer's Journal' was published in the town. By August 1841, the Liverpool Repealers had transmitted £220 to Dublin, and claimed a membership of 3,000. By January 1842 a Repealers' Hall had been opened in Paradise Street. The Liverpool Repealers fully shared in the upsurge of the movement as a whole in 1843. When O'Connell came to speak in February of

---

[29] J. H. Treble, 'The Place of the Irish Catholics in the social life of the North of England, 1829 - 51', unpublished PhD thesis, University of Leeds, 1969; *idem*, 'O'Connor, O'Connell and the attitudes of Irish Immigrants towards Chartism in the North of England 1838 - 1848', in J. Butt and I. F. Clark (eds), *The Victorians and Social Protest: A Symposium* (1973).

[30] C. G. Pooley, 'The Residential Segregation of Migrant Communities in mid-Victorian Liverpool', *Transactions of the Institute of British Geographers*, New Series, 2 (1977), 364-82.

[31] Treble, 'Attitudes of Irish Immigrants'; D. Thompson 'Ireland and the Irish in English Radicalism before 1850', in Epstein and Thompson (eds), *The Chartist Experience*, 120 - 51.

that year, it was again said to be the largest Repeal meeting ever held in the town, with thousands unable to gain admission. The Liverpool Repealers reported that while 'a few months ago the collection of 'rent ' ... averaged only £2 or £3 per week, at the present time it has reached £20'. The movement continued unabated in the early months of 1844. Liverpool shared in the slackening of activity and enthusiasm after the summer months of 1844, though regular meetings continued to be held throughout the next few years.[32] 1848 was to see many in the Liverpool Irish community come close to open rebellion, as is discussed in a further paper in this volume.[33]

There do appear to have been slightly more links between the Irish and the Chartists in Liverpool that Treble's argument would suggest, particularly given the support of the Liverpool Chartists for Chartists in Ireland, and links during the disturbances in 1848.[34] However, these links were nothing like as strong as those demonstrated by Dorothy Thompson in the manufacturing districts. In part this was no doubt a reflection of the particular weakness of Liverpool Chartism, and the unmatched size of the Irish community. The relative lack of involvement of the Irish in local Chartism was clearly not simply a reflection of their largely unskilled status, as this did not prevent them from being involved in politics *per se*. It will be argued below that it can only be fully understood in the light of two further factors: the strength of 'No Popery' agitation, and the support of the unskilled dock workers as a whole, both Irish and English, for free trade politics.

Artisan Freemen:
Peculiarities of the Electoral Franchise in the Chartist Era

In a previous paper, I argued that peculiarities in the local electoral franchise played a large part in explaining the lack of working-class radicalism in Liverpool in the 1815 - 1820 period.[35] A large proportion of the artisans already held the vote, as many as 60 per cent in 1812. As they comprised a majority of the electorate, they were able to use their electoral power to gain not just money in bribes for their votes, but also power at the workplace. The mayor and magistrates were unwilling to act against them in industrial disputes, for fear of losing their support in elections. The artisans who held

---

[32]*Liverpool Mercury*, 9 Nov 1838, 12 Apr and 28 Aug 1839, 26 Feb 1841, 3 Feb, 25 Aug and 15 Sept 1843, 16 Feb and 14 June 1844, and 28 Feb and 12 Dec 1845; Treble, 'Place of Irish Catholics in social life', 321, 331; *Liverpool Journal*, 7 Feb 1843; J. Denvir, *The Irish in Great Britain* (1892), 117.

[33]See ch 4, below.

[34]Moore, thesis, 334 - 343 and ch 6, *passim*.

[35]K. C. Moore, 'Liverpool in the "Heroic Age" of Popular Radicalism, 1815 - 1820', *Transactions of the Historic Society of Lancashire and Cheshire*, 138 (1989), 137-57.

the votes were predominantly from the riverside artisan trades. Trades such as the shipwrights and the coopers had a very high proportion of freemen voters in their ranks. Does this factor explain why these trades were most under-represented in Liverpool Chartism?

With the massive growth of the population in the 1830s, and the nature of the restrictions in the way the freedom could be gained, the proportion of freemen among the artisans fell, to probably just over 20 per cent by 1841. The freeman status was still important, but did appear to be losing its significance. At the same time, the freemen appeared to be losing power at elections. The Reform Act of 1832, by giving the vote to the £10 householders, meant that by 1837 the freemen made up less than 25 per cent of the registered voters, compared with a third in 1834.[36]

However, the working class freemen continued to hold the *balance of power* at Liverpool parliamentary elections, and it was their votes which ensured victory for both of the Tory candidates in 1837 and 1841.[37] Why did the freemen continue to be so markedly Tory in these elections? Bribery and treating was widespread on polling day in 1837, but as both sides resorted to it equally, this provides no answer. However, there were other kinds of bribery which the Tories traditionally undertook and the Liberals did not. The freemen were courted by the Tories with visits by the candidates to the shipwrights' and coopers' club rooms: William Allen, the shipwrights' union's leader, was honoured with a seat in Lord Sandon's carriage after the nomination at the 1841 election. The shipwrights' union was also bribed as a body by the Tories. On their annual parade in 1839 they carried a new banner, 'a splendid silk royal standard, trimmed with yellow silk (which was presented to the society by the members for the borough, and which cost £80)'. When the two Tory candidates spoke at the shipwrights' club room prior to the 1837 election, Alderman John Wright, a former Tory mayor, told them he would 'fit up afresh and beautify the room at his own expense ... It should be fitted up in a style, that would enable them to entertain those gentlemen within its walls (loud applause)'.[38] However, by the early 1840s, the electoral power of the freemen no longer appears to have given them any power in industrial disputes. The Tory shipowners did not feel the need to resort to the kind of political interference in the industrial field that they had made on behalf of the shipwrights in the early 1820s in particular. There was apparently no bribery or treating at the 1841 election; and in any case, it is unlikely that these other, superficial, forms of bribery were in themselves

---

[36]Moore, thesis, 34; *Liverpool Mercury*, 3 Feb 1837.

[37]Moore, thesis, 345 - 48.

[38]*Liverpool Mercury*, 28 July 1839, and 2 July 1841; *Liverpool Mail*, 27 July 1837 and 30 May 1839.

sufficient to account for the continued Toryism of the freemen.

William Shepherd, one of the most prominent middle class reformers, argued that the disfranchisement issue was the prime reason why the artisan freemen supported the Tories in 1841. Shortly after the election he wrote:

> There was no bribery or treating in Liverpool at the last general election. As Walmsley did not begin the practice, the Conservatives did not open their purses, for they were sure of the old freemen, who will never forgive the attempt of some of our party to disfranchise them and always vote against us when no money is stirring to mitigate their resentment.[39]

After their failure in parliament in 1834, the reformers had continued the disfranchisement campaign on a local level.[40] However, while the disfranchisement issue helps to explain why the *Liberals* were so unpopular with the freemen, it does not explain why they did not become *Chartists*. This cannot be explained simply in terms of the fact that they already possessed the vote. There were freemen Chartists in Coventry, Leicester and Nottingham, where at the election of 1842 three hundred freemen Chartists marched to the polls together.[41] These men were anxious to extend the political rights they enjoyed to the rest of the men of their class. The Liverpool Chartists, on the other hand, could not mount a demonstration of any sort at the elections of this period. A further explanation is therefore required to account for the continued Toryism of the freemen in the 1840s.

'No Popery':
the Religious Issue in Liverpool Politics in the Chartist Era

One factor which may appear to explain both the Irish community's rejection of Chartism in favour of Repeal politics, and the English artisans' continuing support for the Tories, is the religious issue in Liverpool politics. It has generally been accepted that the key issue in Liverpool politics in the late 1830s was a religious one. The attempt by the Council to introduce non-denominational education in the two Corporation schools allowed the Tories to raise a cry of 'No Popery!'. This has been seen as the main reason why the Tories regained control of the Council in 1841, and also gained both parliamentary seats in 1837 and 1841, Protestantism becoming their 'electoral

---

[39]William Shepherd to Lord Brougham, 11 Sept 1841, Brougham MSS, University College, University of London.

[40]*Liverpool Mercury*, 13 Oct 1837, 3, 10 and 17 Aug and 7 Sept 1838.

[41]Epstein, 241.

charm'. The Tories, it is argued, were particularly effective in drumming up religious bigotry among the indigenous working class. The net effect was to make 'religious differences the main line of cleavage between the parties', not only in the short term, but for much of the rest of the century, 'with the Liberals indelibly marked as the party of the Irish Catholics and the Tories by contrast a Protestant party with a strong anti-Catholic, no popery, working-class following'.[42] Was this the political reality in the 1830s and 1840s? Was working-class support for the Tories at elections based on 'No Popery'? And did the Tories gain the support of others among the working class, and not just the freemen, on the strength of this bigotry?

The schools issue did not have a long-term influence on local politics, as the Tories soon realized that it was increasing electoral support for the Liberals. By 1839 Reverend Hugh McNeile, the most militant No-Popery crusader in Liverpool, had to admit defeat, commenting that 'he thought the schools had succeeded, and would succeed, for there was not sufficient vital religion in the country to stop them'.[43] This was reflected in the weakness of the No-Popery organizations established by McNeile in Liverpool in these years. The Liverpool Protestant Association which McNeile had set up to fight the schools issue had lost much of its support by 1841. This was largely a middle class organization.[44] McNeile turned his attention to the working class, by establishing a Liverpool Operative Protestant Association in November 1838. Again, however, this gained little support, even its most mild-mannered petitions only receiving 2,000 signatures. In any case, Liverpool was not an exception; there were similar associations in many towns and cities around the country by the end of 1840.[45]

McNeile's Operative Protestant movement continued to exist in the 1840s, but there were fewer reports of its meetings in the press, and apparently none at all after 1845. This was almost certainly because the Orange movement had taken its place. The Orange Order as a whole had been officially broken up after the 'conspiracy' of 1835. It appears to have been revived in Liverpool in 1842: in March, 2 - 300 Orangemen marched in a funeral procession, and on 12 July there were four Orange lodges meeting in the vicinity of Williamson Square alone. The hostility they provoked in the Irish

---

[42]D. Fraser, *Urban Politics in Victorian England, The Structure of Politics in Victorian Cities*, (1976), 134; see also P. J. Waller, *Democracy and Sectarianism. A political and social history of Liverpool, 1868 - 1939*, (1981), 11; B. D. White, *A History of the Corporation of Liverpool, 1835 - 1914* (1951), 23.

[43]Quoted in J. Murphy, *The Religious Problem in English Education. The Crucial Experiment*, (1959), 143. For a revision of the importance of the schools issue, see Moore, thesis, 353 - 367.

[44]Murphy, 219 - 20.

[45]*Ibid*, 170-1, 219-21; *Liverpool Mail*, 24 Jan 1839.

Catholic community was sufficient to lead the authorities to fear that if they marched on that day, public order would be seriously threatened. The Orangemen were only allowed to meet at various places in the town on the 12th, and the entire constabulary of the town, including 60 mounted police, were on duty. A company of troops was also on standby. The Mayor wrote to the Home Secretary the following day that 'Yesterday went off without any material disturbance of the peace', but it is clear from the press and the report of Whitty, the Head Constable, that there had been some very violent clashes, with 24 people arrested.[46]

Orangeism enjoyed a significant upsurge in support in Liverpool in 1843 - probably primarily a reflection of events in Ireland itself. However, it is important to recognise that it remained organizationally small in numbers, despite Frank Neal's contention that Liverpool was the 'centre' of the English Orange movement. His estimate that there were 2,500 Orangemen in the city in 1845 is based on an *assumption*, without any clear evidence, that there were 25 lodges, with one hundred members in each. Harder evidence suggests that there were in fact no more than 5 - 600 Orangemen, belonging to 30 lodges.[47] Given the large size of Liverpool's immigrant Ulster Protestant community (one-sixth of the Irish-born population in 1841), it is conceivable that the indigenous population were not involved at all.[48]

Neal's contention that sectarianism was a significant factor in Liverpool politics in the later 1830s and 1840s is not, however, simply based on the supposed organizational strength of Orangeism. He also contends that 'Orangeism was far more widespread than membership of Orange lodges'. Large sections of the working class, he claims, supported bigots like McNeile who 'won over' the shipwrights and other freemen to support the Tory party.[49] However, as we have seen, largely because of the peculiarities of the local franchise, the freemen already had a tradition of support for the Tories. And if the Tories fought the 1837 election largely on the religious issue, it only served to *reduce* their support among the working-class freemen. The Tories received 3,977 freeman votes in 1835, but only 2,819 in 1837,

---

[46]*Liverpool Journal*, 19 Mar 1842; *Liverpool Mercury*, 24 June and 8 July 1842. On the concern of the authorities, see Public Record Office, Home Office Papers (hereafter HO) 45/249D ff 1 - 15; HO45/249D ff 18 - 19, and HO45/269 f 119, for the military preparations; HO45/249D ff 16 - 17, for the mayor's comment, and ff 20 - 22, for Whitty's report.

[47]F. Neal, *Sectarian Violence. The Liverpool Experience, 1800 - 1914* (1987),70 - 71; *Liverpool Mercury*, 11 and 18 July 1845; *Liverpool Journal*, 12 and 19 July 1845.

[48]*Liverpool Mercury*, 17 July 1846; *Liverpool Journal*, 18 July 1846; Parliamentary Papers 1836 XXXIV (40), *Royal Commission on Condition of the Poorer Classes in Ireland, Appendix G, State of the Irish Poor in Great Britain*, 27.

[49]Neal, 58.

recovering to 3,841 in 1841.[50] There appears to have been a disenchantment with the Tories among a significant section of the freemen in 1837, presumably as a result of the religious issue. Further, the Tories appeared to have received the support of the smaller number of working-class freemen who did vote for them as a result of a range of issues, not just the religious one. Indeed, a meeting of these shipwrights prior to the election suggests that these other issues, particularly disfranchisement and trade protectionism, were far more important in their support for the Tories than the schools question.[51]

If voting patterns tend to counteract the view that the working-class freemen supported Orangeism, violent clashes between the shipwrights and other freemen and Irish Catholics in this era would appear to support Neal's argument. The election riots of 1841, for example, he argues, were 'openly sectarian, Catholic working man against Protestant working man', with the freemen playing a major role among the latter.[52] Back in 1837 there were violent clashes throughout polling day at the parliamentary election, between crowds of up to a thousand supporters of each side, armed with clubs, staves, pokers and other offensive weapons. Six hundred police were on duty all day, and there were a 'great number' of arrests. The *Liverpool Mercury* put the blame firmly on the Tories' use of the religious issue in the campaign: 'need we be surprized that in a town where nearly one-third of the population is Catholic, banners inscribed "No Popery", paraded insultingly through the town, should have led to tumult and outrage?' This, however, meant that it had to admit that the initial aggressors were Liberal supporters - the Irish community. The *Mercury* also inferred that a 'sub-criminal' class, 'the very scum of the population', used the licence which the Irish violence afforded, for their own ends, such as looting and attacks on the police. Once they had been attacked by the Irish, it was inevitable that the working-class Tories would retaliate. Yet much of their violence was directed at the reformers *per se*, rather than specifically at the Irish. A crowd of shipwrights, 'aided by a mob of men and boys' smashed up the reformers' committee room in South Toxteth Ward, and then overturned a coach carrying reformers to the poll.[53]

It can be argued, therefore, that at the 1837 election the religious factor was of only minor importance in the freemen's support for the Tories and as a rationale for their physical clashes with the Irish. However, several violent clashes between the shipwrights and the Irish over the next few years might appear to challenge this view. In March 1839 the *Mercury* commented

---

[50]Moore, thesis, 348.
[51]*Liverpool Mail*, 22 July 1838; see also Moore, thesis, 358 - 61.
[52]Neal, 58.
[53]*Liverpool Mercury*, 28 July 1837.

that 'it is generally known that the Liverpool shipwrights will have a grand display on the 29th of May next, their present prosperity inducing them to make a "show"'. The 29th May was Royal Oak day, traditionally a day of festivity for the shipwrights. The two Tory M.P.s, Lord Sandon and Cresswell, presented them with a new banner for the occasion and about 1,000 shipwrights marched with several of their wives. Before the event, however, there were rumours that Orangemen were to take part in the procession, though this was firmly denied by the shipwrights' secretary when he was summoned before the Mayor. A counter-rumour soon spread that the Irish would attack the parade, but it passed off peacefully. The religious issue was however reflected in two of the many banners carried by the shipwrights on the march: 'The Church and the Altar' and 'The Bible, the whole Bible, and nothing but the Bible'.[54]

The next day, many of the shipwrights, apparently mainly apprentices, gathered in pubs determined 'to make two days of it', and were apparently provided with drinks at the expense of the Tory M.P.s. Fights were provoked with the Irishmen and the situation rapidly developed into a full-scale riot. The riots renewed with even greater ferocity the next day, several pubs where the shipwrights were meeting being attacked, and a crowd of over 500 Irishmen gathering. Those shipwrights who were at work clashed with Irish dock labourers in Canning Dock. The shipwrights then came out of the docks, armed with their adzes and mauls, and attacked the Irish in their own neighbourhoods. One elderly Irish man was fatally wounded after being struck with an adze, and a man with a loaded pistol was arrested. Over 300 police eventually managed to quell the disturbance.[55]

After the shipwrights' parade in 1840 there were again some disturbances, though nothing as serious as the previous year. Again, it was the apprentices who made up a majority of those who were seeking to make trouble. The march in 1841 passed off without any trouble but it was covered by 300 police. It was boycotted by large numbers of the shipwrights, presumably because they did not approve of the events of the previous years. Only about 620 marched compared with around 1,000 in 1839, and this time it included blockmakers and some from other trades connected with ship repair. There were a 'few fights' with the Irish in the evening. A few days later a crowd of largely shipwrights' apprentices, armed with bludgeons, attacked an Operative Anti-Corn Law Association meeting. The police intervened and the meeting was dissolved. The apprentices may well have been hostile to the repeal of the Corn Laws, but it appears that they attacked

[54]*Liverpool Mercury,* 22 Mar and 31 May 1839, and for the rumoured Orange involvement, 24 May 1839; *Liverpool Mail,* 30 May 1839.
[55]*Liverpool Journal,* 1 June 1839; *Liverpool Mercury,* 31 May 1839.

the meeting because of the presence of a large number of Irishmen. At the same time as the meeting was being attacked, other young shipwrights smashed the windows of the schoolroom of St. Patrick's Chapel. The next evening a large crowd of Irishmen retaliated by attacking the pubs where the shipwrights met and also attacked an Anglican church. The following morning 600 shipwrights stopped work and gathered in Canning Dock after hearing that their club-room was being attacked, but the police were able to convince them that this was unfounded.[56]

However, one should be wary of interpreting all this as indicative of a high level of anti-Catholic bigotry among the shipwrights. The shipwrights had supported the Tories at the 1837 election largely for reasons other than religious, but had found themselves under attack from the Irish nevertheless. What was developing therefore was a 'grudge or 'vendetta' between the two sides which had a rationale largely independent of the religious issue, and which increasingly took on a dynamic of its own. It is also clear that those among the shipwrights who started the trouble were the apprentices, and much of the blame for their violence can be put on the 'traditionally' violent behaviour of adolescent males. In addition, other youths, and not just the shipwrights' apprentices, were implicated in the disturbances, which, in 1839, for example, were said to have begun when three shipwrights' apprentices, followed by 'a crowd of blackguard boys' entered an Irish pub in Jordan Street.[57] The general religious toleration of the journeyman shipwrights can be seen from the fact that there were *Catholics* as well as Protestants among them, and that these marched *together* in the parade which preceded the riots in 1839. At the end of the march the 'protestant portion' went to St. Paul's Church, and 'At the same time ... the Catholic members of the procession were listening to a sermon in the neighbouring chapel of St. Mary, in Edmund Street'.[58]

At the 1841 election the religious issue does not appear to have been of any major significance. A colleague of McNeile remarked that he had read the addresses of the Tory candidates, and was 'sorry to see, that though the corn laws, and free trade, and other topics were touched upon, there was not a single syllable about our Protestant interest and institutions'. The address of Lord Sandon, one of the Tory candidates, briefly referred to 'encouraging the spread of religion and education on definite but *tolerant* principles' (my emphasis). While some of the flags of the Tory crowd on polling day referred to the schools issue, the most common banner among them was 'No

---

[56]*Liverpool Mercury*, 5 June 1840, and 4 and 11 June 1841; *Liverpool Chronicle*, 5 June 1841; *Liverpool Mail*, 12 June 1841.
[57]*Liverpool Mercury*, 31 May 1839.
[58]*Liverpool Journal*, 1 June 1839.

Manchester dictation'. Some of the Liberals' banners referred to 'national education' but most were marked 'Walmsley and Free Trade'.[59]

There were, however, violent disturbances at this election, if anything more serious than the riots in 1837. A flagbearer for the Conservatives was killed when his skull was fractured by a brick thrown by an Irish man standing on the roof of his own house; and a 17 year old Irish woman was shot and killed by a publican, when a crowd attacked his pub. Altogether over 175 people were arrested.[60] While it is difficult to assign a motivation to these disturbances, it can be argued that here too religious bigotry or anti-Irish racism played only a minor role. Again, much of the violence of the Tory supporters was directed not specifically at the Irish but at the reformers *in general*. The *Mercury* claimed that 'we saw young girls with Reform Colours chased along the streets, stopped, kicked, and abused in the most brutal manner'. The *Mercury* also again claimed, as in 1837, that a great deal of the disturbances had nothing to do with the election as such, but that certain groups were taking advantage of the licence which it gave:

> Large bodies of low vagabonds thronged the streets, and notwithstanding all the exertions of the police, broke the windows and doors of respectable persons, without the least provocation ... it would appear that party political feeling was not the sole cause of these violations of the peace.[61]

Shops were attacked regardless of their owners' politics. Again, adolescent males were responsible for most of the violence. Indeed, the *Journal* claimed that 'Nearly the whole of the riots have been perpetrated by lads from twelve to twenty years of age'. A great deal of the violence also appears to have been directed solely at the police. Superintendent Murphy reported that 'he was proceeding ... with 40 men, but when he got to Great Crosshall-Street, he saw a crowd of about two thousand men and women. The mob, on seeing them, assailed them with stones and bricks'. The apprentice shipwrights were implicated in the disturbances after the close of the poll in the evening, some of them parading thorough the streets with an Orange handkerchief, before clashing with an Irish crowd. The publican who shot and killed the young Irish woman was also a shipwright. But these incidents were no more than a small part of the riots as a whole and occurred

---

[59]Murphy, 221 - 231; *Liverpool Mail*, 29 June 1841; H. Walmsley, *The Life of Sir Joshua Walmsley*, (1879), 132.

[60]*Liverpool Mercury*, 2, 9, 16 and 23 July 1841.

[61]*Liverpool Mercury* 2 July 1841.

after much of the worst disturbances had already taken place.[62]

Violent clashes between the working-class freemen and Irish Catholics up to 1841 developed into a 'grudge'. How far did this 'vendetta' produce bigotry in the minds of the shipwrights? A large crowd of shipwrights joined the Orangemen in procession on 12 July 1842. While not claiming that the shipwrights were Orangemen, a correspondent of the *Journal* argued that there were strong links between the two groups, a point emphasised by 'XXX':

> it was always their intention to walk with the orangemen on the 12th July, so as to make a greater show, and to awe the Catholics. The whole of the carpenters are nearly all freemen, and both they and the orangemen are all church bigots.[63]

Another shipwright, however, was keen to refute any suggestion of violence. Speaking of a disturbance at a free trade meeting for the shipping trades, by a 'few carpenter boys', he argued

> Most of these lads belong to orange societies, and make it a point to go to the liberal meetings, and make a disturbance there whenever they can. But the respectable shipwrights listened with attention to what was said, and had the chairman given directions, there were quite enough of them in the room to turn the disturbers out. These lads have often brought blame upon the men, but the majority of the shipwrights, however they may be divided in politics, do not countenance such proceedings, and they regard the lads as a great nuisance. I hope these few remarks will do something towards removing the blame to which our character is liable, in consequence of the misconduct of others.[64]

This and other evidence suggests that involvement in Orangeism - particularly after the demonstration of 12 July 1842 - was limited to a few apprentices.

What, in any case, could have produced bigotry among the shipwrights and other working class freemen? The extent to which the Irish posed a threat to their jobs largely governed the success of its appeal, but the Irish were confined for the most part to the unskilled sector. Even here the English were able to keep them out of certain trades - the carters were still overwhelmingly

---

[62]*Liverpool Journal*, 3 July 1841; *Liverpool Mercury*, 2 July 1841.
[63]*Liverpool Journal*, 11 June 1842.
[64]*Ibid*, 15 May 1843.

English-born in 1851. To a large extent then, the Irish competed with each other for work and drove each other's wages down. There was a significant increase in the proportion of the Irish who could be designated as artisans in the 1840s, but this was largely a result of their breaking into tailoring and shoemaking. Far from being connected with 'No Popery', these were the two most markedly Chartist trades. There is little evidence that the Irish were able to break into the riverside artisan trades. In building it was the Welsh who posed the threat to the jobs of the English-born artisans.[65] Neal concedes that 'most of the Irish Catholics were unskilled labourers and did not represent a threat to the jobs of carpenters and shipwrights'. The only reason he can suggest for the supposed bigotry was 'simple xenophobia on the part of sections of the English working class'.[66] The evidence, however, points to a minimal involvement in sectarian violence by the English-born population. While the unprecedented influx of the Irish in the 1840s must have created tensions, 'No Popery' politics had nothing of the force it was to acquire in Liverpool for the best part of the next one hundred years.

Free Traders and Protectionists: the Whig and Tory Working Class

Rather than the religious issue, it was the question of free trade or protectionism which was to dominate Liverpool politics in the 1840s, beginning with the 1841 election. It was this issue which largely divided the working class between support for either the Whigs or the Tories, and explains their relative reluctance to become Chartists. The dominance of this question stemmed from the way in which it fundamentally impinged on the process of capital accumulation by the merchant elite. For many Liverpool merchants the logic in favour of free trade was unimpeachable: free trade meant more trade which equalled higher profits. At a League meeting in 1842 one merchant argued that:

> He had gladly given his £100 for the next year to accomplish the objects of the League; he had hopes he was promoting his own individual good to no small extent by extending free trade principles; he was not ashamed to avow his belief, that his £100 subscription would bring back a hundred times £100, if the objects of the League should happen to be attended with success.[67]

---

[65]Moore, thesis, 68 - 76.
[66]Neal, 41, 55.
[67]N. McCord, *The Anti-Corn Law League* (1958), 25.

This logic was clear to those merchants who owned few or no ships: they did not mind that trade came from foreign countries in foreign shipping as long as they were organizing the transaction. Indeed, there was a long tradition in Liverpool of merchants who specialized in the American trade, using American shipping, who also tended to be of Whig or Liberal politics. It was these who increasingly pressed for free trade in the 1840s.

The logic of opposition to free trade was equally clear for the other great interest group of merchants in Liverpool, those in the West India trade, who were traditionally of Tory politics. Their desire to protect the sugar monopoly stemmed from the fact that many, such as the Gladstones, owned extensive sugar plantations in the West Indies. Trade with the West Indies was largely carried in ships owned by these merchants, and thus free trade also threatened their profits as shipowners. In the light of the risks involved, shipowning may not have been very profitable, but it was vital as part of a chain from the plantations to the sugar refineries of Liverpool. Thus, as well as opposing any relaxation of the duties on sugar, etc., these merchants also opposed the abandonment of the Navigation Acts. This was coupled with a concern over the defence of the country. These merchants also opposed Corn Law repeal in order to protect the agricultural interest of their own party, and because it was seen as the first step towards free trade.

When free trade became a national political issue at the 1841 election, Liverpool became a vital battleground between the two sides. Indeed, the general election was provoked by Liverpool M.P. Lord Sandon's protectionist amendment - relating to the Liverpool West India merchants' interests against proposed Whig free trade measures - which brought about the downfall of the Government by one vote. Was Liverpool to be represented by free traders or protectionists? The freemen, composed mainly of artisans from the riverside trades, held the balance of power, and most Tory and Liberal propaganda to the working class was directed at these trades. The exponents of free trade argued that apart from the general benefit to workers throughout the country in terms of cheaper food and other items, free trade would bring specific benefits to the Liverpool riverside artisan trades. It would greatly increase the shipping using the port and thus increase employment. They calculated that the end of the Corn Laws would mean that there would be one hundred more ships in the corn trade alone: 'Here is employment for thousands of shipwrights, blockmakers, riggers, joiners, ropemakers, and all stopped - for what? ... For dear bread, dear butter, dear beef, and dear cheese'.[68] A shipwright in a letter to the *Journal* accepted the argument:

the depressed state of our trade during the last winter has set

---

[68]*Liverpool Mercury*, 19 Mar 1841.

many of us to think about the cause of it, and we have come to the conclusion that we should have had much more work if vessels came in and went out of the port more frequently than they do at present. Many of us now plainly see that this depression has been caused by the restrictions which foreigners have placed upon our trade, in retaliation for the restrictions which we have placed upon theirs, and that the best way to make all flourish, would be to take off the restrictions, and let nations, like private people, deal with each other as well as they can.[69]

However, few of his fellow tradesmen supported him. They did not believe that free trade would increase employment. Increased foreign trade would be carried in foreign-built ships, which brought little in the way of repair work, the main employment of the Liverpool shipwrights. When he was asked at the 1850 enquiry into Liverpool shipbuilding which class of vessel gave the least repair work, Linacre, the Chairman of the shipwrights' union replied:

Foreigners. If it were not for the colonial-built ships, our men would be in a state of starvation. We should be a good deal better off if you never let a foreign ship come into this port, for they do us no good, and nobody else, I believe.

McNeill, the secretary of the union, added: 'It is a common remark for us to make, when the Queen's dock is full of foreigners, "That is a sign of slack times"'. Foreign ships were no better built, but 'it is their niggardliness that will not allow them to lay any money out'. Only essential repairs were carried out in Liverpool, foreign captains naturally preferring to have their repairs done in their home ports.[70] For this reason a majority of the shipwrights consistently opposed free trade, and in particular strove to uphold the Navigation Acts. By opposing free trade and defending the Navigation Acts, the Tories could appear to be championing the shipwrights. The free traders on the other hand, could be denounced as self-seeking enemies of the working man. According to one shipwright in 1843:

we are, and still remain, quite opposed to the principles of the Radical Anti-Monopoly society. The Shipwrights of Liverpool are

---

[69]*Liverpool Journal*, 20 May 1843.

[70]*Shipbuilding in Liverpool. Evidence taken before the Committee appointed by the Town Council to consider the present state of the Shipbuilding Trade in Liverpool, and the best means which can be adopted for encouraging it* (1850), 134 - 5.

a loyal body of men, and are not to be gulled by a set of men whose only object is to enrich themselves and oppress the industrious working man. We all know cheap bread means low wages.[71]

The logic would have been equally appealing to the other riverside artisan trades that depended on ship repair, such as the ropers, riggers and sailmakers. It may also help to explain why the engineering trades were less involved in Chartism in Liverpool than elsewhere, given the very high proportion of them that depended largely on shipbuilding, but also on ship repair.

We must also consider the free trade and protection issue in relation to the other, unskilled trades, which depended directly on Liverpool's function as a port. There is little direct evidence of the views of seamen. One sailor did speak at an Anti-Monopoly Association for the shipping trades in 1843, commenting that 'Monopolies were evils; but if we abolished our own, other countries would not follow their example'.[72] Free trade might have been an attractive argument to the seamen, simply on the grounds that more trade would mean more work, but if this was carried in foreign ships, would it benefit British seafarers? Certainly, in perhaps the most important sector of Liverpool's foreign shipping, it would. The *Morning Chronicle* reported that 'of crews of American ships out of Liverpool, twelve or fourteen out of the twenty-four are Englishmen or Scotchmen'. American ships appear to have been popular with British crews because of better treatment on board.[73] If seamen were perhaps more likely to be drawn to free trade than protection, this was much more clearly the case for unskilled dockside workers, above all the porters, dock labourers and carters. To them, it did not matter whether trade came in British or foreign ships. More trade meant more work. This support of the unskilled for free trade was reflected in the massive Liverpool petitions in favour of repeal for the Corn Laws, including one of over 40,000 signatures. Working-class involvement in the organized free trade movement, however, was always limited: its supporters were predominantly unskilled dockside workers, who were either without experience of formalized politics or else committed to Irish Repeal organizations.

There is still one factor in this analysis which needs to be resolved. The strong attraction of either free trade or protectionism has been demonstrated. In different ways, both policies offered the possibility of an increase in the total amount of employment available. But so did Chartism through controlling

[71]*Liverpool Mercury*, 5 May 1843.
[72]*Liverpool Journal*, 27 May 1843.
[73]*Morning Chronicle*, 26 Aug 1850.

entry to trades and restricting 'sweating' by legislative means. A small number of seamen, porters and blockmakers were actively involved in Liverpool Chartism. Why did the overwhelming majority of their fellow workers not see things their way?

To a large degree the answer is that the Chartists did not have a coherent policy on free trade and protection . Many Chartists were in favour of repeal of the Corn Laws, as long as measures were taken to ensure that workers enjoyed the benefits of cheaper bread. Others opposed repeal, largely on the grounds that it would reduce employment in agriculture. The editorial comment in the *Northern Star* inclined towards protectionism, but not with any great consistency.[74] From the 1820s onwards radical ideology was inimical to foreign trade. An expansion of the home market was favoured in preference to overseas trade as the solution to low wages and unemployment. Gareth Stedman Jones has argued that 'the evil role of foreign trade' remained a constant feature of the Chartist analysis.[75] Chartism, therefore, could appear to be positively inimical to the interests of all Liverpool's port workers, though it is likely that it was primarily its inability to offer a step forward from the free trade versus protection debate which left it with little appeal to port workers.

As a result of the importance of the free trade and protection issue, the working class of Liverpool in the Chartist period was divided politically against itself, around four main stand points: Tory protectionism, drawing the support of the artisan freemen, particularly the riverside trades; support for the Whigs, largely as a result of the free trade issue, from the unskilled dockside workers, but also from some artisans - tailors often spoke at operative free trade meetings, particularly those who worked exclusively on seamen's clothes; Irish repeal, with considerable overlap, in terms of supporters, with the Whigs; and Chartism, drawing support from the remaining, but not inconsiderable, group of artisans.

The contours of support for Chartism, protectionism and free trade in Liverpool from 1841 onwards demonstrate the validity of this argument. During the 1841 election free trade was the dominant issue, free traders drawing far larger crowds to their meetings than the Chartists had ever attracted. Cobden came to speak at two meetings in the Amphitheatre, attended by up to 5 - 6,000 people, as soon as the government had fallen. An Operative Anti Corn Law Association (OACLA), which was propagated by the

---

[74]L. Brown, 'The Chartists and the Anti-Corn Law League', in A. Briggs (ed), *Chartist Studies*, (1959), 349 - 51.

[75]G. S. Jones, 'Rethinking Chartism' in his *Languages of Class. Studies in English Working Class History, 1832 - 1982* (1983), 115; see also I. Prothero, *Artisans and Politics in Early Nineteenth-Century London. John Gast and his Times* (1979), 228.

middle class liberals, held a meeting in Clayton Square, which was said to be 'filled on all sides', and further meetings in other areas of the town were reported to have drawn crowds of 3 - 4,000.[76] However, the working class freemen held the balance of electoral power, and it was their votes which ensured the return of two Tory-protectionist candidates.

Despite the large interest at public meetings the OACLA had few actual members. Large numbers could be drawn to OACLA meetings only at times when the free trade issue was at the forefront of national politics. At the first annual general meeting of the OACLA in December 1841, the supportive *Mercury* had to admit that 'a considerable number of respectable gentlemen occupied the stage, but the meeting was by no means numerously attended'. The Liverpool Chartists sought to pass their own resolutions at OACLA meetings in 1841 and 1842. The weakness of both movements is demonstrated by the low attendances, and the inability of either side to produce a clear majority a the meetings. However, at a free trade meeting in February 1843, when William Jones, the prominent Liverpool Chartist, attempted to speak, he and his fellow Chartists were attacked and kicked by 'a large body of men consisting principally of dock labourers, lumpers, and loungers, who are generally dependent upon the very men who were about to conduct the performance for the evening'. Yet if this was indicative of the fact that Liverpool Chartism was by now a spent force, so too was the operative free trade movement. Nothing more was heard of the OACLA until January 1844, when a meeting was held 'for the purpose of *forming* an Operative Anti-Corn Law Association' (my emphasis).[77] Yet if there was little organized working-class support for free trade, this was a reflection of the fact that it appealed largely to the unskilled, who were thus also predominantly Irish, and if able to be involved in organized politics at all, were in the Irish Repeal movement. On the other hand, Liverpool petitions for Repeal of the Corn Laws in February 1842 and May 1843 received 36,940 and 42,169 signatures respectively, indicating a considerable degree of support among the working class.[78]

The failure of the operative free trade movement prompted the Liberals' Anti-Monopoly Association (AMA) to switch their efforts towards the shipwrights and the other riverside artisan trades, who had until then been overwhelmingly against them. The continued depression in shipping made

---

[76]*Liverpool Mercury*, 28 May, and 4 and 11 June 1841; *Liverpool Journal*, 12 June 1841.

[77]*Liverpool Mercury*, 10 Dec 1841, 7 and 14 Jan, 22 July and 11 Nov 1842, and 26 Jan 1844; *Liverpool Journal*, 8 and 15 Jan, and 14 May 1842; *Northern Star*, 21 May and 12 Nov 1842, and 4 Mar 1843.

[78]*Liverpool Mercury*, 11 Feb 1842, and 17 May 1843.

them hopeful of winning some of them over - and this of course often meant valuable votes. First signs were encouraging. An AMA meeting in November 1842 for 'ship carpenters, block makers, coopers, ropers, riggers, sailmakers etc.', in the Nelson Assembly Rooms, on the causes of the depression in shipping and how employment could be created, drew an estimated audience of 2,500. A further meeting held in the shipwrights' club-room drew a 'numerous' audience and passed a unanimous resolution in favour of Corn Law repeal, according to the *Mercury*. However, further meetings drew smaller attendances, and by 1844 the AMA was forced to admit failure in its attempts to win over the shipwrights, and switched back to seeking the support of the working class in general.[79] In January 1844 the defunct OACLA was reformed, this time as the Operative Free Trade Society (OFTS). But this new society seems to have attracted little support. A meeting in February of around 300 was disrupted by working-class Tory supporters who apparently managed to get their amendment passed. Further meetings in March and April were also successfully disrupted by Tory supporters. An Operative Free Trade tea party in April drew an attendance described by the *Mercury* as 'not so numerous as was expected', despite the presence of John Bright. In May the *Mercury* described the OFTS as 'this rapidly increasing society', but this is the last that was ever heard of it![80]

When Corn Law repeal became a likelihood, however, the significant level of working-class support, suggested by the large petitions, became something of a reality. At a free trade demonstration organized by and for the working class in January 1846, the Liberal papers put the attendance at over 5,000. The appeal of free trade was not necessarily confined to the unskilled: artisans predominated among the speakers at this meeting, including a tailor, a millwright, a painter, and a Peterloo veteran. Two further meetings were chaired by shipwrights, and another shipwright and a sailmaker also spoke. However, a large body of shipwrights had disrupted a free trade meeting in the Amphitheatre, at which Cobden and Bright were the speakers, just a few days before. The shipwrights were to petition in favour of retention of the Navigation Acts in 1847.[81] If repeal of the Corn Laws gained widespread support in 1846, it can be doubted whether the vast majority of the shipwrights strayed from protectionism.

---

[79]*Liverpool Mercury*, 28 Apr, 25 Nov and 2 Dec 1842, 5 and 12 May and 18 Aug 1843, 1 Mar and 10 May 1844; *Liverpool Journal,* 26 Nov 1842, 22 Apr and 13 and 27 May 1843, 8; *Liverpool Mail,* 29 Apr 1843; *Liverpool Times,* 30 May 1843.

[80]*Liverpool Mercury*, 16 Feb, 22 Mar, 5 and 19 Apr, and 24 May 1844.

[81]*Liverpool Mercury*, 16 and 23 Jan 1846; *Liverpool Mail,* 17 Jan 1846; *The Porcupine,* 8 May 1879; Webb TU MSS, London School of Economics, 'Liverpool Shipwrights' Old Local Society, extracts from old documents etc', ff 346 - 375, 24 June 1847.

The peculiarities of Liverpool's politics in this era were thus only partly a product of structural factors, particularly occupational structure, ethnicity and gender. It is important to recognise that superstructural factors, such as the local electoral franchise, and the particular resonance of the free trade and protection issue, though ultimately rooted in the structural, also had a dynamic of their own. Equally, one must be wary of equating the later history of sectarian-riven Liverpool with the specificities of this era. We must also recognise and evaluate the significance of the fact that Chartism was not a seamless, uniform national movement. Was it not a great source of weakness for the Chartists that the second city of the empire was a 'Whig and Tory ridden town'?

4: Liverpool in the Year of Revolution: The Political and Associational Culture of the Irish Immigrant Community in 1848

John Belchem

The new cultural history of early nineteenth-century Britain has yet to complete its revisionist agenda.[1] Deconstruction has demolished the shibboleth of class, but other social formations await critical scrutiny, not least those groupings which precluded wider class-based behaviour. Gender and skill have been recognised as problematic constructs:[2] other 'differentials' have yet to be deconstructed. Ethnicity is a case in point. No less than class, ethnicity is a cultural and discursive product, a complex and problematic historical process of identity, consciousness and mobilization. By concentrating on the experience of an immigrant community in a year of political excitement, this paper will explore the problems of ethnicity in action. It is part of a wider study in the making of the Liverpool Irish.

In looking at the events of 1848, the focus is on the Irish Confederates, not on the Chartists. Liverpool was never a Chartist city, not even in 1848, the year of official (but counterproductive) Charter-Irish alliance.[3] While the dynamics of working-class politics failed to operate, the Liverpool Irish, faced with otherwise insuperable obstacles to collective behaviour, proved remarkably successful in 'resource mobilization'. By embracing sociological theory and linguistic post-structuralism, historians can begin to understand the achievements of the Liverpool Irish. Like other 'exiles of Erin', they adjusted to the shock of displacement within a sub-culture of their own construction. Their 'coping capacities' were mobilized by a network of voluntary associations which emphasized ethnic identity, while preparing the way - through conformity to the associational norms and conventions of the host

---

[1] For cultural history at its most strident, see James Vernon, 'Politics and the People: a study in English political culture and communication, 1808-68', unpublished Ph.D. thesis, University of Manchester, 1991; and Patrick Joyce, *Visions of the People* (Cambridge, 1991).

[2] See, for example, Joan Scott, 'On Language, Gender and Working-Class History', *International Labor and Working-Class History*, 31 (1987), 1-13.

[3] John Belchem, 'English Working-Class Radicalism and the Irish, 1815-50' in R. Swift and S. Gilley (eds), *The Irish in the Victorian City* (1985), 85-97.

society - for their eventual integration.[4] Mediated through the 'peculiarities' of Liverpool, however, this characteristic immigrant process took a distinctive and protracted form. Assimilation was little in evidence in 1848: indeed, the pattern of ethnic-nationalist associational culture in Irish-Liverpool was to facilitate the most disturbing political challenge in mainland Britain in the year of European revolution.[5]

Historical geographers have located the Irish firmly at the bottom of the local occupational and social hierarchy, a pattern established before the Famine influx rendered Liverpool 'the hospital and cemetery of Ireland'.[6] Factor analysis of the 1841 census - by which time there were already 49,639 Irish-born Liverpool, some 17.3 per cent of the population - has highlighted three major clusters of interrelated variables, a three-class model with an Irish/ unskilled/ lodging/ industrial service/ court house cluster at the base. Predominantly unskilled, the Irish tended to congregate around 'core-streets' in the city's two major working-class areas, close to the docks and the casual labour market: the 'instant slum' of the north end with its purpose-built court housing, and the failed middle-class suburb of the south end, hastily 'made down' into overcrowded and cellared street housing.[7] Strictly speaking, these were not Irish ghettos: outside the 'scale trap' of the core streets the index of segregation was not significantly high; while the persistence rate was remarkably low as the Irish, lacking attachment to particular jobs or dwellings, favoured frequent short-distance movements within familiar territory.[8]

These findings set the Irish in Liverpool apart from their migrant compatriots. The Irish in Britain came from a variety of social, economic and religious backgrounds: they were to distribute (and integrate) themselves

---

[4]L.H. Lees, *Exiles of Erin. Irish Migrants in Victorian London* (Manchester, 1979), 15-21 and *passim*. David Ward, *Poverty, ethnicity and the American city, 1840-1925* (Cambridge, 1989), 180-2. Dale Light, Jr, 'The role of Irish-American Organizations in assimilation and community formation' in P.J. Drury (ed), *The Irish in America* (Cambridge, 1985). For a less positive analysis of ethnic frameworks, see David Fitzpatrick, *Irish Emigration* (Dublin, 1984). For a brief introduction to 'resource mobilization', see John Bohstedt, 'Women in English Riots 1790-1810', *Past and Present*, 120 (1988), 121.

[5]My methods and conclusions differ from two earlier studies: W.J. Lowe, 'The Chartists and the Irish Confederates: Lancashire 1848', *Irish Historical Studies*, 24 (1984), 121; and Louis R. Bisceglia, 'The threat of violence: Irish Confederates and Chartists in Liverpool in 1848', *Irish Sword*, 14 (1981), 207-15. See also ch 1, above.

[6]Quarterly returns of the Registrar General, Third Quarter, 1847, quoted in I.C. Taylor, 'Black Spot on the Mersey: a study of environment and society in 18th and 19th century Liverpool', unpublished Ph.D. thesis, University of Liverpool, 1976.

[7]*Ibid*, 114-15, 213-20.

[8]J.D. Papworth, 'The Irish in Liverpool 1835-71: Segregation and Dispersal', unpublished Ph.D. thesis, University of Liverpool, 1982, ch 10.

throughout the urban hierarchy, taking up a number of occupational and residential opportunities.[9] Liverpool, however, was a case apart. Those who remained in this port of entry were the *caput mortuum* - Father Nugent was later to describe them as 'the dregs'[10] - unable, unsuited or unwilling to take advantage of opportunities elsewhere in Britain or the new world. Here was a breeding-ground of disease and social problems, a nether world surely beneath the bounds of political mobilization.

At this point, the social historian must look beyond census analysis, with its useful snap-shot reconstructions, to consider the complex diachronic process of social formation. In the interests of statistical accuracy, census analysis restricts the Liverpool-Irish to the Irish-born, an exclusion at odds with the inclusive pattern of ethnic associational culture.[11] Furthermore, the statistics, by their very weight, tend to obscure the minority of Liverpool-Irish above the cluster of adverse variables and lowly 'niche' occupations. Although apparently assimilated (in statistical terms at least), this middle-class group - merchants, professionals, publicans and tradesmen - provided an influential and respected leadership cadre for ethnic action, a common pattern in immigrant communities.[12] In Irish-Liverpool, indeed, these middle-class leaders enjoyed greater success than their counterparts in Ireland itself in enlisting their less fortunate fellow-countrymen in the Confederate cause.

In his written report on the Liverpool Irish to the Council of the Irish Confederation in Dublin in January 1848, George Smyth, a successful hat manufacturer in Paradise Street, calculated their numbers - 'including the children of Irish parents' - at upwards of 90,000 and stressed their contribution to the local economy at every level:

> The Irishmen in Liverpool perform nearly all the labour requiring great physical powers and endurance. Nine-tenths of the ships that arrive in this great port are discharged and loaded by them; and all the cargoes skilfully stowed. Out of 1,900 shipwrights 400 are Irish, or of Irish parents; and although Liverpool is a port rather for repairing than building vessels, there is one Irishman of the three or four master builders of the town, and many Irish foremen. In almost every branch of trade Irishmen, notwithstanding the many prejudices with which

---

[9] See the essays by David Fitzpatrick, Colin Pooley and Graham Davis in R. Swift and S. Gilley (eds), *The Irish in Britain* (1989).

[10] Quoted in Taylor, 101.

[11] For an interesting statistical attempt to calculate the size of 'actual Irish communities' using the 'Widnes factor', see W.J. Lowe, *The Irish in Mid-Victorian Lancashire* (New York, 1989), 49-50.

[12] E.J. Ives, 'The Irish in Liverpool. A study of ethnic identification and social participation', unpublished M.Phil thesis, University of Liverpool, 1988.

they have to contend, have risen to the highest promotion ... a large majority of the boot and shoemakers and tailors of the town are Irish, and I know that Irish skill is recognised in the various foundries. Many Irishmen are distinguished for their ability as architects, draftsmen (sic), and clerks of the works.

As the flood of immigration continued, this unacknowledged record of achievement underlined the iniquitous position of 'Famine' Ireland:

... there is an Irish trade with, or through, Liverpool, import and export, equal in value to between eleven or twelve millions a year; and greater than that of any other country of the world, the United States of America alone excepted. Yet a poor Irishman is denied the right to follow the wealth, and labour, and provisions of his country. On landing here, he is cast into prison as an idle vagabond; free trade England wants not him but the produce of his toil, or of the little farm from which, perhaps, he has been sent adrift.

For a nationalist like Smyth, equity for Irish immigrants meant justice for Ireland itself.[13]

A native Ulsterman, Smyth was a gifted organizer and fund-raiser, the founder of the Confederate Club in Liverpool in June 1847, one of the first such clubs of 'Unassociated Repealers', from which remittances reached the Dublin leadership 'with the regularity of the tides'. Previously, his talents had been deployed in support of O'Connell and the local branch of the Loyal National Repeal Association. It seems likely that he attended some of O'Connell's monster meetings in Ireland, travelling in the Liverpool delegation led by Terence Bellew McManus, a forwarding and commissioning agent prominent in the Irish trade. The acknowledged leader of the Liverpool repealers, McManus was another Ulsterman, a friend of Charles Gavan Duffy from early business days together in Monaghan.[14] In line with his current Liverpool interests - he passed £1.5 million in goods per annum - his involvement in repeal politics was two-way. The commander of the delegations to monster meetings in Ireland, Clontarf included, he was also the

---

[13]*Nation,* 15 Jan 1848. For a biographical sketch of Smyth, see 'Forgotten (Almost)', *United Irishman,* 25 Feb 1905, cutting in Clark Compendium, Diocese of Clogher Archives, Bishop's House, Monaghan (hereafter Clark Compendium), envelope D.

[14]T.G. McAllister, *Terence Bellew McManus 1811(?)-1861* (Maynooth, 1972), draws extensively on the Clark Compendium. R. Carleton, a Waterford trader, praised McManus's 'character for great integrity - so high his character that most of the Irish business was transferred to him', see National Library of Ireland (hereafter NLI), Mss 812, Briefs for the counsel in the trial of T.B. McManus.

chief steward at Liverpool gatherings, responsible for security arrangements during O'Connell's visits, when he hired the services of Mick Digney, a lumper on the docks, to recruit sufficient muscle from the waterfront to protect the Liberator from Orange attack. After Clontarf, however, McManus changed tack. Disenchanted by the humiliation, he sought an alternative to O'Connell's constitutional clerical nationalism.[15]

While Smyth continued to collect the Repeal Rent, McManus and his close companion in Liverpool, his second cousin Dr Patrick Murphy, moved closer to the nascent 'Young Ireland' group. An active member (and regular attender) of the elite '82 Club in Dublin, McManus joined Mitchel, Doheny and Meagher in a deputation in May 1846 to Smith O'Brien, imprisoned in Westminster for contempt of the Commons.[16] Speaking at Liverpool *en route*, Doheny publicly declared himself a 'Young Irelander', an incautious remark promptly placed in context on return to Dublin. Reporting back to Conciliation Hall, he deposited the week's Repeal Rent from Liverpool, a sum of £21 out of a total of £148, while 'eulogizing the repealers of that town for their undoubted patriotism and activity and more particularly Mr George Smyth, Dr Murphy and Mr McManus ... observing that Liverpool contributed more than Dublin'. At this stage, Liverpool was at the forefront of the movement, enervated in Ireland itself by dissension and famine - the next week Liverpool contributed (per Smyth) £28.6s (£28.30p) out of a total of £109.14s (£109.70p). A repeal stronghold, Liverpool became contested territory, a crucial site in internecine Irish politics.[17]

Under suspicion of resumed trimming with the Whigs, O'Connell sought to reassert his authority by an absolute proscription of physical force. He demanded the expulsion of George Archdeacon, Repeal Warden of Liverpool, for a speech on the eve of Smith O'Brien's release: 'they were prepared, even with their physical strength, if necessary, to defend their principles. (Cheers) They were a powerful body in Liverpool, and, formed into solid squares, they would beat two millions of Saxons. (Hear, hear)'. Archdeacon, a future Fenian leader, denied the words, but O'Connell insisted on his removal, the first of a number of dictatorial expulsions which finally persuaded Smith O'Brien to

---

[15]John Denvir, *The Life Story of an Old Rebel* (Dublin, 1910), 50; and Bisceglia, 210, which cites Meagher's description of McManus's Liverpool deputation to Clontarf as a '*corps d'armée* of incursive Irishmen'.

[16]M. Doheny, *The Felon's Track* (1914), 86. Richard Davis, *The Young Ireland Movement* (Dublin, 1987), 74-77, 88-90. According to the Rev. Hugh Quigley, McManus used to march along the Liverpool waterfront in the green and gold uniform of the '82 Club 'with the air of a prince, and a rifle on his shoulder', quoted in Bisceglia, 210.

[17]*Liverpool Mercury*, 22-9 May 1846. At its height in summer 1843, the Repeal Rent had topped £2,000 per week.

abandon his neutrality, to sanction the secession of Young Ireland from the Repeal Association.[18]

Smyth was quick to transfer his allegiance, promptly followed by McManus who resigned from the Repeal Association in a blaze of publicity 'to await other men and other times to win for Ireland that boon on which my hopes were so fondly set - the restoration of her power of self-government, whereby she may be entitled to raise her own revenues, and spend them in the development of her resources, and where men of all classes and creeds may be embraced without fear of ascendancy to any'. 'There is scarcely a locality in Ireland', the *Nation* averred, 'where his name will not be recognised, so wide are Mr McManus's commercial and social relations with Ireland; and wherever it is recognised it will suggest a man of the most earnest, laborious and disinterested patriotism - a man, we solemnly believe, who would not sever himself from O'Connell for all the honors and wealth England could bestow, but who is forced to that measure by the unhappy counsels that prevail in Conciliation Hall'.[19] A few months later in January 1847, McManus attended the foundation meeting of the Irish Confederation in Dublin, accompanied by his confidential friend and former clerk, the coal-merchant P. H. Delamere.[20] Next month, McManus, Smyth and Murphy were appointed to the Council: McManus was also to serve on the Trade and Manufactures Committee.[21] Back in Liverpool, Smyth undertook the arrangements for a local Confederate club, a project promoted by Meagher on his visits to the town. The Liverpool Confederate Club was thus firmly established before the Council announced plans for a network of clubs throughout Ireland itself, an exercise in 'elite' politics designed to curb democratic excess, secrecy and sectarianism.[22]

At the outset, the Liverpool Confederates were distinctly middle class. The local leaders - McManus, Smyth and Murphy - were respectively merchant, tradesman and doctor, while across the river in Birkenhead, the leading figure was the architect Martin McDermott, another Council member of the

[18]*Liverpool Mercury*, 5 June 1846. *Nation*, 6-20 June 1846. Lowe, 'Chartists and Confederates', 184; and Davis, ch 3.

[19]*Nation*, 5 Oct 1846. For John O'Connell's regret at Smyth's resignation, see *Liverpool Mercury*, 2 Oct 1846

[20]*National Reformer and Manx Weekly Review*, 30 Jan 1847.

[21]Royal Irish Academy (hereafter RIA), Mss 23H44, Minutes of the Council of the Irish Confederation, ff. 63-6. See also McGee's account of the history of the Confederation delivered at the meeting on 21 June reported in *Irish Tribune*, 24 June 1848.

[22]Clark Compendium, envelope D. 'The Queen against Francis O'Donnell and Others', *Reports of State Trials*, new series, vii, 642. John Denvir, *The Irish in Britain* (1892), 134. Takashi Koseki, 'Dublin Confederate Clubs and 1848', unpublished paper, 2-5.

Confederation, and an occasional contributor to the *Nation*.[23] Some of the Merseyside Irish middle class, however, continued faithful to the Loyal National Repeal Association, most notably the prominent starch manufacturer, John McQuatters. Somewhat disingenuously, Smyth dismissed these residual O'Connellites as 'low in status, persons who are not respectable in any sphere of life'.[24] Others favoured a different course altogether, seeking to promote their interests, to secure assimilation, through mainstream party politics. The Protector Society, established in 1839 to register Catholic voters, was succeeded in 1844 by the Catholic Club promoted by the Irish merchant Richard Sheil (cousin of the Irish Liberal M.P. of the same name) as a Liberal counterweight to McNeile's Protestant Association.[25] Thus, in 1848 there were a number of options for the Liverpool-Irish middle class: Confederate conspiracy; Repeal agitation; or the politics of electoral pressure. An important determinant here, it seems, was the extent of contact - over and beyond charity - with their less fortunate countrymen, the newly-arrived Famine poor. Some were heroic in their professional duties. In recognition of his exertions, Patrick Murphy was invited to preside at a meeting in February 1848 to raise a memorial to the monks of St Benedict who had given up their lives in the typhus epidemic - the 'Irish fever' - of 1847.[26] Significantly, two other members of the medical profession - Francis O'Donnell and Lawrence Reynolds - were among the most militant of the Liverpool Confederates in 1848.[27]

As well as his medical practice, Reynolds, a graduate of the Royal College of Surgeons in Dublin, was involved in journalism, sharing an office at the *Liverpool Weekly News* with John Brady, former secretary of the Regular Trades Association in Dublin. Following a familiar route for Irish artisans - Dublin, Liverpool and Manchester formed an inner triangle within a wider circle of trades' communication from London to Glasgow, Belfast to Cork, Bristol to London - Brady moved to Liverpool after the attempt to revive the Dublin

---

[23]McDermott is listed as Council member 57 in RIA Mss 23H41, Correspondence Book of the Irish Confederation. See also J.D. Balfe's comments on him, undated report, Clarendon Papers, Box 53, Bodleian Library, Oxford. I cannot agree with Frank Neal's assertion that the Confederates were 'men of no standing in Liverpool, indicative of the lack of political or organizational "weight"', F. Neal, *Sectarian Violence: The Liverpool Experience* (Manchester, 1988), 124 note 55. In concentrating on the Orange Order, Neal overlooks the associational and political culture of the Catholic Irish.

[24]*Liverpool Mercury*, 2 Oct 1846.

[25]Lowe, *Irish in Mid-Victorian Lancashire*, 130. P.J. Waller, *Democracy and Sectarianism: A political and social history of Liverpool 1868-1939* (Liverpool, 1981), 29. L.W. Brady, *T.P.O'Connor and the Liverpool Irish* (1983), 27-8.

[26]T.N. Burke, *Catholic History of Liverpool* (Liverpool, 1910), 95.

[27]Note the prominence of another Irish doctor, James Collins, in the early days of the Repeal movement in Liverpool.

guilds collapsed in 1846. The failure of the scheme - the latest attempt by the Dublin trade unionists to conform to the respectability and moderation demanded by O'Connell - caused Brady to question the Liberator's leadership. 'I ever was and ever will be opposed to O'Connell's assuming a dictatorship in political matters', he wrote back to friends in Dublin:

> I don't agree with you as to the young'uns running foul of the "good Ship Repeal". I think they only left when they saw the Commanding Officer & part of the crew likely to run her aground on the shoals of Whig patronage. I am a young Irelander and I believe them honest, hurrah for Repeal and no surrender to Whig or tory Governments.[28]

O'Connellite authority, then, was by no means unchallenged. After the Liberator's death in May 1847, his sons insisted on strict conformity to the constitutional path, but alternative policies proved more attractive in Irish-Liverpool. When the Confederation abandoned the confines of constitutional politics for insurrectionary ways and means, it enrolled the Liverpool-Irish working class in a network of secret clubs supervised by James Laffin, a tailor, one of the sweated trades with a concentration of Irish workers.[29] Here the Confederates built upon long-established 'Ribbon' networks, oath-bound links which had thrived in defiance of both O'Connellite and clerical proscription.

As in Ireland, Liverpool Ribbonism was multi-functional and morally ambiguous: secrecy and ritual served *inter alia* to promote republican revolution, organized crime, sectarian protection and collective mutuality.[30] In some cases, Ribbonism was based on the workplace, a primitive form of trade unionism which sought to control the labour market through threats and violence against outsiders. Irish migrants unaware of the 'goods', the latest secret Ribbon grip and password, often found themselves at painful disadvantage within dockside labour gangs.[31] For the most part, however,

---

[28]NLI Mss 10,511, John Brady to J.M. Kelly, 6 Feb 1847, and to Hunter, 1 May 1847. Fergus D'Arcy, 'Dublin artisan activity, opinion and organization, 1820-50', unpublished MA thesis, National University of Ireland, 1968, 9 and *passim*. See also *idem*, 'The artisans of Dublin and Daniel O'Connell, 1830-47: an unquiet liaison', *Irish Historical Studies*, xvii (1970-1), 221-43; and J.W. Boyle, *The Irish Labor Movement in the 19th century* (Washington D.C., 1988), ch 2.

[29]The Irish accounted for 57.5% of the tailors in Taylor's 1851 census sample, see Taylor, 7.

[30]Tom Garvin, 'Defenders, Ribbonmen and Others: underground political networks in pre-Famine Ireland', *Past and Present*, 96 (1982), 133-55; and M.R. Beames, 'The Ribbon Societies: lower-class nationalism in pre-Famine Ireland', *Past and Present*, 97 (1982), 128-43. A.M. Sullivan *New Ireland* (2 vols, 1877), i, ch 4, is still useful.

[31]Denvir, *Irish in Britain*, 127-31.

Ribbonism was centred on the pub, the focus of male-dominated associational culture.

In this period it was the pub, rather than the parish, which established the identity of Irish-Liverpool. This was achieved in a number of ways: by the character of the landlord; through the facilities for collective mutuality; and by the persistence of an 'underground' political culture. Jack Langan, an ex-champion Irish boxer, ran the most famous 'Irish' pub, strategically positioned across from Clarence Dock, the disembarkation point for most Irish immigrants. A well-known local landmark, it was immediately recognizable by the effigy of St Patrick, shamrock in hand, high on its walls. Langan enjoyed considerable fame and fortune in Liverpool - his estate was valued at over £20,000 on his death in 1846 - appearing on the platform when his hero, Daniel O'Connell visited the town.[32] At the request of Dublin Castle, Langan was kept under close scrutiny by the Liverpool police who concluded that the former pugilist was 'too wealthy and too prudent' to engage in secret Ribbon activity.[33] Lacking such celebrity, other Irish publicans sought to attract custom by offering their premises for various mutualist practices. Here the continuum of convivial and bibulous associational culture extended from 'Hibernian' burial and friendly societies, legally approved by Tidd Pratt and sanctioned by the Catholic Church, to secret Ribbon branches linked to networks across the Irish Sea. In his pub in Crosbie Street, John McArdle, another Ulster Catholic by birth, hosted a number of societies - including the Second Hibernian Friendly Society, the Third Mechanical Hibernian Society and a local lodge of the Ancient Order of Hibernians - some of which were a cover for Ribbon activities. According to an informer McArdle was a 'decent and moderate man who always opposed the continuation of Secret Communication with Ireland'. When appointed Liverpool delegate to the quarterly 'General Board' in Ireland at which the 'goods' were 'passed', McArdle chose not to fulfil his duties and had to be replaced.[34] While McArdle sought to promote Irish interests in an open manner - his public readings from the *Nation* were a regular Sunday night attraction at Crosbie Street[35] - other publicans were less averse to secret activity. The underground tradition was jealously preserved by Widow Hamill. She had been married first to Hugh McAnulty, a Grayson Street publican, the best-known

---

[32]Denvir, *Life Story*, 3-4, 52. *Liverpool Mercury*, 19 June 1846. Langan's featured prominently in 'Liverpool is an Altered Town', Liverpool Record Office (hereafter LRO), Collection of Broadsides.

[33]Public Record Office: Colonial Office Papers (hereafter CO), 904.7 f. 192, letter from Liverpool Police Office, 27 May 1839.

[34]CO 904.7 ff. 188-9; CO 904.8 ff.72-8, informer's reports, May 1840; and CO 904.9, ff. 203-6, Dowling's report, 18 Mar 1842.

[35]Denvir, *Life Story*, 15-16.

and most active Liverpool delegate to the General Board, and then to George Hamill who had continued with the pub and Ribbon connection until he too died, leaving his widow the custodian of the 'general Box'.[36] Similar activity was conducted at certain temperance venues: James Ord's temperance coffee-house in Marybone, venue of the Roman Catholic Total Abstinence Benevolent Society, was Laffin's operational base in 1848 and accommodated at least two Confederate Clubs (see Table 4.1); when in town, Irish delegates were received at James Lennon's Temperance Hotel in Houghton Street, the centre of insurrectionary planning.[37]

Under pressure from prosecution and Catholic and O'Connellite proscription Ribbonism was past its peak by the late 1840s, but its culture of secrecy persisted, enabling the middle-class leaders of the Confederation to penetrate deep into the immigrant community by reviving its network of meeting places in 'sympathetic' pubs, temperance hotels and private houses. Beyond these facilities for collective action, Ribbonism contributed a particular sense of 'national' identity to the Liverpool Irish, a construction - subsequently consolidated by the Catholic Church - in which Irish and Catholic became synonymous. Irish migrants were notorious for their intense regional and local loyalties, for importing their factional feuds, 'Connaught v. Munster... Tipperary v. Limerick ... Leinster Dingers v. Ulster Orangemen'.[38] While these 'private battles' persisted, sectarian violence soon came to the fore, registering a wider sense of national identity. Here the presence in Liverpool of large number of Catholic immigrants from Ulster and adjoining counties, prime Ribbon territory, was the crucial factor. Having imported their fierce sectarian loyalty, they were to rally their fellow-countrymen and co-religionists against the hereditary enemy, the Orangemen. Transplanted in Liverpool, Ribbonism was thus a pro-active force, forging a sectarian national awareness at a time when Orangeism, yet to be appropriated by the local Tory establishment, was an insignificant factor.[39]

Irish Liverpool acquired a northern identity, a character established through Ribbon links to the 'Northern Union'[40] and by the regional provenance of its

---

[36]CO 904.7 ff. 163-70 and CO 904.8 f.78.

[37]Undated report from Balfe, Liscard, Clarendon Papers, Box 53.

[38]*Liverpool Journal,* 25 Nov 1843, quoted in Kevin Moore, '"This Whig and Tory Ridden Town": Popular Politics in Liverpool, 1815-1850', unpublished M.Phil thesis, University of Liverpool, 1988. See also Anne Bryson, 'Riot and its control in Liverpool, 1815-1860', unpublished M.Phil thesis, Open University, 1990.

[39]On the origins of Orangeism in Liverpool, see Neal, 17-32.

[40]Liverpool accounted for two of the original nine committees 'in the north', see Sirr Diaries, 3 Feb 1822, Trinity College Dublin (hereafter TCD), Mss N4.7 f.106.

middle-class Catholic Repeal politicians.[41] Reporting back to Dublin in April 1848, Doheny was impressed by the ardour of 'many northerns (sic) who have acquired rank, and station, and wealth in Liverpool ... If their feeling be an index of the north, you may soon expect to see the province far in advance of the rest of Ireland'.[42] Liverpool, indeed, set the standard for the 'nationalist' north.

This northern complexion produced a sectarian pattern of associational culture and nationalist politics, a formulation established without the aid or blessing of the Catholic Church. Having left Ireland before its 'devotional revolution', the migrants were unacquainted with the discipline of modern Tridentine conformism and thus posed an unwelcome challenge to the church, detracting from the high standard of practice among the small English Catholic community. Non-practising but not indifferent, the Irish approached religion in a 'do-it-yourself' fashion, while attending to their worldly well-being through primary welfare networks operated by women and male-based networks of collective mutuality, protected by secrecy and Ribbon oath. Unaccustomed to such 'client self-reliance', the Church, manned for the most part by English priests, finally mounted a counter-offensive. Ribbonism was proscribed, some Irish priests were appointed, and most important, if not fully in place until after 1850, the church developed its own framework of associational culture, based on the parish, offering sustenance and support for Irish immigrants, male and female, from cradle to grave.[43] It was this cultural provision, subsequently replicated in the United States and Australia, which 'made Irish, Catholic, and Catholic, Irish.'[44]

In 1848 Confederate leaders in Liverpool could appeal to a strong sense of national identity in the ethnic Irish community. However, large groups of newly-arrived Famine immigrants remained beyond their influence: the very poor, for whom politics was not an option in the daily struggle for survival; and the psychologically disorientated, migrants frustrated in their plans to proceed to America, who still persuaded themselves their stay in Liverpool would be temporary and thus eschewed any form of involvement. What follows is an attempt to reconstruct the networks and activities of those

---

[41]Throughout his writings, Denvir repeatedly stresses the prominence in Liverpool of northern Irish Catholics like himself.

[42]*Nation*, 6 May 1848.

[43]G. Connolly, 'Irish and Catholic: myth or reality? Another sort of Irish and the renewal of the clerical profession among Catholics in England, 1791-1818' in Swift and Gilley, *Irish in the Victorian City*, 225-54; Lowe, *Irish in Mid-Victorian Lancashire*, ch 5; J.H. Treble, 'The Attitude of the Roman Catholic Church towards Trade Unionism in the North of England', *Northern History*, v (1970), 93-113; and Papworth, 163.

[44]Light, 13-42; Patrick O'Farrell, *The Irish in Australia* (Kensington, NSW, 1986), ch 5

involved in conspiratorial politics. It has proved possible to penetrate this secret masculine world: the female networks which radiated from the 'core streets' of mid nineteenth-century Irish Liverpool remain, regrettably, hidden from history.

II

Studies of 1848 have overlooked the mechanics of immigrant mobilization. Attention has focused on class-based protest, on the failure of Chartism to integrate its new Irish allies into a successful working-class challenge.[45] The formal alliance with the Irish, long the desideratum of Feargus O'Connor and other Chartist leaders, owed little to Liverpool politics. Manchester, a much stronger Chartist centre, took the lead in this aspect of Anglo-Irish relations. At the first anniversary meeting of the Confederation in Dublin in January 1848 (at which McManus, Reynolds and Smyth were re-elected to the Council), it was not the Merseyside delegation - Reynolds, McDermott and James O'Brien - who spoke most fervently in favour of a Chartist-Confederate alliance, but James Leach, the leading Manchester Chartist, ably supported by another second generation Irish immigrant, Bernard Treanor of Stalybridge one of the expelled Repeal Wardens.[46] Other overtures followed, but the ban on Irish involvement in 'physical force' Chartism remained in place until news reached Dublin of revolution in Paris.[47]

Arrangements were then immediately set in hand through the Trades and Citizens Committee in Dublin and the Repeal Confederates in Manchester for a great demonstration in Manchester on St Patrick's Day to seal the new union.[48] Henceforth, this Manchester-Dublin axis served as the main public channel between British Chartists and Irish Confederates: the Repeal Delegates in Manchester, a regional body of which Treanor was chair, and Archdeacon secretary, coordinated arrangements for an overwhelming public display of

---

[45]Belchem; Lowe, 'Chartists and Confederates'; and John Saville, *1848. The British state and the Chartist movement* (Cambridge, 1987).

[46]*Nation*, 15 Jan, and *Liverpool Mercury*, 18 Jan 1848. Treanor introduced himself as a native of England whose heart 'was as Irish as the hill of Howth'.

[47]For efforts within Ireland to remove the ban, see Takashi Koseki, *Patrick O'Higgins and Irish Chartism* (Hosei University, Ireland Japan Papers, 2).

[48]There is much Dublin-Manchester correspondence in RIA 23H41 and 23H44. See also: State Paper Office, Dublin, Official Papers OP1848/105, correspondence found in Doheny's house after the rising; NLI Mss 442, Smith O'Brien Papers, ff. 2389-2391, letters from Treanor and Halpin; TCD Mss 2040, Trades and Citizens Committee; and *United Irishman*, 12 Feb - 22 Mar 1848.

combined support.[49] By contrast, events in Liverpool took a secret, more insurrectionary and 'Irish' form.

From the outset, there was intense interest in debates in Dublin, where John Mitchel, a militant convert to James Fintan Lalor's social radicalism, abandoned the Confederation and constitutional methods to advocate passive resistance, if not open civil war, in his *United Irishman*. Mitchel was soon welcomed back to Confederate counsels, vindicated by the outbreak of European revolution.[50] Thereafter, militant rhetoric was the order of the day in Dublin, but the Liverpool-Irish grew impatient with its defensive parameters. Having rejected O'Connellite constitutionalism, they were keen to proceed further, to begin active preparation for civil war.

Revolution in France convinced the Liverpool Confederates of the efficacy of physical force. Henceforth, they were to operate simultaneously at different levels, public and secret. In public, the aim was a strong united front: here McManus, Murphy and Smyth sought to enrol repentant O'Connellites and renegade Orangemen, while Reynolds and Matthew Somers, a provisions dealer, canvassed support, somewhat incautiously, among local Chartists. In secret, plans were laid for diversionary activity, to set the docks and town ablaze once Ireland was 'up'.

Large crowds flocked to the weekly Confederate meeting at the George IV Assembly Room on 27 February, encouraging the leaders to convene a public meeting to congratulate the French.[51] Placards were posted, printed by Thomas Kenny, a local printer in Whitechapel and Liverpool agent for the *United Irishman*, under the slogan 'France and Liberty! Ireland and Repeal!' 'The power of Irishmen for good or evil, is now felt in Liverpool', the *Nation* averred: 'They divide the interest in public events at this moment with the people of Paris'. The meeting on 5 March, chaired by Dr. Murphy, was packed to capacity, but the magistrates accorded it little attention.[52] Within a few days, however, they were to place the town under a state of alarm. Two factors prompted this dramatic change in attitude: disorder on the streets; and secret intelligence reports that the St Patrick's Day festivities in Manchester, ostensibly to seal the Confederate-Chartist alliance, were a cover for more sinister designs.

---

[49]*Nation,* 6 May 1848, and *United Irishman,* 6-13 May 1848.

[50]Davis, 140-52.

[51]*Nation,* 4 Mar 1848. Smyth to Halpin, 27 Feb in *State Trials,* vii, 662, and Halpin's reply, 1 Mar 1848, RIA 23H41.

[52]*Nation,* 4-18 Mar 1848. Public Record Office: Home Office Papers (hereafter HO) 45/2410B, Rushton, 6 Mar 1848. Unfortunately, this large file has recently been renumbered, although the material in it is clearly marked as HO45/2410A. Furthermore, the contents are now in a state of total disorder, hence it is impossible to give folio numbers. All references to this file are dated 1848 unless otherwise stated.

The prevention of street disorder was a police priority in Liverpool.[53] There was a thriving 'secondary economy' of the streets to service the needs and requirements of seamen and casual labourers, a boisterous arena of hawkers and costermongers (trades in which the Irish enjoyed something of a monopoly),[54] of bookies, pawnbrokers and prostitutes. The police were engaged in constant battle to keep such activities out of 'respectable' public view. In March, unemployed porters, many Irish among them, demonstrated outside the Exchange, prompting fears of street disorder throughout the city centre. The magistrates, not unsympathetic to the porters' grievances against the recent de-regulation of the trade, issued a placard advising the men to petition Parliament, while assuring them that licences were to be withdrawn from master porters who kept pubs or lodging houses, or paid their men in pubs:

> The Magistrates most earnestly implore the Workmen to abstain from continual large Assemblies either on the Exchange or elsewhere. Such meetings have the effect of inducing disturbers of the peace to interrupt the tranquillity of the town.

While most of the porters heeded the advice, crowds continued to assemble daily on the Exchange. Irish orators apparently 'urged them to call for "bread or blood", and to break open any place in the event of their wants not being supplied'. Amid rumours of an influx of strangers and of a secret delegate meeting in town, the police took decisive action on 13 March after Head Constable Dowling was jostled by an unruly crowd - 'instead of respectable working men', the *Mercury* reported, 'he had the blackguards from Vauxhall Road and Toxteth Park to contend with'. Streets around the Exchange were cleared by baton charges and water cannon.[55]

In these circumstances, the magistrates, supported by the Catholic Church, decided not to allow the annual St Patrick's Day procession through the streets.[56] The procession was abandoned with little demur. Repeal leaders in Liverpool were anxious to present a united and disciplined public

---

[53]M. Brogden, *The Police: Autonomy and Consent* (1982), 43-73.

[54]Smyth noted the 'remarkable inclination which they (the Irish) manifest in this town for dealing, if it were only on a capital of sixpence', *Nation*, 15 Jan 1848.

[55]See the daily correspondence from Horsfall, the mayor, and Rushton, the town clerk, 7-15 Mar HO45/2410B. See also: Proceedings of Magistrates, Liverpool Corporation, Special and Sub-Committee Minute Books, LRO 352 MIN/SPE, vol. ii, ff. 332-36; and *Liverpool Mercury*, 10 and 14 Mar 1848. The porters' petition campaign continued for the rest of the year, see *Liverpool Mercury*, 4 and 14 Apr, and 26 Dec 1848.

[56]Horsfall, 15 Mar, HO45/2410B. See also J. Boyle's letter in *Liverpool Mercury*, 17 Mar 1848.

front, to dissociate the Irish cause from the violent disorder of poor law and income tax riots elsewhere in the country. Crowded weekly meetings of both the O'Connellites and the Confederates were held at their respective venues on 12 March, the Repeal Hall, Paradise Street, and the Assembly Rooms, Hood Street. 'All present' the *Nation* reported, 'seemed to feel that Ireland's opportunity was at hand, and that union among all Repealers was not only desirable but essential to the success of their cause':

> Both meetings deprecated all violence and outrage; they characterized the outbreaks in Glasgow, London and Manchester as wicked, and injurious to the progress of democratic reform. They advised the Irishmen of Liverpool to be observers of the peace on St Patrick's day.[57]

As the day approached, however, the authorities received alarming intelligence reports. Colonel McGregor at Dublin Castle, writing on Lord Clarendon's instructions, and an anonymous informer in Glasgow both warned that repealers in Liverpool, Manchester and Glasgow were 'concocting mischief and even entertained the idea of setting fire to these towns possibly on the 17th'. Given the vulnerability of the unenclosed dock and warehouse system to arson attack, the magistrates took every possible precaution: extra troops were drafted in on both sides of the river; over 5000 Special Constables were enrolled; movement of gunpowder was prohibited throughout the town; gatemen were stationed on permanent guard at all dock bridges; dock masters were ordered to ensure that every ship in dock was equipped with a hose and kept constantly manned, to be supplemented if necessary by seamen on special alert in the Sailors' Home; the borough engineer was instructed to keep the water pressure high and turncocks at the ready; and bell-ringers were put on guard at strategic churches to raise the alarm. In the event, the day passed without incident. Doheny and Meagher arrived on the morning packet from Dublin, *en route* for the Manchester festivities, but contrary to McGregor's information, there was no sign of Mitchel.[58] Clearly the authorities had over-reacted to alarmist and unsubstantiated intelligence, prompting the Chartists to lampoon the 'Dogberry Mayor'.[59] However, few

---

[57] *Nation,* 18 Mar 1848.

[58] LRO 352 MIN/SPE, ii, ff. 340-6. Horsfall and Rushton, 16-20 Mar, HO45/2410B. Lowe makes no reference to these alarms and precautions when he describes St Patrick's Day 1848 as the quietest for many years in Liverpool, see 'Chartists and Confederates', 176.

[59] See Edmund Jones's remarks, Abstract of Speeches, 31 Mar, HO45/2410B.

of the precautions were to be relaxed. Within a few days, information from a more reliable source confirmed the worst fears of the mayor and magistrates.

In late March, the Sallyford journalist, J.D. Balfe, a prominent Council member of the Confederation, much involved in liaising with the Chartists, stopped off in Liverpool. Balfe was Clarendon's most reliable and highest-placed informer, able to obtain 'exact information of the proceedings of the "War Leaders"'.[60] On arrival at Lennon's Temperance Hotel -'the rendezvous of all the Republicans, Chartists, Infidels and Insurrectionists in Liverpool' - Balfe was invited to an upstairs room in which McManus, Murphy and Smyth were studying the latest communication from Dublin, where Mitchel, Smith O'Brien and Meagher had been arrested after the demonstration on 21 March. McGee's letter advised that Smith O'Brien and Meagher, having been released on bail, were shortly to visit Liverpool *en route* for Paris to congratulate the revolutionary government. In preparation, McManus and colleagues were instructed 'to take the immediate steps to organize the Repealers and Chartists in Liverpool for an insurrection which might be now considered as certain "to take place"':

> This Organization and arming I can now give you a practical assurance is going on most rapidly here and I have only to invite you to direct the authorities to this House, for the purpose of ascertaining the truth of what I say. That the towns in England are to be made the prey of flames and devastations by the joint cooperation of both Chartists and Repealers is looked upon as a fact as certain to be accomplished, that it occupies all Chartists and Repealers minds. This line of proceeding is one of the most "sure resources" upon which the Confederates in Ireland rely for success in the insurrection which is now resolved upon.

When Smith O'Brien and Meagher arrived in Liverpool they received Balfe 'rather coldly'. In fear that his cover had been blown, Balfe retreated to a safe haven on the Wirral, and was thus unable to report in full on the lengthy discussions between Smith O'Brien, Meagher, McManus, Murphy and Smyth.[61]

In public, the Liverpool leaders continued to construct a united disciplined front. Smyth developed a common despatch network, sending identical

---

[60]Balfe, 7 Apr 1848, Clarendon Papers, Box 53. Kevin B. Nowlan, *The Politics of Repeal* (1965), 210.

[61]See Balfe's reports from Liverpool and Liscard, 20 Mar -7 Apr, and undated, in Clarendon Papers, Box 53.

resolutions to 'Old and Young Ireland Repealers' in Dublin.[62] Meetings were held in close proximity, as the Confederates, denied the use of regular venues in Hood Street and Hunter Street, transferred their public operations to an empty shop and ware-room in Paradise Street, adjacent to the Repeal Hall. Thousands thronged the vicinity on 26 March, unable to gain entry to crowded meetings which 'rejoiced at the practical union of Old and Young Ireland'. At the Confederate meeting, McManus, Smyth, O'Brien, Laffin and other speakers 'ran rapidly over the overthrow of thrones and of principalities which the last week's news has brought' raising the question, 'Shall Ireland continue the only slave state in Europe?' The meeting separated peaceably, with 'every man resolved to be scrupulously exact in his conduct, so as to afford no excuse to those whose object it might be to goad them into riot or disorder'.[63] On the following Sunday, union was sealed by an interchange of personalities at the neighbouring meetings: McManus was welcomed onto the O'Connellite platform while Brennan joined the Confederates 'in the spirit of true patriotism and fraternity'. 'The Liverpool Repealers of both parties are now, thank God, united', the *Nation* reported.[64]

The Confederate meeting attracted other allies, encouraging McManus on return from the Repeal Hall to boast that England was 'in a state of siege, they (the English) did not know what point we would attack them in'. Williams, an Ulster Orangemen, pledged his support, claiming he could 'muster 100 men of his own stamp' from his local lodge. Edmund Jones, a Liverpool delegate to the forthcoming Chartist Convention attended to recommend 'the arming of the people … all hope of any good result from petitioning Parliament had for ever fled from him, and the only hope he had was in good strong arms and God above'.[65] His appearance was a reciprocal gesture. In the build-up to the presentation of the Petition on 10 April, Confederate orators had come to the fore on the Chartist platform.

Somers led the way, assuring the 'Brother Chartists' of the active support of 'no less than 50,000 brave Irish hearts in Liverpool', as he underlined their common interests: 'You see 20,000 Porters at your Docks driven from their own country by misrule depriving you the artisans of Liverpool of your bread but I ask you Democrats of Liverpool to assist us as our cause is one'. Moral force, he insisted, was nonsense: they should petition 'on the point of a bayonet … with a musket over the shoulder and a pike in the hand', implements available from the new 'ironmongery business' opened by his

---

[62]Smyth to Halpin, 21 Mar 1848, *State Trials*, vii, 662-3.
[63]*Nation*, 1 Apr, and *Liverpool Mercury*, 4 Apr 1848.
[64]*Nation*, 8 and 15 Apr 1848, which includes a letter from McManus.
[65]*State Trials*, vii, 652-3.

colleague, Dr Reynolds.[66] On the Chartist platform, Reynolds introduced himself as a 'Young Irelander - one of that class of men who detested and hated, and spurned the word "petition"'. Nevertheless, he remained committed to 'forcible intimidation', looking to the mass platform to mount a combined and irresistible display of strength: 'Let the Chartists of England and Irish Repealers unite in one grand body, and all the powers of England, and foreign assistance to help them, could make no impression upon the phalanx they would present'.[67] While Reynolds rejuvenated the time-worn language of pressure from without, Somers appealed to a different revolutionary tradition: 'I boast no higher than a plebeian birth', he proudly proclaimed, 'and I can trace my genealogy no further back than to that of two men who died on a gibbet on Vinegar Hill, in 1798, and I am prepared to share the same fate, if need be, but determined to improve on their mode of action'.[68] In a particularly emotive speech, he gave warning of an insurrectionary 'organization' which extended from Liverpool and Manchester to 'the foot of the very throne itself':

> I tell the Merchants of Liverpool that as I think I see Warsaw in flames to take care that the spark of ignition may not reach the very town and spot on which we are standing. And at the same time I tell them that before the news is four hours in Liverpool of an attempted massacre of my Countrymen ... the Martyrs dying on the Scaffold or on the plain would have the Consolation in giving their last throe, of looking up to Heaven, and seeing the skies reddened with the blaze of the Babylons of England!!!![69]

At the next Confederate meeting, Smyth questioned the wisdom of 'hyperbolical speaking' but he had no wish to return to O'Connellite moral force.[70] Much influenced by the mood in Liverpool, Dunne and Leyne, an official delegation from Conciliation Hall, stretched O'Connellite constitutionalism to the limit as they praised the spirit and unity of the local repealers at a meeting in the Concert Hall: 'Let it be distinctly understood that they would stand upon the constitution to the last, but they were resolved not to be put down by brute force'.[71] The local authorities, preoccupied with

---

[66]Abstract of Speeches, 31 Mar, HO45/2410B.

[67]Reports enclosed in Horsfall, 8 Apr 1848. *State Trials*, vii, 664.

[68]Chartist meeting, 14 Apr reported in *Liverpool Mercury*, 18 Apr 1848.

[69]Reports enclosed in Horsfall, 8 Apr, HO45/2410B.

[70]*Nation*, 15 Apr 1848.

[71]McQuatters chaired the meeting on 6 Apr, see *Liverpool Mercury*, 7 Apr 1848. See also Leyne's report back to Dublin, *Nation*, 15 Apr 1848. Leyne was soon to join the insurgents.

rumours and reports of unscheduled arms shipments for Ireland (including a consignment of pikes apparently ordered by McManus on a recent business trip), dismissed the militant rhetoric as 'the mere language of Irish exaggeration'. 'I am satisfied there is no regular organization in Liverpool', the Mayor reported on 8 April, oblivious of developments a few days earlier.[72]

On 5 April, the Confederates adopted a new structure of four sub-committees - organization, arming, propaganda and finance - which were to report weekly to the general committee in Preeson's Row. In the first weeks, discussion concentrated on finance, accommodation and other practicalities, including the appointment of Laffin, chair of the local organizational sub-committee, as representative to the Repeal Delegates in Manchester.[73] While implementing this internal reorganization, the Confederates continued to enliven the Chartist platform, encouraging their allies to escalate their agitation, the Kennington Common 'fiasco' notwithstanding. Reynolds openly advised Chartist audiences that 'he had given himself up to the cause of the people, and opened a shop ... he would be happy to furnish good "short" swords at 6½d each'.[74] Convinced of his right to sell arms, he brought an action for trespass against an over-zealous policeman who raided his premises.[75] The darling of the crowd, Larry the ironmonger was soon obliged to moderate his language, however, when the Crown and Government Security Act introduced the offence of felonious sedition, a charge which extended to 'open and advised speaking'.[76] Thereafter, the Confederates concentrated on internal organization, using their committee structure to develop a network of secret clubs.

The fate of John Mitchel added urgency to the task. There was great excitement when Mitchel arrived in Liverpool in late April on a 'fraternal' visit with Doheny. Much to the disappointment of the thousands who thronged Queen's Square, hoping to greet their hero, he was immediately called back to Dublin to face new charges under the 'Felon Act'.[77] Following the acquittal of Smith O'Brien and Meagher, Mitchel's trial, the first under the new

---

[72]Horsfall, 4, 6 and 8 Apr, HO45/2410B. The Home Office ordered a close inspection of the docks, see letters to Horsfall, 3 and 5 Apr, HO41/19, ff. 71 and 78.

[73]Extracts from Confederation Minute Book, 5-27 Apr 1848, *State Trials*, vii, 653-5. *United Irishman*, 6 May 1848.

[74]*Liverpool Mercury*, 14 Apr 1848.

[75]*Liverpool Mercury*, 25 and 28 Apr ;*United Irishman*, 29 Apr; and Horsfall, 24 Apr, HO45/2410B.

[76]See report of 25 Apr meeting, *Liverpool Mercury*, 28 Apr 1848.

[77]*Nation*, 29 Apr ; *Liverpool Mercury*, 28 Apr ;Rushton and Horsfall, 25-6 Apr, HO45/2410B. Doheny advised the disappointed crowds to 'arm, arm, arm'. In his report on the visit, Balfe claimed that 'numbers of the Chartists wish Mitchel to become their leader, and to shake off <u>Feargus</u>', see his letters 25-8 Apr 1848, Clarendon Papers, Box 53.

Act, was a crucial test case. The Liverpool committee went into permanent session, awaiting news of the verdict and subsequent instructions from Dublin.[78] McManus was in Ireland when Mitchel's sentence - 14 years' transportation - was finally announced. Outraged, he immediately contacted his old friend Gavan Duffy, who now abandoned his conservative stance to join Father Kenyon and a small group of radicals in a secret junta committed to active insurrectionary planning. It would seem that McManus returned to Liverpool before the junta convened, but Duffy was able to inform his co-insurrectionists that come the day of the rising, McManus had promised to seize a couple of the largest Irish steamers at Liverpool, load them with arms and ammunition taken from Chester Castle, and proceed to Ireland. As regards diversionary activity, he intended to cripple the port by setting blaze at low-tide to quayside cotton warehouses, 'filled with material as inflammatory as the dried grass of a prairie'.[79]

On his return, McManus held private discussions with Murphy, Reynolds, Somers, Smyth and O'Hanlon at Delamere's house in Gloucester Place, his new lodgings. He had decided to vacate his Seacombe villa to be ready at hand on the Liverpool side of the river.[80] Reflecting the new mood of anger and resolution following Mitchel's conviction, local organization was reviewed and tightened: public statements were vetted by the general committee to prevent loose talk; and members without arms or ammunition were declared ineligible for committee service.[81] Meetings, however, remained semi-public, allowing the police to gain uncontested access. Two undercover policemen were sent to Circus Street on 6 June, where plans were discussed to extend the club network under the supervision and instructions of a new central council. The purpose, as one unnamed speaker explained, was to emulate revolutionary Paris where district clubs facilitated rapid action, as 'word could be passed with the quickness of electricity. He hoped there would not be a Street of any importance in Liverpool without its Club'. Laffin announced that fourteen clubs were already in existence in town with plans for six more. Reynolds reported on his successful missionary tour to Birkenhead, Runcorn and Warrington. Robert Hopper, a joiner adept at making staves for pikes, provided further details of extensive arming and organization in Birkenhead, before announcing himself a Protestant who 'would prefer being tyrannized by

---

[78]Extracts from Minute Book, 26 May 1848, *State Trials*, vii, 656.

[79]Charles Gavan Duffy, *My Life in Two Hemispheres* (2 vols, 1898), i, 277-8. McAllister, 11-12. Clark Compendium, envelope D, f. 610. Davis, 158. Prior to his trip to Ireland, McManus addressed the Roderick o'Connor Club in Manchester, see *United Irishman*, 27 May 1848, which also reports a Stockport meeting addressed by Reynolds and Archdeacon.

[80]Clark Compendium, envelope D, f. 636.

[81]Extracts from Minute Book, 29 May 1848, *State Trials*, vii, 657.

the Roman Catholics rather than by the English Government'. McManus, who 'appeared to be under the influence of Liquor' said 'he had no doubt that before he cut his Christmas Dinner, he would have his hands bloody with fighting or Ireland free'. He promised 'every man who fights with us shall have a piece of land allotted to him in his own country, which he can call his own'.[82]

To promote the club network, Confederate orators commandeered the Chartist Whitsun demonstration on the North Shore, their last appearance on the public platform. Reynolds set the tone, dismissing issues of class - 'I would not set class against class, and I would not join you if I thought you would have any hatred of the middle class' - to concentrate on the struggle to free the martyred Mitchel, exiled on Bermuda:

> There is only one way of restoring him; that is, not at public meetings, but at club houses. Every street in Liverpool and every town ought to have its club; every club its president, and other commanding officers; every club ought to take care to have every power of defending itself; every officer ought to have his rifle, every committee man his musket, and every member ought to have his pike. (Great cheers)[83]

The club system expanded rapidly assisted by a streamlined committee structure introduced by McManus,[84] but Confederate organization was still vulnerable to police infiltration. Superintendent Redin obtained a detailed report of secret activities from an informant who enrolled as number 111 in the Bagenal Harvey Club. The club met every week day evening (except Wednesday, 'Finance night') to read the Irish newspapers and 'receive Instructions how to <u>construct barricades,</u> with Lorries, floats, Carts, etc, etc, which no Cavalry can get over'. Arms, supplied by Reynolds, were obtainable for members either by raffle or by weekly subscription schemes, 1s. (5p.) a week for a gun, 6d. (2½p.) a week for a pike.[85] Other undercover agents kept watch on Joseph Cuddy, Reynolds's assistant, as he toured the clubs to

---

[82]Reports enclosed in Horsfall, 8 June, HO45/2410B. This speech figured prominently in the prosecution case against McManus, see *Liverpool Mercury*, 13 Oct 1848, but at the later trial of the Liverpool nine, P.C. Willock admitted his notes were unclear and that most of the words had probably been uttered by Dr O'Donnell, see *State Trials*, vii, 680 and 693.

[83]*Liverpool Mercury*, 13 June 1848. *State Trials*, vii, 668-76. Somers and Hopper also spoke in favour of armed clubs. For reports of drilling at Farrell's Temperance Hotel, Cazneau Street, in preparation for this meeting, see Horsfall, 8 and 11 June, HO45/2410B.

[84]Extract from Minute Book, 26 June 1848, *State Trials*, vii, 659-60. McManus chaired the new committee to procure arms.

[85]Report enclosed in Horsfall, 30 June, HO45/2410B.

exhibit specimens. Reynolds himself was more cautious: he ordered reporters to leave and placed guards on the door before brandishing a pike-head, sixteen inches long, at the foundation meeting of the Bermuda Club.[86] Arming, the informers reported, was accompanied by regular drilling, as the local Confederates prepared for a disciplined and decisive show of force in August to coincide with harvest-time action in Ireland where the export of grain was to be prevented. The plan was to assemble up to 10,000 armed men in a local square to deter the authorities from despatching troops across the Irish Sea.[87]

Approaching the point of no return, McManus decided to spell out the odds, to test the resolve of the rank and file. 'It was no foolish game they were about to play', he advised the meeting in Circus Street on 27 June:

> They would have to contend with the best disciplined troops in the world, and with a dreadful and dangerous foe, it was no trifling matter to deluge a Country in blood, nor for the leaders of a party to put their necks into a halter and then be deserted by their men. The question was would they be firm? Would they fight with their leaders? And when Ireland required them to act would they stand firm?

Reassured by Smyth, O'Donnell, Hopper and others, McManus insisted on tighter security: henceforth, admission to meetings was strictly by membership card. Laffin announced other measures to prevent further police infiltration into the clubs, now nearly 40 in number: new members were to be admitted only on the personal recommendation of two existing members.[88]

The local authorities immediately informed the Home Office of these ominous developments. 'It is not a question of Chartism which as far as this town is concerned, may be considered as completely extinct', Horsfall explained: 'Clubs are being formed here now in a manner which has not been attempted before'.[89] A committee of magistrates was appointed to investigate the danger. There were at least 100,000 Irish in Liverpool, they reported, out of a total population estimated at 375,000:

> The great mass of this Irish population consists of unskilled labourers and the bulk of it is Roman Catholic. Your Committee fear that among

---

[86]P.C. Javett's evidence at the committal of Cuddy, *Liverpool Mercury,* 18 Aug 1848.
[87]Reports enclosed in Horsfall, 28 and 30 June, HO 45/2410B.
[88]Reports enclosed in Horsfall, 28 June, HO45/2410B. Extract from Minute Book, 27 June 1848, *State Trials,* vii, 660.
[89]Horsfall, 8 July, HO45/2410B.

this enormous amount of people the Irish leaders would find a very great number who would ardently join in any attempt to aid the progress of Repeal, even though that progress led to open rebellion and servile war.

There were already between 30 and 40 secret clubs (see Table 4.1), capable of assembling 2,000-4,000 armed men, unannounced on the streets. Armed insurrection in Liverpool was 'very probable and indeed almost certain if there be an Insurrection in Ireland ... though a political, might (in the outset) be the ostensible motive - the real one would soon appear; a triumphant armed mob in a rich town would not respect property or life'.[90]

The Home Office promptly agreed to military reinforcements, but refused to sanction the arming and drilling of Special Constables in a local national guard. Whitehall proposed to send police from London, but Dowling declined the offer, explaining that it would be impossible for them to infiltrate the clubs as new applicants, Irish to a man, were now carefully vetted on regional provenance, religion, occupation and the 'known political feelings' of their family. Dowling was forced to rely for information - none of which could be used in court - on informers who 'live in a constant state of alarm that the least discovery would consign them to death'.[91] Through these channels, the authorities learnt of the election of an Executive Council to co-ordinate plans for a great display of force on 1 August, in preparation for which there was target practice on the North Shore, and the distribution of hay-forks to those unable to afford pikes: 'For God's sake let Mr Dowling leave nothing undone for if we only get possession of the Town for one hour, no one knows the consequence.'[92] Developments in Ireland, however, were to alter these plans.

Much delayed by O'Connellite attempts to exclude the club network from a public reunion of the repealers, the Irish League finally held its first public meeting on 11 July. Dr Murphy wrote to offer apologies that 'none of us from Liverpool will be able to attend', adding that 'the Club system is the most

---

[90]Report of the Committee of Magistrates appointed at a General Meeting of Magistrates held on 8 July 1848, HO45/2410B. On 8 July, *Nation* reported the number of Liverpool clubs 'in working order' at 33, the *Irish Tribune* at 'no less than 30'. *Liverpool Mercury*, 1 Aug 1848, lists 14 clubs. In the absence of the missing Minute Book, I have succeeded in identifying at least 23 clubs, see Table 4.1.

[91]Letters to Horsfall, 10, 13, 19 and 20 July 1848, HO41/19, ff. 240, 242-5, 248, 250. Dowling to Horsfall, 15 July, HO45/2410B.

[92]Report enclosed in Horsfall, 19 July, HO45/2410B. Extract from Minute Book, 17 July 1848, *State Trials*, vii, 661, lists the members of the elected Executive Council: Drs Reynolds and O'Donnell, Messrs Laffin, McManus, Smyth, Delamere, O'Hanlon, Jones and Somers. The informer's report also listed Murphy, O'Brien and Hopper.

effective move ever yet made for righting Ireland'.[93] Behind the constitutional facade of the League, the secret junta proceeded with plans for the clubs to take action after the harvest. They were forced into a premature rising, however, when the government, having instituted a number of arrests, announced the suspension of Habeas Corpus in Ireland. Reluctant to the last, Smith O'Brien was now persuaded that insurrection was the only option.

Within hours of the introduction of the Habeas Corpus Suspension Bill on 22 July, the mayor, magistrates and other leading citizens petitioned for its provisions to be extended to Liverpool, where there were fears of a rising that very night.[94] William Rathbone, a celebrated Liberal, explained the circumstances to his daughter:

> 100,000 Irish in Liverpool unemployed, and Chartists to join, are fearful materials for mischief ... our open docks and warehouses leave us much at the mercy of the incendiary ... The English law is defective, we cannot search for arms when we know where they are; we cannot incarcerate the leaders, though preaching rebellion or virtually such, though not legally; nor can we enter the houses where clubs we <u>know</u> meet, and the most inflammatory and rebellious language is used; yet Liverpool is the high road to and from Ireland, a post which a general would say the <u>country's safety</u> required to be guarded; yet her majesty's Ministers leave us very much to ourselves, and in some degree tie our hands by their reserve.[95]

At 6 p.m. on 22 July, Henry Banner, a porter, was apprehended in Byrom Street, carrying a sack of 31 pike-heads. Joseph Cuddy, Reynolds's 'salesman', immediately appeared on the scene to claim possession of the goods. Although worried about the legal grounds, Rushton, the stipendiary magistrate, decided to remand them both, pending Home Office instructions. At first, Whitehall ordered their discharge, but this was countermanded by a telegram: 'Detain Cuddy till further orders'. By next post, the Liverpool authorities received instructions from the Home Secretary to take action

---

[93]*Irish Felon,* 15 July, and *Nation,* 15 July 1848 which reported that McManus was in Scotland on 11 July, addressing the United Repealers of Glasgow.

[94]C.B. Banning, Post Office, Liverpool, 22 July, and Horsfall, 24 July, HO45/2410B. *Liverpool Mercury,* 25 July and 1 Aug 1848, for the counter-petition of those who thought suspension would be 'an unnecessary interference with the liberty of the subject ... an indelible stain on the town of Liverpool'.

[95]W. Rathbone to Mrs Paget, 23 July 1848, quoted in E.A. Rathbone (ed), *Records of the Rathbone Family* (Edinburgh, 1913), 223-4. The Attorney-General had just advised against prosecuting Reynolds and Hopper for sedition and unlawful assembly, see Horsfall, 22 July, HO45/2410B.

against those who supplied arms and those who assembled with arms in secret clubs.[96] A number of raids quickly followed. Fourteen pike-heads, 23 sword-knives, five pike staves and some ammunition were seized from Reynolds's warehouse in Vauxhall Road.[97] Packets containing powder, ball cartridges and percussion caps were found in the garret above James O'Brien's news-room in Hurst Street, along with four pikes, specially recommended by O'Brien as 'the implements that frightened the bloody Orange tribe in the year '98'.[98] It was another week, however, before the major arms cache was discovered, 500 cutlasses and some canisters of gunpowder concealed in a cellar.[99] By this time, the clubs were in retreat - and the leaders in flight - as the Confederate minute book, a detailed record of committee membership and meetings, had fallen into police hands, captured in an arms raid on the premises of Edward Murphy, secretary of the Sarsfield Club. The town was 'perfectly tranquil', Horsfall reported on 31 July: 'Our head Constable does not think that they are broken up but ashamed at the discovery of the Book and the double patrol which we have had for the last three nights'.[100]

Confederate conspiracy collapsed in the face of rigorous police action and in the absence of effective leadership. Horsfall outlined the measures taken - including a round the clock watch on McManus and Murphy - in one of his letters to Lord Clarendon. 'I am not without hopes', he wrote, 'that letting the Insurgents see that we are prepared will have the effect of preventing a crisis'. This direct Liverpool-Dublin correspondence - supplemented in emergency by telegraph - was a vital channel of communication, a means of keeping watch on suspicious movements of arms and men across the Irish Sea and the Atlantic, whence the arrival of an American 'Irish Brigade' was expected imminently.[101] Throughout the period, Liverpool was placed under a virtual state of seige, although press reports of 2,000 troops and 20,000 Special Constables were nearly double the effective numbers.[102] At some expense to standards and efficiency, the police force was increased from 800 to

---

[96]Horsfall, 23-4 July, HO45/2410B. Waddington, 24-5 July, HO 41/19, ff. 256-7. *Liverpool Mercury*, 25 July 1848.

[97]Horsfall, 26 July, HO45/2410B. *State Trials*, vii, 648.

[98]*Liverpool Mercury*, 28 July and 22 Aug 1848. *State Trials*, vii, 684-5.

[99]Horsfall, 3 Aug, HO45/2410B.

[100]Horsfall, 31 July-1 Aug, HO45/2410B. *Liverpool Mercury*, 22 Aug 1848. *State Trials*, vii, 649. See the letter from the Secretary of the PRO, 24 Apr 1893, confirming that the Minute Book was missing, in Clark Compendium, envelope F.

[101]Horsfall to Clarendon, 20, 22 and 30 July 1848, Clarendon Papers, Box 16. I am currently preparing a paper on the American 'Irish Brigade' of 1848.

[102]Moore, 460-1. For the arguments over who was to pay for the military reinforcements and the large tented camp at Everton, see Saville, 155.

1,300,[103] while in the absence of a suitable warship, armed marines were put aboard the 'Redwing', a government tender boat on the Mersey.[104]

McManus, the 'generalissimo of the conspiracy', might have defied these odds to rally the rank and file for a diversionary outbreak. He had apparently subscribed £500 to the clubs, but at the decisive moment he was suddenly called away, not to return to take the lead. Summoned by Duffy, he set sail for Dublin on 24 July, taking only a tin box containing his '82 Club uniform and a brace of pistols. What happened next is difficult to establish. The policeman who tailed him on board the 'Iron Duke' lost contact in Dublin before McManus reached Duffy in Newgate gaol. Contrary to expectations of his prompt return, he took Duffy's advice, setting off for south Tipperary, the area chosen for Smith O'Brien to make his stand.[105] He may well have tried to summon aid from Liverpool. On 26 July, according to a reliable Dublin police informant, '400 of the Felon or Mitchel Club came over from Liverpool, but they would do more good by staying at home, they were about going back, he did not know who ordered them over'.[106] The next day, rumour was rife on both sides of the Irish Sea. Liverpool was thrown into alarm by false reports of a successful outbreak in Ireland, while in Dublin placards appeared announcing serious disturbances in Liverpool, during which, according to local rumour in Thurles, 500 police had been killed.[107] Emboldened by such reports, two members of the 89th Regiment, part of the vast military encampment at Everton, advised their drinking companions: 'Now boys is the time to turn out for Ireland'.[108] At the docks, 500 Irish labourers were dismissed from employment, having refused to be sworn in as special constables.[109] But the armed support upon which McManus relied failed to materialize, even though he had previously chartered three small steamers to be on standby, ready to sail to Wexford.[110] When he finally made contact

---

[103]LRO: 352 POL 1/2 Watch Committee Orders to the Head Constable, 20-27 July 1848; and 352 MIN/WAT 1/4 Minutes of the Watch Committee, ff. 478-82, 20 July 1848, and ff. 644-48, 29 Apr 1849, Dowling's Statistical Return for 1848, which noted a large increase in constables reported for drunkenness and neglect of duty 'attributable to the sudden and considerable augmentation of the Force subsequently to July last when it was found impracticable to take the usual precautions for enquiry into the characters of candidates'.

[104]Horsfall, 25 July, HO45/2410B.

[105]Horsfall, 25-26 July, HO45/2410B. McAllister, 12-13. Clark Compendium, envelope D, f. 610.

[106]C.D.'s report, 27 July 1848, TCD Mss 2039, f. 45.

[107]Horsfall, 27 July, HO45/2410B. *Liverpool Mercury*, 28 July 1848.

[108]Clark Compendium, envelope D, ff. 609-10.

[109]Horsfall, 29 July and 2 Aug, HO45/2410B.

[110]McManus's account in Fitzgerald's *Narrative* cited in Dennis Gwynn, *Young Ireland and 1848* (Cork, 1949), 254.

with Smith O'Brien at Ballingarry, he could not conceal his disappointment at his failure to procure even 200 men from the Liverpool clubs. Two days later, the rising collapsed in widow McCormack's cabbage patch on Boulagh Commons. Amid the ignominy, McManus emerged with dignity and integrity. Throughout the whole day, the Rev Fitzgerald recorded, he 'showed more courage and resolution than any one else'.[111] Bitterly disappointed by the failure of his Liverpool plans, McManus was to prove himself 'the boldest fellow among the entire body of insurgents'.[112]

When news arrived of the collapse at Ballingarry, the Liverpool authorities decided to maintain the alert. 'Parties here speak of Smith O'Brien's movement being precipitated', Horsfall informed Grey, 'and it must not do to relax in any precautionary measure until after the Harvest'.[113] A few weeks later, an informer reported that the Felon's Hope Club was about to be reorganized at Ord's Temperance Hotel, following instructions from Ireland received by Ord, Kenny, the printer, and a dangerous man called Foster:

They are determined to keep up the agitation, there is plenty of money moving amongst the Confederates in Ireland, Reynolds, McManus, Laffan(sic) and Hopper, are in or near Waterford, they are unknown to the Constabulary there, so pass unnoticed, they are actively engaged with Two Frenchmen, organizing Clubs, to use upon the conviction of 'Smith O'Brien'.[114]

By this time, however, the Grand Jury at Liverpool had found a true bill for seditious conspiracy against the leading Confederates. As Table 4.2 shows, several of those indicted succeeded in eluding arrest, including Thomas O'Brien, secretary of the central committee, and James Laffin, in charge of local organization. Reynolds fled to America, where he was to serve with distinction as surgeon (and poet-laureate) of the 63rd Regiment, New York Volunteers (Irish Brigade) in the civil war.[115] Patrick Murphy spent sixteen years in exile in Rouen before returning to his medical practice in St Paul's Square[116] - his namesake, Edward Murphy, away in Ireland (with

[111]Rev. P. Fitzgerald, *Personal Recollections of the Insurrection at Ballingarry in July 1848* (Dublin, 1861), 25.

[112]J.O'C's report (Balfe), 5 Sept 1848, Clarendon Papers, Box 53. For McManus's own narrative of events, see Gwynn, Appendix 3.

[113]Horsfall, 31 July, HO45/2410B, and Horsfall to Clarendon, 30 July 1848, Clarendon Papers, Box 16.

[114]Reports enclosed in Horsfall, 24 Aug, HO45/2410B

[115]See the biographical sketch of Reynolds in M.Cavanagh, *Waterford Celebrities* (Waterford, n.d.), 1-15. See also Treasury Solicitor's Papers, 11/137 part 1.

[116]Clark Compendium, envelope D contains much material on Dr. Murphy.

McManus?) when the crucial minute-book was seized from his premises, surrendered himself to the Liverpool police on 18 August.[117] Matthew Somers hoped to turn Queen's evidence, an offer rejected by the Home Office because of his 'prominent part' in proceedings.[118] Delamere was acquitted and soon entered the army as a distinguished commissioned officer.[119] George Smyth was less fortunate. At the trial in December, he failed to dissociate himself from the militant oratory of the Chartist platform, despite his counsel's contention that Confederates 'have no sympathy with Chartists ... and deprecate as strongly as they can the false position that Chartism had taken up in the country'. When Smyth left prison his business was ruined. He enjoyed a long life, but never regained his former prosperity: he died in poverty and obscurity in Brownlow Hill Workhouse in 1887.[120] McManus had already been declared bankrupt before the authorities finally apprehended him in Cork at the end of August.[121] Convicted of high treason at the Clonmel Special Commission, he was transported to Australia, whence he escaped to California. After his death in 1861, his corpse was carried to Dublin for a public funeral. It was a stage-managed affair, the first public demonstration of a movement in which the Liverpool-Irish would soon be prominent, Fenianism.[122]

---

[117]Horsfall to Clarendon, 18 Aug 1848, Clarendon Papers, Box 16.
[118]Cornewall Lewis to Messrs Lowndes and Co., 25 Oct 1848, HO 41/19, f. 323.
[119]Clark Compendium, envelope D, f. 636.
[120]*State Trials*, vii, 689. *United Irishman,* 25 Feb 1905.
[121]Clark Compendium, envelope F, ff. 411-12.
[122]McAllister, chs.5-8.

Table 4.1: Confederate Clubs in Liverpool and Birkenhead, 1848

	Name	Venue	Officer/Delegate
	Liverpool		
1:	Bermuda	Gt Howard St	-
2:	Oliver Bond	46 Naylor St	-
3:	Brian Boru	40 Gilbert St	Patrick O'Hanlon
4:	Byrne	-	-
5:	Connaught Rangers	Addison St	-
6:	Davis (formerly Faugh a Ballagh)	-	Peter Ryan
7:	Emmet	32 Rose Place	-
8:	Lord Edward	-	-
9:	Erin's Hope	-	-
10:	Felon's Brigade	-	-
11:	Felon's Hope	Ord's Temperance Hotel	Murphy
12:	Bagenel Harvey	Bevington Bush	Dr. O'Donnell
13:	Liberator	Newsham St	-
14:	John Mitchel	47 Thomas St	Farrell and Perkins
15:	Roger O'Moore	-	-
16:	Owen Roe O'Neill	Ord's Temperance Hotel	Williamson
17:	William Orr	-	-
18:	Hamilton Rowan	-	-
19:	St. Patrick	New Bird St	Martin Boshell
20:	Sarsfield	-	Edward Murphy
21:	Tom Steele	-	John Clifford
22:	Wolfe Tone	-	-
23:	'82 Club, Liverpool	-	T. B. McManus
	-	Eldon Place	-
	-	52 Hurst St	-
	-	Milton St	Dr. Reynolds
	-	Limekiln Lane	Matthew Somers
	-	Dublin St	Matthew Somers
	Birkenhead		
	John Frost	-	-
	John Mitchel	Davis St	Robert Hopper

NOTE: This list has been compiled from a wide variety of sources as the Minute-Book of the Confederation is missing in the Public Record Office. However, there are lengthy extracts which give some details of the clubs in *Reports of State Trials*, new series, vi, 637 - 71.

Table 4.2: List of Confederates indicted for seditious conspiracy, August 1848

Name	Occupation	Sentence
T. B. McManus	Shipping Agent	Transportation
Lawrence Reynolds	Surgeon	Not tried
Patrick Murphy	Surgeon	Not tried
Francis O'Donnell	Surgeon	2 Years
P. H. Delamere	Coal-agent	Acquitted
Joseph Cuddy	Porter	1 year
Matthew Somers	Provision dealer	2 years
Robert Hopper	Joiner	2 years
Edward Murphy	Book-keeper and collecting clerk	3 months
James Laffin	Tailor	Not tried
Martin Boshell	Clerk	1 year
Thomas O'Brien	Labourer	Not tried
George Smyth	Hat manufacturer	2 years
Patrick O'Hanlon	Labourer	Not tried
James O'Brien	Linendraper	6 months
James Campbell	Labourer	Not tried

NOTE: The occupations have been established from a wide variety of sources. The names appear in the same order as in *Reports of State Trials*, new series, vii, 638, which simply lists McManus, Reynolds, Murphy, O'Donnell and Delamere as gentlemen, and the rest as labourers.

5: Riotous Liverpool, 1815 - 1860

Anne Bryson

Introduction

Liverpool in the mid nineteenth century was a disorderly town. Although political dissent and political riot were less common here than in industrial towns such as Manchester, there was frequent use of collective violence in other ways: at elections, in trade disputes, in the course of private quarrels, against the police, as an expression of sectarian loyalties, and as a direct response to minor grievances.

Riot is not a neglected topic; many important studies have been published over the years.[1] However, two tendencies can be identified. The first is to concentrate on the motives for riot, and to neglect the way riot was controlled; the second is to identify most riot as a rational mechanism of protest. By collecting information mainly from major protest-based riots, the riots of smaller and less reputable groups of people can be obscured. Reliance on centralised official sources can encourage deceptive parallels between geographically separate riots arising out of differing local conditions.[2] This approach can concentrate on disturbances seen as dangerous by the government of the day, while neglecting minor or apolitical incidents. This in turn can support an assumption that riot and protest are identical. Where riots include casual pub brawls, the use of raw statistics as an indicator of protest is unsafe, but not unknown. Control of riot has of course received some attention, but has usually been secondary to the study of protest. Even

---

[1] A selection would have to include G.Rudé, *The Crowd in History 1730-1848* (1981) and *Ideology and Protest* (1980); M.Beloff, *Public Order and Popular Disturbance 1660 - 1714* (1938); F.O.Darvall, *Popular Disturbances and Public Order in Regency England* (1969 [1934]); F.C.Mather, *Public Order in the Age of the Chartists* (Manchester, 1959); E.J.Hobsbawm, *Primitive Rebels* (Manchester, 1978) and 'The Machine Breakers', *Past and Present*, 1 (1952), 57-70; E.J.Hobsbawm and G.Rudé, *Captain Swing* (1973); E. P. Thompson, *The Making of the English Working Class* (1962) and 'The Moral Economy of the English Crowd in the Eighteenth Century', *Past and Present,* 50 (1971), 76-136; J.Stevenson, *Popular Disturbances in England, 1700-1870* (1979); J.Bohstedt, *Riots and Community Politics in England and Wales, 1790-1810* (Cambridge, Mass., 1983).

[2] Introduction to J.Stevenson and R.Quinault (eds), *Popular Protest and Public Disorder* (1979).

histories of the police often deal only incidentally with operations against riot, although there are honourable exceptions.[3]

By concentrating on Liverpool, this research project takes in riots of all kinds, pub brawls as well as protests.Ten participants was taken as a minimum, large enough to exclude close kinship, and pre-arranged partnership. All incidents were considered where there was violence, real or potential, which happened in a public place.

The motives of rioters have normally formed part of the definition of riot: problems arise from the lawyers' distinction between riot for 'public' motives and affray for 'private' motives. While there is a clear difference between a drunken brawl outside a public house and, for example, Chartist-inspired crowd activities, there are gradations between the two. What of resistance to police interrupting a brawl? What about violent loyalist demonstrations? What about fights as entertainment? If boxing is sport, then it is possible that men may fight for motives other than protest. Studies of crowds at football matches support this.[4] There are dangers in applying modern studies to earlier periods, but football violence shows considerable similarity to riotous behaviour at elections. The problem of drawing this line can best be avoided by considering all collective violence without distinction.

If riots of all kinds are thus considered, the way in which mechanisms of control were applied can be compared. Clearly, riots were perceived differently by the authorities according to their apparent origin. The authorities' interpretation of the riot is more accessible than the rioters', and it would be this rather than the 'true' motivation which influenced control and punishment. One might ask whether the handling of incidents related to severity in terms of danger to life or property, or whether the apparent motive for the riot was more important. Maybe some types of riot were tolerated more readily than others.

There is little direct evidence to show how the magistrates regarded riots, but press reports show certain assumptions. A number of categories seem to have been meaningful to writers and, presumably, to their readers.

---

[3]Works on police history which deal with riot include R.D.Storch, 'The Plague of the Blue Locusts', *International Review of Social History*, 20 (1975), 61 - 90, and 'The Policeman as Domestic Missionary', *Journal of Social History*, 9 (1976), 481 - 509; C.Emsley, *Policing and its Context* (1983), 68-71; T.A.Critchley, *The Conquest of Violence* (1970); J.Stevenson, 'Social Control and the Prevention of Riots in England, 1798-1829' in A. Donajgrodzki (ed), *Social Control in Nineteenth-Century Britain* (1977); D.Philips, 'A New Engine of Power and Authority' in V.A.Gatrell et al (eds), *Crime and the Law* (1980); L.Keller, *Public Order in Victorian London*, unpublished PhD thesis, University of Cambridge, 1976.

[4]SSRC/Sports Council, *Public Disorder and Sporting Events* (1979); P. Marsh, E. Rosser, and R. Harré, *The Rules of Disorder* (1978).

The most notable is *political protest*. Among the Tory press the ideas of protest and disorder were clearly linked: it was assumed that a protest meeting needed strong policing, in case of riot; speeches at such meetings could typically be described as 'calculated to inflame the passions of the multitude'.[5] The more liberal press can be seen to have implicitly accepted the same interpretation by its stress on the peacefulness of such meetings.

The treatment of *elections* was very different. The violence so feared at protest meetings was largely accepted at elections. Until the 1830s, it was so normal as to be scarcely newsworthy. In 1816, electoral rioters were tried at the assizes, yet the only record in the press of disorder is about three lines.[6] Later in the period, when election riots were seen as more important, it was still deemed sufficient to state that supporters of opposing parties were involved; no further explanation of fighting was required.[7]

In contemporary terms, *sectarian* disorders were very similarly regarded. These were at least as much concerned with political allegiance as with religion, as contemporary references to 'rage of party' suggest. The first such riot was in 1819;[8] they became well-known during the 1840s. As with elections, the political allegiance of the press affects the allocation of blame, but fighting surprised nobody when Protestant and Catholic met.

These were not the only groups of whom this could be said. In a sense, sectarian battles were a special case of a kind of riot we might call *private battle*. This was expected of Irish immigrants: 'natives of the sod, to have trodden which in youth seems to communicate a certain eccentricity to the character somewhat unfriendly to peace'.[9] Similar behaviour was also expected of navvies and schoolboys.

In other styles of riot, the press stressed the reason for the use of violence rather than the identity of the rioters. The cause given can range from protest at the dismissal of an actress to lack of food.[10] This group has been termed *direct action* riots. Two types of grievance, however, have been separated from this group because they were clearly viewed differently. The first of these is *trade disputes*. Most common was intimidation of workmen not on strike, and considerable space was devoted to magistrates' remarks about interference with fellow-workers. The other special case was the *anti-police* riot. This was usually either resistance to arrest or the rescue of

---

[5] *Saturday's Advertiser*, 18 Nov 1826.

[6] *Liverpool Mercury*, 14 June 1816; Public Records Office (hereafter PRO), Palatinate of Lancaster papers (hereafter PL)26.79, Indictments, Lancaster Summer Assizes, 1816.

[7] *Saturday's Advertiser*, 17 June 1826; *Liverpool Courier*, 7 July 1841.

[8] *Liverpool Mercury*, 30 July 1819; *Saturday's Advertiser*, 21 Feb 1829; *Liverpool Times*, 22 Mar 1842.

[9] *Saturday's Advertiser*, 23 Sept 1826.

[10] *Gore's General Advertiser*, 6 Dec 1824; *Liverpool Mercury*, 20, 27 Feb 1855.

prisoners; there was normally little news-space devoted to either. Often enough, riots were reported only incidentally, perhaps when a constable was seriously injured. In comparison with trade disputes, there was a noticeable absence of moralising comment: such riots were made by the incorrigibly corrupted who, unlike decent working men, would not be open to reason.

There remain, of course, a number of cases where evidence is lacking. These have been termed riots of *unknown origin*. Either accidents of survival or lack of contemporary interest can account for this: perhaps the incident happened in a street where it was 'only to be expected' by the newspaper-buying public.

The reporting of different types of riot is interesting. Crowds at political protest meetings were given considerable attention by reporters who would be present primarily to report speeches; elections were similarly reported, but here crowd violence was often discounted as 'only to be expected', at least before about 1830. Sectarian riots were reported very differently by different papers, but the major incidents occurred normally on 12 July, and for most of the period even a peaceful 12th was worthy of report. Trade disputes were also fairly comprehensively reported, considerable detail of trials being given. In all these types of incident, the same incident would often be reported in several newspapers. In contrast, reports of direct action riots, private battles, and anti-police riots often owed their news-space to factors such as humour, perhaps that of Irish witnesses reported in 'quaint' dialect, such as:

> I niver offended Mary Mallowney in me life, plase yer worships, but she shtruck me tree times and offended me very bad entirely[11]

Clearly the number of unrecorded cases, whilst unknown, is very much higher in these types of incident than in elections, political or sectarian riots, or trade disputes. The relative frequency of different types cannot be measured. However, comparisons of the nature and handling of different types do not rely on knowledge of frequency, so long as there is a sufficient sample of each type, and chances of survival do not significantly bias these samples. The most obvious comparison to consider is between the concluding decades of the unreformed oligarchic corporation and the years after the 1835 Municipal Corporation Act, the periods just before and just after the foundation of the town's first modern police force: 1815 to 1835 and 1836 to 1860.

---

[11] *Liverpool Chronicle*, 24 Sept 1839.

Mechanisms of Control under the Old Corporation

Before 1835, responsibility for policing the town was shared between three bodies: the town constables, the dock police, and the nightly watch. The town constables were directly under the control of the mayor. In 1815 they numbered 26, and in 1835, 53. They did not patrol the streets, and were mostly occupied in connection with the courts and the execution of warrants. Their efficiency was not remarkable. In 1829, unfit men were dismissed, and in 1831 a superintendent was appointed who had been an inspector in the Metropolitan Police.[12] Neither of these changes produced much improvement. However, the constables could be reinforced by paid special constables, enrolled in advance for elections, or appointed at short notice when needed.[13]

At night, the town was patrolled by the nightly watch; they answered to commissioners elected by the vestry. Active commissioners were usually men debarred from local government by lack of family connection, by not being freemen, or by religious or political persuasion; their energetic approach ensured considerable improvement. In 1815, 83 watchmen were employed; and a resident's memoirs describe the feebleness of the 'Old Charleys', employed to be kept off the parish. Later men '... looked as if they would stand no nonsense, and could do a little fighting at a pinch'.[14] In 1826, and again in 1828, the force was purged of unfit men, and in 1830, a superintendent was appointed who brought with him the Metropolitan Police rule book.[15] He had two successors, the second being M J Whitty, an Irish journalist without police experience who was to be a great success as head constable of the Liverpool police for its first eight years. By the time the watch were subsumed into the new police force their number had increased to about 150.[16]

Standards of discipline are difficult to evaluate. Drunkenness was common, and the turnover of men was fast. It was unusual for the watch to be used against daytime riots, or at public meetings or elections. However,

[12]Liverpool Record Office, Minutes of the Corporation (hereafter Town Books) vol 14, 488, Oct 1814; Vol. 16, 156, 7 Oct 1829; Report of Commissioners on Municipal Corporations in England and Wales (hereafter Munic.Corp.Report), 2715; *Liverpool Courier*, 22 July 1831.

[13]Town Books, vol 15, 90, 5 Apr 1820;Parliamentary Papers 1833 (344.) XIII.589,Munic.Corp.Report, 2723.

[14]Munic.Cor Report, 2715; *Liverpool Mercury*, 17 Feb 1815; 'An Old Stager' (Aspinall); *Liverpool A Few Years Since* (Liverpool, 1885 [1852]), 104-107.

[15]Liverpool Record Office, Minutes of Commissioners of Watch, Scavengers and Lamps (hereafter Min.Com.Watch), 2 June 1826, 26 Sept 1828, 20 Aug 1830.

[16]Min.Com.Watch, 10 Aug 1830; *Liverpool Mercury*, 24 Jan 1834.

they routinely dealt with many riotous affrays; they patrolled in strength in areas like Vauxhall Road on Saturday nights and on the night of St. Patrick's day when drunken riots were expected.

The third force, the dock police, was occasionally used against riot. It was established in 1811: by 1824, it consisted of 32 men; as the docks expanded, so did this force, totalling 155 by 1833. Less is known of their efficiency than of that of the constables. In 1833, following the example of the nightly watch, a metropolitan police officer was appointed as superintendent.[17] All three forces had now had chief officers with metropolitan experience.

There were frequent clashes between these forces, often when members of one arrested members of another. Relations between their superiors were little better: there were frequent petty disagreements, and in 1834, the council came into conflict with the commissioners over plans for a new day police force. There had been experimental daytime patrols in 1828 which came to nothing.[18] In 1834, the common council drafted a bill to appoint a new day force. This was delayed by disagreements between council and vestry, and was overtaken by municipal corporation reform. Its preamble does not mention riot or disorder, merely 'offences against persons and property'. The size of the force is not stated: in view of the reluctance of the council to increase the number of constables, it would probably have been small.

In emergencies, the mayor could reinforce the police with troops, with the approval of the Home Office. In practice, approval sometimes came after the event. At first men were brought from Chester or Manchester when needed, which before rail transport meant a delay of about 24 hours. These troops withdrew as soon as the immediate danger had passed, as the council would not pay to provide barracks. In 1831, accommodation was provided in a former lunatic asylum, and a permanent military presence was maintained thereafter.[19] Between 1815 and 1835, troops were called for nine out of seventy-nine incidents.

The police increased both in numbers and efficiency over these years. In 1815 there were probably about 140 police of all kinds, with troops available only after considerable delay. By 1835, the police numbered 336,

---

[17]Munic.Corp.Report, 2752, 2768; Home Office Papers, Kew PRO (hereafter HO),40.18, f 98, Mayor to Hobhouse, 22 Apr 1824; *Liverpool Courier*, 20 Mar 1833.

[18]Min. Com. Watch, 3 Oct 1828; Town Books, vol 16, 71, 5 Nov 1828; *ibid*, 83, 3 Dec 1828.

[19]HO43.32, f 257, Dawson to Mayor, 24 Mar 1824; HO79.4, f 124, Hobhouse to Byng, 1 May 1826; HO40.26/1, f 61, Bouverie to Peel, 3 Sept 1830. Town Books, Vol.15, 97, 7 June 1820. *Saturday's Advertiser*, 26 Nov 1831; HO41.11, f 235, Phillipps to Mayor, 29 Mar 1833.

with troops also permanently stationed in the town. Riot was never quoted to justify increases to the police forces; theft seemed much more dangerous. Nevertheless, the commissioners for municipal corporations reported that 'this force has been found perfectly adequate to the preservation of the peace of the town...the inhabitants consider themselves a very well protected community'.[20] There were undoubtedly those who disagreed, yet on the whole Liverpool was probably as well policed as any town outside London.

Riots, 1815 to 1835

For the years between 1815 and 1835, 79 incidents were identified, actual violence (sometimes minimal) occurring at 74 of them. Many were small brawls of unknown origin, but there were others (including one sectarian riot, one anti-police riot, and one trade dispute) which convulsed the town for over 24 hours; the type which most frequently caused such disorder was election riot.

Elections

Elections in the early part of the century were convivial. Music, processions, banners, all helped the festive air, but drink was the most powerful influence. Voters were received only in groups of ten ('tallies'), which were formed up in public houses and entertained until needed. Bribery was usual; in some years the sum was only that lost in wages by taking time off to vote, in other years it was much more.[21] The holiday atmosphere of processions, of musicians accompanying 'tallies' to the poll, the fact that today the gentleman canvasser bowed to the artisan, all eased restraint. The feeling of misrule was probably more productive of disorder than any desire to influence the outcome of the election, and much more serious violence would have been necessary to do so. The formation of partisan groups was helped by the presence of clubs with freemen among their members. They were very active: candidates approached artisan voters at their clubs, trade-based or convivial, and both types marched in the 'chairing' processions of the winners.

---

[20] Munic.Corp.Report, 2715.

[21] PP 1826-7 (394) IV.1114, *Report from Select Committee on Electoral Polls for Cities and Boroughs*; LRO *Report of Proceedings before the Select Committee of the House of Commons appointed to try the matter of the petition against the return of William Ewart for the Borough of Liverpool, Session 1830-31* (Liverpool, 1831); *Result of Evidence given before the Select Committee appointed to enquire into the petition on Liverpool Borough* (n.d. [1833]).

Nine elections led to fears of disorder during this period. The extent of disturbance is hard to estimate because it was considered normal: in 1826, one paper reported 'A very few acts of outrage only, and not of an aggravated character'.[22] Such disturbances as are described include large noisy gangs parading through the town, breaking windows where party emblems were displayed, or carrying effigies of unpopular local personalities. Party insults sometimes led to fighting, and candidates were often insulted, and occasionally assaulted. This was all fairly normal for the times; earlier Liverpool elections had been, and later ones were to be, even more riotous.

Few preventive measures were used. Special constables were posted at the hustings and the candidates' lodgings; more were enrolled if there were serious riots. In 1816 the dock police were used, and rioters tried at Lancaster assizes; seven men were imprisoned for eighteen months.[23] These sentences must reflect fears of working-class radicalism in Manchester and other areas rather than Liverpool concerns. Few other arrests are recorded, and no sentences. It is probably safe to assume that trials would normally be summary, and sentences short.

Two changes in the 1830s reduced disorder. In 1831, the use of booths, with voters divided alphabetically, meant the end of tallies. And the practice of 'chairing' winning candidates ended in 1832; this had always been a chaotic ceremony. Both changes were brought about by the Reformers, for whom, unlike the Tories, tradition was not enough to justify even moderate riot.

Political Protest

More than any other occasion, political meetings led to unjustified fears of riot. Six incidents were found: four times, precautions were taken but no disorder resulted; once, windows were broken, and once there was minimal disorder.

Even while the Six Acts were in force, the mayor of a corporate town could permit public meetings, and Liverpool's mayor did so without apparent fear that disturbances would develop. Processions such as those of trade societies were permitted, and did not need a large police presence. There is no evidence that special constables were appointed. When permission was refused, as it was if parliamentary reform was involved, the meeting might still be held: in the handful of such cases, there were neither preventive measures

---

[22]*Saturday's Advertiser*, 17 June 1826.
[23]*Liverpool Mercury*, 14 June 1816, 9 Jan 1835. Town Books, vol. 14, 613, 5 Feb 1817; PRO PL26.79, Lancaster Assizes, Indictments, Summer 1816; *Gore's General Advertiser*, 25 Nov 1830.

nor arrests. Working men did not seek approval, but met outside the town boundary; no such meeting led to significant disturbance. There was minor disorder, shouting and jostling, during a visit of William Cobbett. The *Liverpool Mercury* reported that the peaceful majority overcame trouble-makers and 'shouldered them out of the square'.[24] The mayor had decided to intervene only against an actual breach of the peace.[25]

Despite this trivial measure of actual violence, however, the mere idea of political protest could produce quite disproportionate measures of prevention. While strong precautions were not invariable, they were enforced after serious rioting at similar meetings elsewhere. In August 1819, a meeting was held to protest about Peterloo. The Home Office advised the mayor to observe the meeting and provide legal evidence of seditious speeches; there was implicit approval of the decision not to stop the meeting, which was held without permission. The yeomanry stood by (in heavy rain), and all passed off quietly.[26] In 1820, when local reformers wanted to celebrate the Queen's acquittal, the mayor threatened to use troops, negotiating a compromise whereby a procession was held (peacefully, as it turned out) and an illumination was replaced by a firework display in Mosslake Fields.[27] The lack of trouble is remarkable: ultra-loyalists tried to 'introduce into the procession carriages containing their frail female friends'.[28] And in 1831, after severe riots in Bristol over parliamentary reform, the mayor asked that troops be sent to Liverpool, even though a recent reform meeting attended by a crowd estimated at ten thousand had been peaceful.[29] The disproportion between precautions and disturbance was typical of this type of potential riot.

Trade Disputes

These disputes also caused considerable alarm. Thirteen riotous incidents were recorded during these years, and precautions were taken on one further occasion. Many trade associations existed: as Clive Behagg argues, beside its official rules each had unwritten rules determining its

---

[24]*Liverpool Mercury*, 3 Dec 1819.

[25]*Billinge's Advertiser*, 29 Nov 1819.

[26]HO41.4, f 267, Hobhouse to Mayor, 28 Aug 1819; *Gore's General Advertiser*, 2 Sept 1819; HO41.5, f 1, Hobhouse to Mayor, 1 Sept 1819.

[27]HO40.15, f 135, Drake to Byng, 13 Nov 1820; *Billinge's Advertiser*, 21 Nov 1820.

[28]*Liverpool Mercury*, 24 Nov 1820.

[29]HO52.13, f 274, Mayor to Lord Melbourne, 2 Nov 1831; HO40.29/2, f 303, W.Banning, Postmaster in Liverpool, to Sir F.Freeling, 12 Oct 1831.

attitude to the use of violence.[30] Some specialised in individual violent acts. The shipsawyers, vulnerable to competition because of their relative lack of skill and powerless because their apprenticeship was too short to qualify for freemanship, were particularly noted for extreme individual violence, including murder and arson. Other trade associations tended towards collective violence. The most serious riots were among the shipwrights, but ropemakers, shoemakers, ironfounders, and builders used similar methods during these years.

Violence in protecting the interests of workers must be seen in context. In most cases, wage rates were agreed peacefully: petitions, advertisements, and even the law were used. Strikes, which resulted most often from the reduction of wages, did not necessarily involve violence, nor was violence always collective. Its victims were usually strikebreakers. In some riots, often the smallest, considerable injuries were inflicted.[31] In larger riots, there might be only rough handling. Some used the ceremony of 'rough music', where shame encouraged conformity to group norms, as when ropemakers carried two men around the town in a cart, their coats inside-out and placards around their necks,[32] or when shipwrights burned the effigy of an apprentice who (instructed by a magistrate) did work traditionally done by journeymen.[33] There might also be a threat of future violence. The object was to make strikes effective by preventing the use of blackleg labour. This worked best in trades where a seven-year apprenticeship limited supply of skilled men; since a man could qualify for the franchise by serving a 7-year apprenticeship to a freeman, these trades also had the greatest political influence.

The Shipwrights' Club was the most powerful trade organisation. It had about 900 members; almost half were freemen, and at election times the club was lavishly entertained by candidates. Royal Oak day, known as Shipwrights' Day, was celebrated with a procession in which other trades joined, followed by club dinners. Up to 400 men could be mobilised from the shipyards at short notice, by ringing the yard bells.[34] No other club had such power or prestige, but several functioned similarly. Some had links with national unions in the same trade, but links between trades seem not to have been formed until

---

[30]Clive Behagg 'Secrecy, Ritual and Folk Violence: The Opacity of the Workplace in the First Half of the Nineteenth Century' in R D Storch (ed), *Popular Culture and Custom in Nineteenth Century England* (1982), 154-179.

[31]PP 1825 (417.437) IV.499.565, *Report of Minutes of Evidence from the Select Committee on Artisans and Machinery* (1824), 184; *Gore's General Advertiser*, 29 Jan 1824.

[32]*Gore's General Advertiser*, 17 Nov 1825.

[33]*Liverpool Courier*, 18 Apr 1827.

[34]*Liverpool Mercury*, 2 June 1820 and 1 June 1827; *Gore's General Advertiser*, 7 June 1827. See also ch 3 above.

1833-34, when most if not all of the building trades joined a general trades union, probably the Operative Builders' Union.[35]

As the nature of trade associations developed, so did methods of control. At first the police were ineffective: in the case of the ropers' 'carting' it took more than an hour to find constables. For years, little action was taken against the largest bodies, the shipwrights and shipsawyers. Strong action was first taken in 1824: master shipwrights and sawyers asked the mayor for troops to protect their premises from strikers.[36] In 1827, further riots were caused by a campaign by employers to destroy the Shipwrights' Club. Troops were again requested, to protect strikebreakers at work.[37] Troops were used also during a national building strike in 1833.[38] Such requests were granted without hesitation. The maintenance of order in trade disputes seems to have had high priority for both local and national government.

The need to prevent intimidation in strikes sometimes also influenced sentences on strikers, occasionally although not usually long; the prisoners were normally also lectured about the 'true' interests of the working man.[39] In the case of the ropemakers' ceremonial, it seems to have been thought necessary to show that even relatively non-violent behaviour would not be tolerated: the prisoners were committed to the assizes 'in order that they might hear the law of the land propounded to them by the highest authority'.[40] Both in prevention and punishment, trade disputes were severely treated. This was not because of violence: sentences almost as high were passed on apprentices who gave way to intimidation and stopped work.[41] It was the attempt of workmen to exert economic control at all which produced so disproportionate a reaction.

Direct Action

These riots were fairly frequent, but usually rather small. Of 14 cases, nine happened during the cholera epidemic of 1832.[42] Here as elsewhere,

---

[35]*Liverpool Courier*, 14 Aug 1833; *Liverpool Journal*, 22 June 1833; R.W.Postgate, *The Builders' History* (n.d.), ch 3, 55-76.

[36]HO40.18, f 53-58, Petitions of master sawyers, master shipwrights, and Mayor to Peel, 22 Mar 1824; HO43.32, f 257, Dawson to Mayor, 24 Mar 1824.

[37]HO41.7, f 232, Hobhouse to Mayor, 16 Apr 1827; HO40.22/1, f 80, Eckersley to Hobhouse, 20 Apr 1827; *Liverpool Courier*, 2 May 1827; *Liverpool Albion*, 16 July 1827.

[38]HO40.31/1, f 35, Bouverie to Phillipps, 30 June 1833.

[39]*Gore's General Advertiser*, 29 Jan 1824 and 12 Sept 1833.

[40]*Gore's General Advertiser*, 23 Mar 1826.

[41]*Liverpool Courier*, 18 Apr 1827; *Gore's General Advertiser*, 17 Nov 1825.

[42]*Liverpool Journal*, 2 June 1832; *Liverpool Times*, 5 June 1832; *Liverpool Courier*, 6, 13, 20 and 27 June 1832.

riots arose from fears of 'burking' - that doctors would dissect the bodies of cholera victims, and perhaps murder them in order to do so.[43] In Liverpool, doctors were assaulted, and the 'palanquin' used to take patients to the temporary cholera hospital was destroyed. Those involved were described as 'chiefly composed of low Irish'.[44] These riots were taken very seriously by both press and authorities. Catholic priests were prevailed upon to call for restraint.[45] There were exemplary trials at the quarter sessions, where magistrates declared that they would 'visit such offences with the utmost severity'.[46]

Other cases were very varied, including the rescue of a child from a drunken mother, theatre riots, and an attack on a temperance meeting.[47] The response to direct action riots was flexible, depending partly on the intentions of the rioters. Sentences might be severe, or there might be implicit approval of the crowd's action as in the case of the drunken mother; she rather than her attackers was arrested. It is this use of discretion which typifies the official reaction to these incidents.

Sectarian Conflict

In the early nineteenth century the difference between Protestant and Catholic was largely seen as one of 'party'. Conservatives were Anglican; Radicals were identified with Catholicism and Nonconformity.

The first 12 July celebration in Liverpool, in 1819, produced the first Orange riot. About 100 Orangemen marched through the main streets of the town carrying banners bearing Protestant devices, usually provocative to Catholics. Eleven attackers were arrested, and troops called out to prevent a recurrence.[48] Sentences were substantial. A march in the following year ended similarly, with eight arrests. The mayor attempted to prosecute the order for breaking the peace. This prosecution failed, and charges against the attackers were (presumably as a result) not pressed. Thereafter, only minor

---

[43]M.J.Durey, *The Return of the Plague: British Society and the Cholera, 1831-2*, (Dublin, 1979), 158-9, 183-4; Ruth Richardson, *Death, Dissection and the Destitute* (1987) 223-230.

[44]PP 1836 (40) XXXIV.427, *Report on the State of the Irish Poor in Great Britain* (hereafter *Poor Inquiry (Ireland)*), Appendix G, 18.

[45]*Poor Inquiry (Ireland)*, 18.

[46]*Liverpool Courier*, 13 June 1832.

[47]*Liverpool Mercury*, 7 June 1822; *Gore's General Advertiser*, 16 Dec 1824 and 27 Jan 1825; *Saturday's Advertiser*, 26 Aug 1826; *Liverpool Mercury*, 9 Oct 1835.

[48]*Gore's General Advertiser*, 22 July 1819 and 29 July 1819; *Billinge's Advertiser*, 19 July 1819 and 26 July 1819.

incidents occurred before 1835; the fortunes of the order were generally in decline.[49]

Liverpool had few Orangemen before the 1830s; many in the 1819 procession came from elsewhere. There is no evidence yet of sympathy towards the Order among leading Tories. Senior says that English members then were mainly Irish immigrants, and working-class, and this seems to have been true of Liverpool.[50] It is possible that opposition to the 1819 march may have been organised by a 'ribbon' society, one of a number of Catholic societies linked by a tenuous central organisation whose main function was the coordination of passwords. They were not terrorist organisations, although they were often confused with agrarian secret societies which were. Ribbon societies were usually urban, and sometimes acted as trade societies.[51] Their main purpose was opposition to Orangemen, often in battles which were announced in advance.[52] Such societies did meet in Liverpool at this period.[53]

On 12 July 1835 there was a serious riot when rumours of a procession caused crowds to collect in the Irish areas of town.[54] At first the crowds were not dispersed, but about 10 pm a small disturbance caused the watchmen to make an arrest. An attempt to rescue the prisoner became a mass attack on the bridewell by a crowd armed with sticks and axes. The outer door was broken down, and those besieged inside rang a bell intended as a fire-alarm. Help soon arrived, first the watchmen then the mayor with 200 troops, 100 dock police, and several constables. Later, 500 special constables were sworn in to prevent the rescue of the 51 prisoners. Forty three were convicted, and sentenced to up to six months.[55]

These sentences were influenced by the large scale of disorder, yet other sectarian riots were also taken more seriously than more casual battles, perhaps because they tended to happen in the centre of town. There were also fears that increasing Irish immigration would produce greater disorder.

---

[49]PP 1835 (603) XVII.1, *Report of Select Committee on Orange Lodges in Great Britain and the Colonies*, Ap II, 3; H.Senior, *Orangeism in Ireland and Britain, 1795-1836* (1966), 175 and 199.

[50]Senior, 152,154,158,176; *Poor Inquiry (Ireland)*, 20.

[51]G.Broeker, *Rural Disorder and Police Reform in Ireland, 1812-1836* (1970), 1-13; Lynn Hollen Lees, *Exiles of Erin: Irish Migrants in Victorian London* (Manchester, 1979), 213-4, 223-4. See also ch 4 above.

[52]Broeker, 15.

[53]PRO CO904.8.8, M'Gloin to Drummond, 4 Jan 1840; *Billinge's Advertiser*, 27 July 1819.

[54]*Liverpool Courier*, 5 July 1835; *Gore's General Advertiser*, 16 July 1835; *Liverpool Mercury*, 17 July 1835.

[55]*Liverpool Courier*, 4 Oct 1835.

Directly or indirectly, this was to prove true over the later years of the century.

Private Battles

Ten incidents have been found where violence was directed neither against authority nor towards any clear objective, but resulted from the sense of identity of those who formed one or both sides. Children, navvies, and some Irish immigrants were among groups involved.

In the case of the Irish, private battles were fully expected. The more adventurous Victorian tourist might even attend an Irish fair in the hope of seeing a faction fight. Broeker describes how fights were used in rural Ireland to settle local feuds, and Lees describes similar fights among London Irish at about the same time. Ribbon societies provided passwords specifically in case of fighting.[56] Irish immigrants were often unjustly blamed for more than their share of crime, yet they do seem to have been involved disproportionately often in assaults and affrays. Finnegan's study of the Irish community in York found that these crimes, together with drunkenness, led to the Irish contribution to total crime being higher than that of other sections of the city's population.[57]

The information available about these private battles is usually slight. Those involving navvies aroused considerable concern, those among children were often ignored. The treatment of Irish fights fell mid-way: the watch or other police attempted to stop them, but the only measure against recurrence was strengthened patrols on Saturday nights. They clearly came low on the local authorities' scale of priorities.

Rescues and Anti-Police Riots

Fourteen riots were of this type. Only two were unprovoked attacks,[58] suggesting little generalised resentment of policing. Most responded to police actions, many being attempts to rescue prisoners. On one occasion, the watch attempted to arrest two women, and a crowd collected which was estimated at some thousands. It was rendered unusually formidable by the chance presence of Irish recruits en route for South America to fight as mercenaries. This mischance was balanced by the fortuitous presence of English troops just disembarked from Ireland, who were used to disperse the crowd and prevent

---

[56]Broeker, 15-16; Lees, 167, 213-4; PRO Colonial Office Papers CO904.7.77-92, Statement of John Kelly, 6 Dec 1839.

[57]F.Finnegan, *Poverty and Prejudice* (Cork, 1982), 132-154.

[58]Min Com Watch, 28 May 1824; *Liverpool Courier*, 23 Jan 1826.

recurrence.[59] Other cases in this category were much smaller. Typical were rescues of prisoners arrested for fighting, or resistance to the seizure of an illicit still.[60]

The cases reported are almost certainly a very small proportion of actual occurrences. Preventive measures are known only for the watch, whose commissioners tried whenever possible to prosecute after any assault, collective or individual. Patrols were strengthened on Saturday nights in disturbed areas.[61] This measure was felt by the superintendent in 1833 to be unnecessary; fights, he claimed, often started with the arrest of drunks who could otherwise have found their way home: 'On Saturday nights, the Watchmen are Bullies, and the extramen their seconds'.[62]

Rescues were a serious problem; one measure against them was a vehicle fitted with chains to transport prisoners. In 1820, the mayor and magistrates deliberated on the problem of rescues,[63] but unfortunately their decision is not known. From the early 1820s, there were many improvements to courtrooms, bridewells, and gaols. These measures, of course, were not directed solely to the prevention of riot: the taking and securing of prisoners was essential to the rule of law.

Riots of Unknown Origin

Seven incidents remain in this category, and in the absence of more evidence, little can be said. They serve to demonstrate the limited press coverage of minor riots; it is certain that many more cases were completely unreported. One case was described as 'one of those disgraceful riots of so frequent occurrence in that neighbourhood';[64] only this one, among so many, was recorded. Such riots troubled the authorities little. As with private battles, only the commissioners of the watch appear to have taken any action, and this was mainly to protect watchmen from assault. The main measures, extra patrols and prosecution, have already been mentioned. Prosecution must have been at best chancy among overcrowded courtyards and back-alleys, if rioters outnumbered the watch, and identification after the event even harder.

---

[59]*Billinge's Advertiser*, 28 June and 2 Aug 1819. HO41.4, f 157, Hobhouse to Mayor, 26 June 1819.

[60]*Gore's General Advertiser*, 25 Jan 1816; *Saturday's Advertiser*, 23 Sept 1826; *Liverpool Mercury*, 23 Aug 1833.

[61]E.g.Min. Com. Watch, 23 Jan 1824, 20 May & 24 Sept 1824, 10 Jan 1826, 30 May 1835.

[62]Min. Com. Watch, 5 Apr 1833.

[63]Min. Com. Watch, 26 Dec 1823, 29 May 1829, and 28 Mar 1834. Town Books, vol 14, 597, 6 Nov 1816; vol 15, 95, 7 June 1820.

[64]*Gore's General Advertiser*, 28 Nov 1833.

New Corporation and New Police

The new Reformist corporation of 1836 was quick to take up its task. Law enforcement was very important to them; their first meeting discussed the appointment of magistrates, including a stipendiary police magistrate. Two days later a watch committee was set up; within two months a new police force took to the streets.

While routine policing was delegated to the watch committee, the handling of serious riot was not. This was made clear at the 1841 election when the watch committee's offer of help was rebuffed: '...the conservation of the peace of the Town being the peculiar duty of the magistrates, they had ... taken such measures as seemed to them desirable'.[65] The head constable's reports on major riots were normally addressed to the mayor, the watch committee receiving copies.

Home Office interest in disorder was slight to begin with; they first showed interest after warnings of an Orange Day procession in 1842.[66] From then on, such intervention became more frequent, usually because of sectarian and election riots. Nevertheless, the official view of the town, as politically peaceful, is shown by a report during the 'plug plot' riots that Liverpool was the one northern town from which troops could be withdrawn.[67]

The new police force first went on duty on 29 February 1836. Its 290 constables and 60 reserves, were supervised by 24 inspectors and 4 superintendents. In June 1837, this force amalgamated with the dock police, bringing the total number of police to over 500, and in 1838, the 88 dock gatemen were also sworn in as constables.[68] The police instruction booklet printed in 1836 gives only one page out of 68 to the handling of riot, which was assumed to be small and nocturnal.[69] Riot control was expected to be an important police function nevertheless, ranking with fire as a hazard, yet the danger to property was usually paramount: 'perhaps millions worth of property [at] the mercy of depredators'.[70]

The police were responsible jointly to the magistrates, and to the council by way of the watch committee, which met weekly; until 1851 there

---

[65]LRO 352 MIN/WAT 1/2 (Liverpool Record Office Watch Committee Papers), 414-5, 19 June 1841; *ibid*, 419, 26 June 1841.

[66]HO43.62, f 355, Phillipps to Mayor, 23 June 1842

[67]HO45.268, f 66, Warre to Phillipps, 10 Aug 1842.

[68]LRO 352 MIN/WAT 1/1 16, 28 Jan 1836; 41-44, 24 Feb 1836, 294 ff, 8 Apr 1837; 327, 10 June 1837; 589, 24 Nov 1838; *ibid* 1/2, 156.

[69]*Instructions for the Liverpool Constabulary Force*, 3 Feb 1836 in HO73/3, papers of Commissioners on County Police.

[70]LRO 352 MIN/WAT 1/5, 251-2, copy of letter, Dowling to Mayor, 12 Dec 1850.

was also a daily board dealing with disciplinary charges and requests for police attendance. Both transmitted commands via the head constable, whose powers rapidly increased as he inspired more trust. Head Constable Whitty was charged as early as 1836 with selecting constables on isolated beats to be armed with cutlasses; his decision to issue them during the Carpenters' Day riots in 1839 was discussed by the watch committee after the event, but legal opinion vindicated his action.[71]

The newly-appointed stipendiary magistrate was particularly important in the supervision of the police, because he was in a position to see the results of police activities. An editorial in the *Liverpool Journal* shortly after Whitty became its editor shows his awareness of this, arguing that, unlike the Irish Constabulary, '...our force is local and unambitious, responsible to two public bodies, and obliged to take instructions from both .... all actions [are] soon brought out into open police court'.[72]

Police methods against riot fall into two distinct categories, dictated to a great extent by prevailing circumstances. When serious disturbances were expected, precautions could be taken. The force was mobilised on military lines, with constables in squads under strict discipline. In smaller or unexpected riots, the first men on the scene had to respond as individuals, relying upon their own discretion as in day-to-day policing. In both cases, only two methods were legally permitted: the dispersal of crowds, and arrest. The law permitted the use of force in self defence, and of 'reasonable' force in dispersal and arrest. It did not permit either police or troops to make war on rioters, aiming to kill or disable them merely to stop them.

It is very difficult to establish whether the police misused force. Up to 1844, bodies of police were usually kept out of sight until needed; and the senior officer might attempt to disperse a crowd by negotiating with its leaders. Mounted police were used to maintain communication: senior officers often used horses. When confrontation was unavoidable, the foot police might charge, presumably (although this is not stated) using their staffs; they might stand firm to repel an attack; they might pursue small groups of rioters to prevent their forming larger bodies. Water was occasionally used to disperse crowds: this happened first when a fire-engine was present by chance.[73]

In contrast to the policy of the Metropolitan Police, there was no hesitation about allowing the police to take on a military appearance.

[71]LRO 352 MIN/WAT 1/1, 225, 24 Dec 1836; *Liverpool Mercury*, 7 and 14 June 1839; *Liverpool Courier*, 8 June 1839.

[72]*Liverpool Journal*, 15 June 1844.

[73]*Liverpool Courier*, 22 May 1839; LRO 352 MIN/WAT 1/1, 350-1, 29 July 1837; 1/2, 408-12, 12 June 1841; 417-8, 26 June 1841; 421-7, 5 July 1841; 408-12, 12 June 1841; *Liverpool Mercury*, 31 May 1839; *Liverpool Chronicle*, 16 Sept 1843.

Cutlasses were used by squads of men rather than individuals, for deterrence rather than self-defence. Armed police were sometimes also mounted; at the election of 1841 a troop (many of whom were said to have military experience) were used to clear streets by what can only be described as a cavalry charge, even though arms they carried were not used.[74] Arms were sometimes issued and even drawn during riots, but were rarely if ever reported to have been used. Constables were also equipped with a staff, meant both as a weapon and to signal for assistance by rapping on the pavement.[75] This could bring together up to twelve constables, depending on the area. Special constables were rarely used. They were not trusted by the regular police. At the 1841 election, the police found the specials 'excited' and, to prevent their causing more disorder, imprisoned them in the market until late at night.[76]

Early opposition to the police was slight, but after Whitty's resignation in 1844 there were problems. The second head constable, Miller, was a failure: in October 1844, when his inefficiency was already under investigation, he directly disobeyed a watch committee order, and was required to resign.[77] Dowling, Whitty's deputy, at first passed over, now became head constable. He was a poor choice to inherit a damaged force, being already in bad health.[78] Under his leadership standards continued to decline. Unwarranted assaults by the police increased. Randomly selected cases include two constables tried for an assault on a carter; an assault on a woman which the magistrate described as 'atrocious'; and two constables tried for quelling a riot by randomly hitting heads with sticks. The magistrates expressed concern: in 1852, they warned that police sticks would be withdrawn if such practices continued.[79] The watch committee were apathetic, or at best slow. Occasions of public disorder provided ample evidence of the state of the force. Orange Day 1850 saw serious riots for which the police were unprepared: an intervention of Liverpool police in a riot in neighbouring Birkenhead was disastrous, with many injuries to both rioters and police;[80] yet in 1851 the daily board ceased to sit, delegating

---

[74] Thurmond Smith, *Policing Victorian London* (1985), 113-120. LRO 352 MIN/WAT 1/1, 350-1, 29 July 1837; *ibid*, 1/2 408-12, 12 June 1841; 421-7, 5 July 1841; *Liverpool Chronicle*, 3 July 1841.

[75] *Liverpool Chronicle*, 26 Mar 1836; *Liverpool Journal*, 20 Aug 1836

[76] LRO 352 MIN/WAT 1/2, 421-7, 5 July 1841.

[77] *Liverpool Mercury*, 19 Apr 1844; LRO 352 MIN/WAT 1/3, 382-5, 25 Oct 1844.

[78] LRO 352 MIN/WAT 1/3, 89, 10 June 1843; *ibid*, 97, 24 June 1843; *ibid*, 133, 2 Sept 1843; *ibid*, 178, 25 Nov 1843.

[79] *Liverpool Journal*, 14 Feb 1846; *Liverpool Mail*, 25 Sept 1847, 21 Feb 1846, 10 Jan 1852; *Liverpool Mercury*, 2 June 1848; *Liverpool Chronicle*, 2 Feb 1850.

[80] HO45.3118, Mayor to Home Secretary, 13 Aug 1850. LRO 352 MIN/WAT 1/5, 237-9, 30 Nov 1850; HO45.3472 J&K, f 3, Brotherton to Waddington, 27 Dec 1850; HO45.3472 J&K, f 19, Williams to Home Secretary, 16 Apr 1851.

responsibility to the head constable. In 1852, after a police assault on Catholic Irish worshippers, senior officers tried to suppress evidence. Dowling was implicated, and dismissed.[81]

Only the watch committee could investigate general discipline; the magistrates were restricted to individual cases brought to their notice. After the Tories regained control of council, the Committee revealed two disturbing sources of influence. First, a Reformist attempt to exclude brewers from the watch committee was defeated. Second, members of the Orange order were also elected. Orangeism was not yet the power in local politics that it became later in the century, but in areas such as Toxteth it was of great influence. Councillor James Parker intervened to protect Orangemen from police activity; another Orangeman, H.G.Harbord, marched openly at the head of Orange processions while serving on the watch committee.[82] In 1844, the magistrates had attempted to forbid membership of Orange or Ribbon clubs. The watch committee objected and obstructed, saying they alone might issue such a regulation. It was claimed that the few men concerned had resigned from their lodges, but there were rumours of many secret members. Certainly by 1852 it was felt necessary to renew the prohibition.[83] The degree of influence is uncertain, yet to permit any involvement of either drink or sectarianism argues a very lax approach to policing.

The experience gained under Whitty in handling riots was lost along with force discipline under Dowling. His replacement, Captain Greig, set about recovering standards. Introducing this new leader to the men, the chairman of the watch committee spoke of the unnecessary use of violence. In August, at Greig's recommendation, the heavy bludgeon used by the police was replaced by a lighter stick. In December he again addressed the men about unnecessary force, threatening dismissal.[84] During his first year there were 161 dismissals out of a force numbering 806. With 153 resignations, this meant a turnover of nearly 40 per cent. From 1853 onwards, discipline improved, but police violence was not eliminated: in 1854 day patrols lost even the lighter stick.[85]

---

[81]*Liverpool Mercury*, 21 Nov 1851; LRO 352 MIN/WAT 1/5, 486, 28 Feb 1852; 494, 4 Mar 1852; 546 ff, 1 May 1852.

[82]*Liverpool Mercury*, 7 Apr 1843 and 28 Apr 1843; *Liverpool Journal*, 4 May 1844; *Liverpool Mail*, 4 May 1844 and 30 Nov 1844; LRO 352 MIN/WAT 1/3, 388, 9 Nov 1844, 410 ff, 30 Nov 1844, 627, 10 Nov 1845.

[83]LRO 352 MIN/WAT 1/3, 276-9, 27 Apr 1844; 349, 31 Aug 1844; *ibid*, 1/5 516, 27 Mar 1852; *Liverpool Journal*, 4 May 1844.

[84]*Liverpool Mercury*, 28 Apr 1852; LRO 352 MIN/WAT 1/5, 654, 7 Aug 1852; *ibid*, 1/6, 54-5, 24 Dec 1852; 298, 21 Jan 1854; 308, 11 Feb 1854; *Liverpool Mercury*, 28 Dec 1852.

[85]LRO 352 MIN/WAT 1/5 148-152, 28 May 1853, 680, 25 Sept 1853; *ibid*, 1/6, 298, 21 Jan 1854, 301, 28 Jan 1854, 305, 4 Feb 1854, 308, 11 Feb 1854, 311, 18 Feb 1854.

By the time of the first visit of inspection in 1857, the force, now numbering just under 1,000, had apparently recovered. The Inspector's reports were uniformly favourable: the force's military drill was often singled out for praise:[86] in 1860, it was stated that the force had a 'knowledge of military movements sufficient to admit of their being brought to bear with precision and decisive effect'.

By then occasions for such expertise were rare. Under Whitty, military-style action was relatively common. Under Dowling, police discipline was ragged, the response to riot a mere attack with bludgeons on nearby heads. Under Greig there were few occasions when the police acted in bodies, but his methods were similar to Whitty's; his plan for the election of 1852 shows similar dispositions. In general, the efficiency of the force in handling riots varied over the years in parallel with its overall efficiency.

Riots, 1836 to 1860

While 79 incidents were found for the years 1815 to 1835, there were over 300 between 1836 and 1860. It is not always possible to decide whether reporting or underlying incidence had increased. However, one type which certainly became more frequent was sectarian riot.

Sectarian Riot

This typically Liverpudlian form of riot occurred at least 41 times, and was feared another 18 times. Frank Neal's book gives a valuable and detailed account, stressing the association with working-class Toryism.[87] The Tories in opposition found the theme of 'the Church in danger' valuable, and sectarian issues were repeatedly raised at municipal elections. They drew upon anxiety at the increasing proportion of Irish in Liverpool. Popular fears were strongest in 1847-8, when Irish famine victims overwhelmed relief agencies. The press also contributed, particularly during the debate over the Maynooth Grant in 1841-2, and the 1850s agitation over 'papal aggression'. The most prominent Protestant activist was the Rev. H. McNeile, an Ulsterman, noted for oratory and manly good looks, who never hesitated to involve himself in party politics or sectarian dispute. His language was

---

[86]PP 1857-8 XLVII.657, *Reports of the Inspectors of Constabulary for the year ended 29 Sept 1857*, 54 (712); PP 1859 XXII.399, *Reports.....29 Sept 1858*, 65 (436); PP 1860 LVII.527; *Reports.....29 Sept 1859*, 61 (587); PP 1861 LII.641; *Reports.....29 Sept 1860*, 61 (701); PP 1862 XLV.433, *Reports .....29 Sept 1861*, 58 (490).

[87]Frank Neal, *Sectarian Violence: the Liverpool Experience, 1819 - 1914* (Manchester, 1988).

extreme: '....are you to be deposed and murdered as heretics?' He was prominent in the Operative Protestant Association whose membership included many working men.[88]

Throughout the 1840s and 50s, local membership of the Orange Order grew. In 1849 about 40 lodges met in the town; by 1860, there were 100. While there were links with respectable Tories, most members were workingmen.[89] During the time of the Reformist council, no Orange procession was attempted. The magistrates opposed all such parades, and even prevailed upon the Welsh to give up their peaceful celebrations of St.David's Day to avoid giving an excuse to others. In 1839, though, the shipwrights' procession, disused for 8 years, was revived.[90] As Kevin Moore has described, the procession was peaceful despite the presence of Orange banners, but later there were serious riots. Similar processions in subsequent years were strongly policed.[91] In 1841, a Protestant teetotallers' procession was planned for 12 July and Whitty took the precaution of ascertaining his legal powers. The town clerk's opinion that the police could only act if there was an observable tendency to a breach of the peace determined policy for some years, limiting magistrates to advising rather than ordering that processions should be avoided, and forbidding arrest until disorder was imminent. The council asked repeatedly but unsuccessfully for powers to ban processions, perhaps by the extension of a law used in Ireland.[92]

Processions on St. Patrick's day, 17 March, were also feared as a possible occasion for sectarian riot. False analogies were drawn which identified this as the Catholic equivalent of 12 July. In fact, while drunken disorder was frequent, sectarian riot was almost unknown. Orangemen's ideas of legitimacy made it unlikely that they would attack unprovoked, nor did Irish nationalists use provocative symbolism. Protestants and Catholics could and did share this celebration at least until about 1840, in both Liverpool and Ireland.[93]

---

[88]*Liverpool Journal*, 6 Aug 1836; *Liverpool Mail*, 26 Nov 1839, 26 Sept 1840; *Liverpool Chronicle*, 12 Dec 1842

[89]*Liverpool Mercury*, 16 July 1841, 20 Oct 1849; *Liverpool Courier*, 6 Mar 1860; *Liverpool Journal*, 28 May 1842; LRO 352 MIN/WAT 21/6, 479-80, 16 July 1842.

[90]*Liverpool Chronicle*, 12 Mar 1836; *Liverpool Mail*, 30 May 1839; *Liverpool Mercury*, 31 May 1839.

[91]*Liverpool Mail*, 30 May 1840; *Liverpool Chronicle*, 5 June 1841. See ch 3 above.

[92]HO45.249D, f 7, headed 'Queries put by Mr. Whitty, 10th July 1841'. HO45.670, Resolution of Liverpool Magistrates, 15 Apr 1844; HO43.66, f 354, Phillipps to Mayor, 19 Apr 1844; f 292, Waddington to Mayor, 14 July 1851; HO45.3472M, f 22, Mayor to Home Secretary, 19 July 1851.

[93]*Liverpool Journal*, 19 Mar 1836; Jacqueline R Hill, 'National Festivals, the State, and 'Protestant Ascendancy' in Ireland, 1790-1829', *Irish Historical Studies*, vol xxiv (1984), 30-51.

Early in 1842, soon after the Tories regained control of the council, a large Orange funeral procession took place without police intervention. The Order next asked permission for a procession on 12 July. The mayor consulted the Home Office. Although some lodges agreed not to march, troops were made available.[94] A procession was held, masquerading as a 'postponed' shipwrights' procession.[95] Strong policing kept order; for the next eight years precarious peace was maintained. Abstention from processions could be negotiated but not enforced, and cooperation was usually conditional upon there being no St. Patrick's procession. Nor could the Order always control its members, particularly the young.[96] Disorder was small until 1850, when there was a death by shooting.[97] The next year, a procession was permitted despite warnings; the head constable, Dowling, said he had no reason to fear riot. Police did not accompany the marchers, and serious disorder broke out. This prompted Home Office accusations of inefficiency to which the mayor replied by again quoting the need for greater legal powers.[98] An anonymous letter alleged that Dowling's reluctance to act was a result of Orange influences. Such rumours were extremely persistent. Since the attempt in 1844 to prevent police belonging to Orange lodges had been defeated, the matter had been ignored, and known Orangemen had been allowed to become watch committee members. Relations between the police and the Irish were bad; and recently Liverpool police had shown during a riot of Catholic Irish in Birkenhead that they would meet violence with violence.[99] Significantly, it was immediately after Dowling's resignation, brought about by his attempt to cover up a violent attack by police on Irishmen, that the magistrates renewed their attempts to outlaw Orangeism from the force, the watch committee this time assisting.[100]

---

[94]LRO 352 MIN/WAT 21/6, 254, 7 Mar 1842. HO45.249D, f 2, Mayor to Graham, 28 June 1842; HO45.269, f 117, Wemyss to Phillipps, 14 July 1842; *ibid*, f 119, Town Clerk to Falconer, 12 July 1842.

[95]*Liverpool Mercury*, 3 June 1842.

[96]*Liverpool Mercury*, 18 July 1848; *Liverpool Times*, 14 Mar 1843; HO45.670 Minutes of Magistrates Meeting, 11 Apr and Mayor to Graham, 16 Apr 1844; *Liverpool Journal*, 14 June 1845; *Liverpool Chronicle*, 19 July 1845.

[97]*Liverpool Mercury*, 16 July 1850; *Liverpool Mail*, 20 July 1850; *Liverpool Chronicle*, 17 July and 3 Aug 1850; *Liverpool Courier*, 7, 24 and 31 July 1850.

[98]HO45.3472M, f 26, Petition of Arthur McEvoy, 2 July 1851; *ibid*, f 10, Dowling to Mayor, 7 July 1851; *ibid*, f 18, Dowling's report, 14 July 1851. HO43.79, f 292, Waddington to Mayor, 14 July 1851; HO45.3472M, f 22, Mayor to Home Secretary, 19 July 1851.

[99]HO45.3472M, f 16, Anon to Home Secretary, 19 July 1851; LRO MIN/WAT 1/5, 5 and 28 July 1849; HO45.3140, Statements of complainants re police actions at riot of November 1850.

[100]LRO 352 MIN/WAT 1/5, 382, 9 Aug 1851; *Liverpool Chronicle*, 6 Sept 1851; LRO 352 MIN/WAT 1/5, 516, 27 Mar 1852.

In August the following year, 1853, a procession was held, against the advice of magistrates. Although no greater legal powers were available, the Home Office recommended firm action. The new head constable, Greig, led the police out in force to meet the marchers. Several arrests were made, and trouble averted. After this date, processions were held only outside the borough, the police guarding the boundaries.[101] For the moment, these riots were successfully contained.

Political Protest

As in the first half of the period, violent political protest was often anticipated but rarely amounted to much. Disorder occurred on eleven occasions; precautions were taken on a further nine. Attacks on protest meetings by Conservative working men were frequent; disturbance rarely resulted from protest. The attackers would probably have claimed religious justification. The Operative Conservative Association gave an indication of popular political views when in 1837 they objected to government by 'papists, infidels, socinians'. At elections, 'the pulpit beat its 'drum ecclesiastick', with vigour.[102] When support for Tory candidates was a Protestant duty, it was predictable that sectarian riot disrupted Radical meetings. Kevin Moore has described the activities of the 'old freemen'; they were noticeable, for example, at a protest meeting in 1839, 'linking themselves together, and pushing, swaying the crowd in different directions'.[103] He has also described how apprentice shipwrights too became involved in such attacks. Soon after, the sectarian demagogue McNeile spoke against reform of the corn-laws; the police stood by and Catholic priests urged calm.[104]

Major public meetings were of course routinely given a police presence, whether controversial or not. Meetings were also more often held indoors, with admission by ticket. Both helped ensure quiet. The peculiarities of Liverpool's popular politics have been dealt with elsewhere in this book. Chartists scolded the locals for apathy; the Irish were a different matter.

---

[101]HO45.4085, f 85, poster; *ibid*, f 86, Mayor to Walpole; HO41.20, f 22, Jolliffe to Mayor, 11 Aug 1852; HO45.4085F, f 88, extract from N & S Division Report Books, 10 Aug 1852; *ibid*, f 93, Town Clerk to Walpole, 12 Aug 1852; PL 27.13/2; *Liverpool Albion*, 16 Aug 1852; *Liverpool Mercury*, 13 Aug 1852, 14 July 1854, 13 July 1858, and 13 July 1859; *Liverpool Chronicle*, 28 Aug 1852 and 14 July 1860; LRO 253 MIN/WAT 1/6, 46, 27 Nov 1852; HO45.5128, f 552, police report of the events of 28 June 1853; *Liverpool Courier*, 18 July 1855

[102]*Liverpool Mail*, 25 July 1837; *Liverpool Chronicle*, 4 Apr 1837.

[103]*Liverpool Mercury*, 24 May 1839.

[104]*Liverpool Mercury*, 18 June 1841; *Liverpool Chronicle*, 12 June 1841; *Liverpool Mail*, 12 June 1841; LRO 352 MIN/WAT 1/2, 408-412, 12 June 1841; *Liverpool Mercury*, 18 June 1841. See also ch 3 above.

Daniel O'Connell's appearances drew enthusiastic crowds. A Liverpool branch of his Repeal movement existed by January 1841, with perhaps about 5,000 members.[105]

John Belchem has described the events of 1848; all that need be done here is to underline the strength of the official reaction. In March, 500 special constables were sworn in; soon afterwards, the enrolled pensioners were alerted. As usual, the main fear of the merchants was for their goods; particularly after messages from Dublin Castle that the Chartists and Young Irelanders meant to start fires on St Patrick's Day. The Irish readily sacrificed their parade in the interests of public safety, but panic was unabated.[106] For the next five months the authorities were watchful. Large number of troops and special constables were at hand. Meetings of Chartists and Repealers were watched openly and covertly. Some Confederate meetings were prevented. The police were armed, and their numbers increased from 830 in July to 1,090 by 16 September.[107] A petition, signed by many, to extend the suspension of Habeas Corpus from Ireland to Liverpool is an important indicator of local panic.[108] The outcome was anticlimactic. A flurry of preventive activity accompanied the arrest of a handful of activists and the press began to minimise the scale of the affair;[109] estimates of potential revolutionaries fell from thousands to scores.[110] The Liverpool authorities were anxious, however, to keep their additional powers. The Home Office insisted that the police should be disarmed, and later had to request the release of marines protecting the docks. Even so, large numbers of troops were retained.[111] The mayor wrote plaintively '....I understand that we have

---

[105]*Liverpool Mercury*, 19 Jan 1836, 1 Jan 1841, 12 Aug 1842 and 22 Nov 1844. K B Nowlan, *The Politics of Repeal: A study in relations between Great Britain and Ireland, 1841-50*, (1965), 22; *Liverpool Journal*, 29 Aug 1840, 24 Oct 1846 and 1 May 1847; *Liverpool Chronicle*, 16 Sept 1843

[106]HO45.2410B, f 891, Mayor to Home Secretary, 9 Mar 1848; *ibid*, f 1170, Mcgregor (Constabulary Office, Dublin Castle) to Dowling, 15 Mar 1848; HO41.19, f 42, Phillipps to Mayor, 14 Mar 1848; *Liverpool Journal*, 18 Mar 1848. See ch 4 above.

[107]HO45 2410B, ff 498-507, Abstract of Speeches at a Public Meeting, held at the Music Hall in Bold Street, ... 31 Mar 1848; *ibid*, f 619, Report of T.A.Redin, 29 June 1848; *ibid*, f 639, Report of Magistrates, 8 July 1848. *ibid*, f 1054, Mayor to Home Secretary, 10 June 1848; *Liverpool Mercury*, 14 Apr 1848; LRO 352 MIN/WAT 1/4 518-9, Report of Sub-committee on Increase in Police Force, 16 Sept 1848.

[108]*Liverpool Journal*, 29 July 1848; J.Saville, *1848: The British State and the Chartist Movement* (Cambridge, 1987), 154-5.

[109]HO45.2410B, f 721, Mayor to Home Secretary, 23 July 1848. HO45.2410D, f 621, Warre to Asst. Adjutant General, 1 Aug 1848.

[110]PL26.176 Indictments, Liverpool Assizes, Summer 1848; PL27.12/1 Depositions, ditto.

[111]HO41.19 f 276, Waddington to Mayor, 4 Aug 1848; *ibid* f 304, same to same, 31 Aug 1848; HO45.3131, f 54, Cathcart to Waddington, 27 Nov 1850.

the character of being unnecessarily alarmed here...'.[112] This was by far the most dramatic case of protest-directed activity during the first half of the century in Liverpool; it exhibits in full measure the excessive alarm and easy recourse to troops which characterised the treatment of political disorders.

Elections

Of nine contested parliamentary elections, only two were apparently completely orderly. Both freemen and householders voted, and the freemen appear to have been trustees of the old heritage of election violence, and their increasing dilution a moderating factor. There is no record of disturbance at municipal elections, at which only householders voted. In 1835, freemen formed just over one-third of the electorate; by 1841 they were only a quarter. Their proportion continued to fall thereafter.[113]

Shorter elections, using polling booths, were easier to police, and precautions were extensive, but not foolproof. Sectarian riot was expected in 1837; troops were brought to the edge of the borough in readiness.[114] Despite inexperience, the police coped, without using the cutlasses with which they were armed. Injuries occurred, but riot never became widespread.[115] Armed police were even more prominent in 1841, when mounted men with drawn cutlasses in four squads charged simultaneously down four streets in a close copy of a cavalry charge.[116]

In both these years, many rioters were arrested. 1841 saw heavier sentences, rioters having caused two deaths. The election of 1852 was particularly troubled. Stockport had recently suffered severe anti-Irish rioting, and Liverpool Conservatives had again raised the sectarian cry. Beforehand, the police seized a cache of weapons said to have been prepared for use in sectarian riots. The Tories insisted on using party colours,[117] although they had been sacrificed in 1847 with good effect. Trouble started as the Tory procession passed an Irish enclave, but police acted quickly. Two deaths

---

[112]HO45.2410B, f 811, Mayor to Home Secretary, 5 Aug 1848.

[113]*Liverpool Times*, 29 June 1841; *Liverpool Chronicle*, 19 Aug 1837.

[114]E.g. LRO 352 MIN/WAT 1/1, 350-1, Head Constable's Report following election, 29 July 1837; *ibid,* 417-8, Report prior to election, 26 June 1841; HO52.34, f 210, Mayor to Ld J Russell, 28 July 1837; HO52.35 f 135, Wemyss to Phillipps, 26 July 1837; *ibid,* f 137, Campbell to OC 7th Fusiliers, 25 July 1837; *ibid,* f 142, Wemyss to Phillipps, 29 July 1837.

[115]LRO 352 MIN/WAT 1/1, 350-1, 29 July 1837; *Liverpool Mail*, 25 July 1837; *Liverpool Mercury*, 26 July 1837; *Liverpool Journal*, 29 July 1837; *Liverpool Courier*, 24 July 1837; *Liverpool Chronicle*, 29 July 1837.

[116]*Liverpool Chronicle*, 3 July 1841.

[117]*Liverpool Journal*, 24, 31 July 1847.

occurred, both probably resulting from police action although inquest verdicts exonerated the force.[118] In other years, however, police action prevented widespread disorder, although there might be small outbreaks. In general, the police gained control of electoral riots quite quickly, as had been the case for sectarian riots.

Trade Disputes

Collective violence during trade disputes was recorded 26 times, and police precautions on three other occasions. The relative scarcity of industrial violence during this period is remarkable in view of the changes affecting workers: mechanisation, imposition of London working hours, increase in the use of apprentice labour, all produced dissent. Other changes, though, reduced chances of conflict; docks replaced shipyards, and roperies were forced outside the borough to find space - both ropers and shipwrights had been frequent users of violence.

The approach of trade organisations to violence was as disparate as before 1835: the same trades continued to be responsible for the majority of violent incidents, with less violence from growing trades such as engineering. The shipwrights' society claimed priority in employment for local men, and assaults on outsiders were frequent.[119] However, the numbers involved in these attacks were lower than in 1815-35, rarely over 50. Serious injury was reported only once.

In comparison, dock porters were restrained. When threatened by major change in 1846, their methods were entirely peaceful, although in 1848, a meeting caused alarm by coinciding with fears of Irish revolt, and troops were called in.[120] In another dock strike, in 1853, the police claimed to have maintained order; the credit is probably due rather to the strikers' moderation.[121]

---

[118]*Liverpool Journal*, 3 July 1852; *Liverpool Albion*, 5 July 1852; *Liverpool Chronicle*, 26 Jun and 10 July 1852; *Liverpool Times*, 8 July 1852; *Liverpool Mail*, 24 July 1852.

[119]*Liverpool Mercury*, 21, 28 Oct 1853; *Liverpool Times*, 15 Dec 1842, 8 Sept 1846; *Liverpool Courier*, 7 July 1852; *Liverpool Chronicle*, 29 July 1854.

[120]*Liverpool Mercury*, 10 Mar 1848, 22 Mar 1850; *Liverpool Mail*, 11 Mar 1848; HO45.2410B, f 979, Rushton to Home Office, 6 Mar 1848; *ibid*, f 859, Mayor to Home Office, 7 Mar 1848. HO41.19, f 22, Phillipps to Mayor, 9 Mar 1848; *Liverpool Mail*, 11 Mar 1848. See also ch 4 above.

[121]LRO 352 MIN/WAT 1/5, 169, 11 June 1853; HO45.5128, f 543, Mayor to Home Secretary, 13 June 1853; HO43.83, f 29, Waddington to Mayor, 22 June 1853; LRO 352 MIN/WAT 1/5, 331, 1 Apr 1854.

Police protection was readily given to strike-breakers, and at least once plain-clothes police crossed a picket-line as provocateurs.[122] The police supported employers without question despite the often minimal levels of violence.

Private Battles

Thirty-two such battles were found: as before, they involved schoolchildren, Irish immigrants, and navvies. At least one fight happened by arrangement: a barrel of beer was provided, and 300 men joined in 'what the Americans call a free fight'.[123]

Schoolboys were not taken seriously: 2s 6d (12½p) fines might be imposed.[124] There was similar tolerance for the snowball fights which three times broke out among merchants (grave and serious businessmen, as a rule) on Exchange Flags. Windows were broken, and the head constable himself struck by snowballs; some gentlemen were even taken into custody, but almost immediately released.[125]

The Irish were pre-eminent, but not alone, among those forming fighting alliances. Apart from regional loyalties, and Ribbon clubs, there were family groups such as the 'Kellys, Fitzpatricks and Murphys', and clubs like the mysterious 'Molly Maguires', first mentioned in 1853.[126] They were reputedly sworn to give mutual help, 'an insult..... to one being taken as an insult to all'.

Resulting prosecutions got little attention from magistrates, who might decline to act if there were faults on both sides. There were probably many unrecorded riots of this type. Constables were content to stop disorder, without necessarily making arrests. For example, police had dealt with a series of riots which had been 'agait [sic] for a fortnight' before making any arrest.[127] Many disturbances were private also, in a sense, in their location.

---

[122]*Liverpool Mercury*, 5 Feb 1841 and 28 Apr 1853; *Liverpool Courier*, 4 May 1853.

[123]*Liverpool Daily Post*, 10 May 1859; *Liverpool Albion*, 16 May 1859.

[124]LRO 352 POL 1/1, 63, 30 Apr 1836; *Liverpool Mail*, 3 Feb 1849. *Liverpool Chronicle*, 2 June 1849.

[125]*Liverpool Mail*, 7 Jan 1854 and 3 Feb 1855; *Liverpool Albion*, 9 Jan 1854; *Liverpool Mercury*, 6 Jan 1854, 30 Jan 1855; *Liverpool Chronicle*, 7 and 14 Jan 1854 and 3 Feb 1855; *Liverpool Times*, 1 Feb 1855; *Liverpool Courier*, 31 Jan 1855; *Liverpool Daily Post*, 13 and 20 Feb 1860.

[126]*Liverpool Mercury*, 10 May 1853; *Liverpool Albion*, 27 Mar 1854; *Liverpool Journal*, 17 Apr 1858.

[127]*Liverpool Journal*, 16 July 1853.

The poorer areas of town were warrens of courts and alleys.[128] The courts, which could be entered only via a narrow tunnel, were not part of the official police beat. It is not surprising that little attention was given to these riots until they spilled onto a main street, where they were taken slightly more seriously.

Direct Action Riots

Thirty-four recorded cases were found, all more or less violent, with varying degrees of spontaneity. Some would engage in riot for payment: 50 men were hired to prevent the USS 'Victoria' from leaving port before she could be arrested.[129] The form of traditional demonstration known as 'rough music' was recorded once, when Irishwomen crossed town to shame the mistress of a well-known Irish publican.[130] A similar imposition of group norms can be seen in the case of a shipwright, subjected to a punishment known as 'dozening' for failing to contribute towards the shipwrights' procession.[131] He was told that 'we must serve thee as any other person for the violation of rule'. The magistrate declared that he 'must' impose a fine, but made it small. The Evangelical movement also led to riots when open-air preaching caused annoyance. Clergy expected the police to ensure a quiet audience, but lowlier evangelists might find that they, not their audiences, were arrested.[132]

The traditional cause of direct-action riots was lack of food. In several years a soup-kitchen - at which a single constable maintained order - was the only resource of many. This complacency was shaken in 1855. Bread had been dear all summer; the winter was extremely severe, the usual charities quite inadequate. In February, people clamouring for food were dispersed by police.[133] The next day, crowds milling about in the streets coalesced into a mob. Bread-shops were attacked, loaves and money being demanded or taken. Very few other targets suffered. The police made little impression on the rioters, who dispersed in front of them only to re-form elsewhere. Two hundred 'respectable' porters were sworn in as special constables; mounted

---

[128]I.C.Taylor, 'The Court and Cellar Dwelling; the Eighteenth Century Origin of the Liverpool Slum', *Transactions of the Historic Society of Lancashire and Cheshire*, 122 (1970), 82.

[129]*Liverpool Journal*, 23 May 1840.

[130]*Liverpool Mercury*, 12 Nov 1855.

[131]*Liverpool Mercury*, 25 June 1841; *Liverpool Journal*, 19 June 1841.

[132]*Liverpool Mercury*, 16 Mar and 1 July 1857; *Liverpool Courier*, 15 Apr 1857 and 14 Apr 1858. See also ch 7 below.

[133]LRO 352 MIN/WAT 21/6, p154, 7 Jan 1842; *Liverpool Mercury*, 21 July 1854, and 9 and 20 Feb 1855; *Liverpool Journal*, 24 Feb 1855.

police and enrolled pensioners were called out; order was restored by the end of the day.[134]

Over 100 were arrested, the vast majority being Irish in origin.[135] Many were committed to the Assizes, where sentences were harsh. The press justified severity against starving people by labelling them 'Manchester desperadoes', 'pickpockets and prostitutes': 'This was not a riot of the working men'.[136] Yet one of these papers admitted that out of 65 tried in one day, only two were known to the police, and these for drunkenness.

Following this riot, the authorities became more sensitive for a time to the threat of hungry men, and a group were arrested in 1857 for going about in gangs, begging. The Stipendiary Magistrate in sentencing them remarked that 'whether people were suffering or not, ... order should be maintained in this town'.[137] On the whole, however, direct action riots were left to the police to deal with as they saw fit, and police priorities were decisive.

Anti-Police Riots

These were by far the most numerous, no less than 90 being found. Most were rescues of prisoners: the police also risked assault when they interfered in popular pastimes like dog-fighting and Sunday cricket. In 1838 an inspector was killed when attempting to stop a prizefight.[138] There were also revenge attacks.[139]

The frequency of recorded attacks on the police rose around 1844-50, when force discipline degenerated seriously.[140] There is little direct evidence of police aggression, but the incident which brought about Dowling's dismissal showed the police attacking indiscriminately an Irish crowd whom they took

---

[134]*Liverpool Courier*, 21 and 28 Feb, and 4 Apr 1855; *Liverpool Times*, 22 Feb 1855; *Liverpool Journal*, 24 Feb, 3 and 31 Mar, and 7 Apr 1855; *Liverpool Mercury*, 20 Feb 1855; *Liverpool Chronicle*, 24 Feb 1855; *Liverpool Mail*, 17 and 24 Feb 1855; HO41.20, f 92, Waddington to Mayor, 19 Feb 1855; *ibid*, f 93, Fitzroy to Mayor, 22 Feb 1855; *ibid*, f 95, same to same, 24 Feb 1855; PL27 13/1 & PL27.13/2, Depositions; PL26.204 Indictments, Liverpool Assizes, Spring 1855; LRO 347 QUA, Quarter Sessions Indictments, Mar 1855.

[136]PP 1854-5 XIII.313, *Report of Select Committee on Poor Removal*, 297.

[136]*Liverpool Courier*, 21 Feb 1855; *Liverpool Chronicle*, 24 Feb 1855.

[137]*Liverpool Daily Post*, 4 Dec 1857.

[138]*Liverpool Mercury*, 15 June 1838, 16 Apr 1852, 18 July 1854 and 22 June 1858. LRO 352 MIN/WAT 21/1, 52, 27 May 1836; *ibid*, 21/3, 82, 15 June 1838; *ibid*, 1/2, 152-3, 15 Feb 1840; *Liverpool Journal*, 4 June 1838 and 15 June 1839; PL 26.130; *Liverpool Albion*, 12 Sept 1836

[139]*Liverpool Courier*, 28 Apr 1852; *Liverpool Albion*, 30 May 1859.

[140]1836-44: 16 cases, 20.8% of known riots; 1844-52: 40 cases, 37.4%.

to be already rioting; they were in fact escaping from a collapsing church building.[141] Under Greig's regime, rescues continued to be frequent, and there were also battles between the police and troops, in which both sides joined with some alacrity.[142]

Preventive measures were few, beyond increasing patrols in troublesome areas, and the individual constable's response and the availability of men nearby were mainly responsible for deciding the outcome.

Riot of Unknown Origin

Forty-three incidents have no known cause. Many of them occurred in areas recognised as disorderly, such as Vauxhall Road, Scotland Road, or St James Street. The character of the public houses was probably relevant. The publican of one in Vauxhall Road, shown to have harboured prostitutes and pickpockets, kept his licence because every house in the road was as bad.[143] Drink was often blamed, but no systematic data is available. Drunken men, and women, might fight in the street; the event was of no great interest.

Conclusions

There were clearly differences in the pattern both of riots and of their control between the two periods 1815 - 1835 and 1836 - 1860. The most obvious is that many more cases of riot were found in the later period in almost every category. Figure 5.1 shows the annual mean number of riots for each period. The only type to become less frequent was election disorder, where the number of opportunities is limited by number of contests.

---

[141]*Liverpool Journal*, 28 Feb 1852; *Liverpool Mail*, 28 Feb 1852; LRO 352 MIN/WAT 1/5, 486, 28 Feb 1852; *ibid*, 516, 27 Mar 1852.

[142]*Liverpool Chronicle*, 23 Dec 1848 and 5 July 1851; *Liverpool Mercury*, 12 Jan 1849 and 8 July 1851; *Liverpool Albion*, 7 July 1851; *Liverpool Daily Post*, 14 Sept 1858; *Liverpool Courier*, 15 Sept 1858; *Liverpool Journal*, 18 Sept 1858.

[143]LRO 352 MIN/WAT 1/5, 546, 1 May 1852.

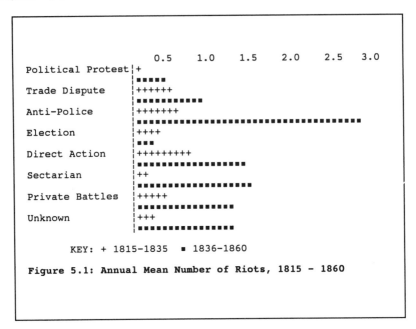

KEY: + 1815–1835 ■ 1836–1860

Figure 5.1: Annual Mean Number of Riots, 1815 – 1860

The relative frequency of different types of riot is no safe basis for conclusions, when the probability of a riot being reported cannot be established. The increase in recorded cases probably reflects better reporting. It is clear, however, that disorder was extremely persistent. On a national scale, political protest declined; locally crowds were still ready to use violence for a wide range of other purposes.

How does the differentiation in handling compare? This can be considered under three headings: preventive measures, policing of actual riots, and punishment. Preventive measures were possible only where there was advance warning, as with elections, trade disputes, and political protest meetings. The most extreme measure was the provision of military force in advance of need. Before 1835 this was restricted to trade disputes and political protest. After 1836 it was found in six out of the eight categories. Of course, the general level for preventive measures increased for all types of anticipated riot; there was more manpower available for policing. Political protest in both periods attracted the most extreme measures, but after 1835 election and sectarian disorders were also taken seriously. On the other hand the approach to trade disputes grew more tolerant; extreme measures had not been unusual before 1835. This evening-out of preventive measures suggests an underlying belief in the equal illegality of riot of all kinds, regardless of its target. Where disorder and even violence had been apparently taken less seriously than interference with trade, or with peace officers, it seems that violence and disorder in themselves came to be considered as worthy of attention.

Police activity during riots is harder to analyze. The size and violence of the mob, their location, the practical difficulties in bring police to the scene, all limited the possible measures. There could be little differentiation in reactive measures unless the police were able to prepare in advance. It is true that between 1836 and 1860, troops were never used against rioters; they had been used in nearly 10 per cent of cases in the earlier period. This, of course, reflects the growing strength of the police; we are talking about two different things.

Punishment - arrest, trial and sentence - is a different matter. Like policing, numbers of arrests were affected by practical considerations, and thus are of little help. There was a reduction in the mean number of arrests per incident probably due to the reporting of smaller incidents with fewer arrests rather than to a change in policy.

The distribution of trials between police courts, quarter sessions, and assizes shows more interesting alteration. Before 1835, the probability of trial at quarter sessions or assizes varied greatly with the type of riot. Trials at the assizes were relatively unusual. The majority arose from trade disputes: three quarters of such trials were at the assizes, compared with about one-eighth of trials for attacks on the police. This was presumably to obtain publicity as a warning to others. Where the popular view might have condoned riot, the theatre of the trial underlined the illegality of such methods of protest.

After 1835, the probability of being sent for trial at assizes or quarter sessions was more uniform. The chance of summary trial was a little higher for those taking part in private battles; in sectarian riots, it was a little lower. This reflects the events of 1852, when 15 prisoners were sent to the Assizes to mark the new policy of preventing Orange processions. This method of demonstrating official disapproval was clearly still valued.

The sentences resulting from these trials, of whichever type, are of greatest interest. For each period, sentences were ranked in order of length. The median rank for each type could then be plotted in linear form, as in figure 5.2. One type was omitted for the first period: the only known sentences for riot at elections were those at the Lancaster Assizes in 1816; it is almost certain that the normal treatment of electoral rioters was summary trial followed by a fine or a short sentence.

The possibility of sentence-length being determined rather by the severity of violence than by type of riot was also tested; no important correlation was found for either period either between sentence and severity (in terms of damage or injury) or between sentence and size of riot (in terms of numbers taking part).[144] Before 1835, it is clear that the type of riot was important in determining the punishment of those arrested. After 1835, closer grouping is very clear. Political riot is obviously a case apart; otherwise, sentences are applied more evenly across all types of riot. Such differentiation as remains is still statistically significant, but is very much smaller. Statistical tests show that the possibility of such differences arising by chance was extremely small.[145] Clearly, the data on sentences shows that punishment for riot of any type except political protest became much more uniform. Those arrested while taking part in collective violence were to be punished, it would seem, purely for having rioted. Neither their motive, nor the outcome of the riot, was likely to affect their sentences.

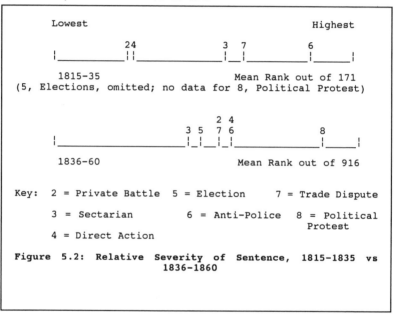

Figure 5.2: Relative Severity of Sentence, 1815-1835 vs 1836-1860

When all aspects of control are combined, it appears that the authorities before 1835 distinguished between riots of different type, on a scale with political protest at the upper end. Sectarian riots, anti-police riots, and trade

---

[144]Spearman Correlation Coefficients: Sentence vs Severity; 1815-35, .0476 (N = 163, sig = .273); 1836-60, .0039 (N = 828, sig = .456); Sentence vs Size; 1815-35, .0326 (N = 161, sig = .341); 1836-60, .0140 (N-787, sig = .348).

[145]Kruskal-Wallis One-Way Analysis of Variance: significance <0.0001 for both periods.

disputes were highly placed; election disorders, direct action riots and private battles were ranged towards the lower end. Can any underlying theory be sketched in to account for this pattern? By some, or perhaps in some contexts, violence was seen as merely a natural property of the 'lowest of the low'; and sometimes not only of the lowest. Before better policing, even a well-to-do young man might be expected to engage in 'nocturnal brawls, riots and dissipations'.[146] The Irish in particular were understood to enjoy a good fight, the race 'who broke each others' heads as an amusement'.[147] This explanation can be referred to as 'brutishness'. Disgraceful though it might be, such fighting was thought to be of no great consequence. Mere injury was unimportant. It could be written at election time that 'there may have been a broken head or two', yet 'never, perhaps, was an occasion of this sort less deformed by any ill-humour'.[148] Even the Recorder, speaking about unprovoked assaults on passers-by, explained that the danger was that the attackers might turn to robbery.[149]

Injuries, then, did not make a riot a matter for concern. However, disorder could provide an opportunity for theft. This explanation could be called 'criminal motivation'. For example, disturbances were explained as a ruse to permit pocket-picking.[150] Between them these two theories were predominant in private battles, election riot, anti-police riot and riot of unknown origin. Both brutishness and criminality would be expected to be intractable, the best measure of prevention being severe punishment for serious cases, such as attacks on peace-officers.

In contrast, some riot might be recognised as rational: violence might even occasionally be justified, as when a crowd rescued a child from a drunken woman. More often, the crowd was held to be misguided: moderate punishment, accompanied by explanation, might be beneficial. This can be seen in the cholera riots, and more frequently in trade disputes in the magistrates' set speech on the right of men to sell their labour without intimidation. Such lessons might be even more effective at the Assizes, where it would have maximum publicity.

None of these three explanations, caused serious anxiety, apparently. This was reserved for the most alarming rationale, 'subversive riot'. This was so much feared that it was rarely openly named. The 'demagogue' wishing to 'marshal a formidable host, and make a physical demonstration for carrying

---

[146]Brooke, *Liverpool in the Last Quarter of the Eighteenth Century* (Liverpool, 1853), 298-300.
[147]*Liverpool Times*, 11 Mar 1834.
[148]*Saturday's Advertiser*, 27 Oct 1827.
[149]*Saturday's Advertiser*, 24 Jan 1829.
[150]*Liverpool Courier*, 27 Oct 1831.

some popular doctrine' or 'a few ill-disposed persons' stealing gunpowder from a magazine were typical bogeymen.[151] 'Inflammatory' was a much-used word; the populace, well-known as tending to brutish or criminal riot, was seen as tinder, ready to be ignited by any stray political spark. For some, subversive riot was the only 'real' riot; there can be no other explanation for the startling statement by the head of the Dock Police, that 'there have been no riots at Liverpool while I have been in office'.[152] Riot to coerce the authorities into yielding political power was insubordinate, disruptive of the social fabric, to be prevented at all costs. It was to guard against this that political meetings were so highly policed. Perhaps trade disputes owe their severe handling to the direct self-interest of the corporation in the maintenance of the trade of the town, but the stress on insubordination suggests links with this most dangerous category.

After 1835, sentences were no longer much influenced by the category of riot, nor were its size or severity relevant, yet individual sentences still varied. Now the individual's actions seem to have been the most important determinant. Incitement was more punishable than following a ringleader. Assaults on bystanders outweighed fighting between 'willing' participants. The legal idea of collective guilt of rioters was replaced by an approximation to individual guilt.

The varied sentences and precautionary measures of 1815-35 had been decided by magistrates who owed their legal function to their position as mayor or alderman. They were amateurs in law enforcement. After 1836, there was also a professional stipendiary magistrate who presided over the vast majority of trials for riot or assault, and advised on questions of public order; there was also the advice of the head constable. In less serious cases, the police acted without magisterial advice. The keynote for this period was professionalism. The statistical evidence shows the result. To the professional law enforcer, a riot was a riot; it was a disturbance of the peace which he was required to maintain. In writing of the whole range of crime during this period, Emsley has identified a tendency for it to be perceived as 'a national and impersonal problem ... perpetrated ... against respectable people'.[153] The result found in the case of riot in Liverpool supports this.

There is no reason to suppose that growing uniformity of handling meant that any new theory of riot took over from the ideas of brutish, rational, or criminal motivation of earlier years. The Irish in particular were, as the Stipendiary Magistrate put it, apparently 'activated by a spirit as ungovernable

---

[151]*Liverpool Courier*, 21 Aug 1833; HO44.26/1, f 114, Jordan to Bouverie, 5 Nov 1830.

[152]*Poor Inquiry (Ireland)*, 20.

[153]C.Emsley, *Crime and Society in England, 1750-1900* (1987), 42.

and reckless as .... savages'.[154] According to Head Constable Dowling, Irish districts 'but for the presence of the police would be a scene of constant uproar and bloodshed'.[155] It was not the Irish alone, however, who were held to be so wild. Increasing references to 'roughs' occur. Pearson[156] points out that fears of 'roughs' were to increase over the next twenty or thirty years, culminating in the 1880s, the decade when Stedman Jones[157] has identified a crisis in public confidence caused by fears of 'the residuum'. Stevenson notes that after 1848 the Irish and the 'roughs' between them increasingly took the blame for disorder.[158] Storch's claim that the lower orders were feared because they 'aimed somehow at the utter unravelling of society' is rather too dramatic, but Emsley's picture of more rational fears of the residual 'dangerous classes' fits much better.[159] 'Instead of respectable workingmen', the police were on one occasion confronted with 'the blackguards from Vauxhall Road and Toxteth Park'.[160] And there were frequent cases where 'brutish' and 'criminal' ideas are linked. Criminality was mentioned more frequently in reports of riot. The Bread Riots of 1855 were in this way blamed on 'the lowest and vilest ... those who are not in the habit of working honestly for a livelihood'.[161] The harping on the criminal nature of the crowd was so laboured that it displayed an insistent anxiety to deny that the rioters had any reason to steal bread. It suggests a need to answer an argument which nobody in fact put forward: that starving people might be justified in stealing bread. Between the lines, the theory of rational riot peeps through, only to be forcibly obscured by insistence on the brutality and criminality of the rioters, justifying heavy sentences.

The use of violence in trade disputes was also commonly seen as understandable although misguided, as the frequent explanations by magistrates show. Yet such cases were relatively infrequent. In the main, although all three theories of motivation - brutal, criminal, and rational - were still recognizable, they were merging into one idea of a 'brutish and criminal' section of society which was to blame for the majority of cases of disorder. This had the advantage that the measures of punishment seen as necessary to the maintenance of order could also be seen to be deserved.

---

[154]*Liverpool Mail*, 13 July 1844.

[155]LRO 352 MIN/WAT 1/5, 5, 28 July 1849.

[156]Geoffrey Pearson, *Hooligan: a History of Respectable Fears* (1983).

[157]G Stedman Jones, *Outcast London* (Harmondsworth, 1984), ch 16.

[158]John Stevenson, *Popular Disturbances in England, 1700-1870* (1979), 300.

[159]R D Storch, 'Blue Locusts', 87; C.Emsley, *Crime and Society in England, 1750 to 1900* (1987), ch 3.

[160]*Liverpool Mercury*, 14 Mar 1848.

[161]*Liverpool Mercury*, 20 Feb 1855.

There was still one great exception to this approach. Political protest still had the power to create panic. The events of 1848 were the most notable example: demands for troops, and even for a gunboat; constant communication with the Home Office; a petition for the suspension of Habeas Corpus; rumours of a conspiracy to destroy shipping; the draconian dismissals of hundreds of workmen who refused to enrol as special constables. The 'Plug Plot' problems of 1842 had provoked similar although more muted reaction.

Subversive riot, then, was still feared in 1848 as it had been earlier. Nor did the idea of its dangers die quickly. In 1853, the mayor still argued for the maintenance of a military force in the town because troops 'would if an emergency should arise have a powerful effect in overawing the disaffected and designing'.[162] Nevertheless, other types of riot were being taken more seriously than previously, and it is uncertain which type of riot, criminal or subversive, was in the mind of the Inspector of Constabulary Forces in 1859 when he remarked that the military skills of the Liverpool Police Force were proof against 'disturbers of the public peace, howsoever numerous'.[163]

---

[162]HO45.5128, f 540, Mayor to General Viscount Hardinge, 21 Feb 1853.
[163]PP 1860 LVII.527 *Reports of Inspector of Constabulary .... 1859*, 61 (587).

6: False Dawn of New Unionism? Labour Unrest in Liverpool 1871 -1873[1]

Eric Taplin

I

From late 1871 to mid 1873 Liverpool experienced a period of sustained labour unrest. Many occupational groups, both skilled and unskilled, with or without formal union organization, expressed their discontents over wages, hours and conditions of work by demanding improvements from their employers. If petitions failed then strike action took place. Industrial militancy on this scale had not been witnessed in Liverpool before and the purpose of this essay is to give an account of these events, to offer an analysis of their causes, and to examine their wider implications.

Before doing so, however, some brief comments on labour in nineteenth century Liverpool require examination. For much of the century organised labour in Liverpool was weak, fragmented, unstable and largely ineffective. This was, in part, a reflection of the city's economic and social structure. Manufacturing industries that had been developing in the eighteenth and first half of the nineteenth century such as pottery, watchmaking and shipbuilding steadily declined as commerce and trade expanded. By the second half of the century there was no strong diversified manufacturing base in Liverpool to match that found in ports like Glasgow and Newcastle-on-Tyne where shipbuilding and heavy engineering employed large numbers of men. It was the docks, wharves and quays; ships, railways and canals; and service industries to maintain and improve these facilities that absorbed entrepreneurial resources in Liverpool.

This does not mean that manufacturing disappeared from the city. A whole range of enterprises existed to supply the needs of an expanding urban community; and the building industry and food processing were of major importance. But such enterprises tended to be relatively small scale; workshops rather than large factories predominated, and the labour force reflected this economic structure. In the second half of the century the major

---

[1] I am grateful to Pat Hudson of the Department of Economic and Social History, University of Liverpool, who read a draft of this essay and made a number of valuable suggestions.

sources of employment were to be found at the waterfront, in building and other urban industries and in commerce. There was an inexorable trend towards unskilled employment in occupations where militancy or effective trade union organization was unpromising.

As the imperious march of trade elevated Liverpool to the second port of the country so the docks expanded along the banks of the Mersey and an increasing army of seafarers, dock labourers, carters, tugboatmen, flatmen (bargemen) and warehousemen were required most of whom were unskilled and employed on a casual basis. To be sure there were expanding work opportunities for artisans such as shipwrights engaged in ship repair work and marine engineers to maintain and develop the dock system but they were a small proportion of those who laboured at the waterfront.

The building industry though requiring craftsmen such as carpenters and joiners, masons and the like employed large numbers of casually employed unskilled labourers and the emergence of jerry-built housing encouraged the use of less skilled, cheaper labour. Other urban industries such as tailoring and shoemaking became less skilled and less localized with technological and transport advances.

As the casual system of employment expanded so a rising proportion of the workforce was condemned to live on the margins of poverty. Casualism limited horizons to the daily struggle for work; fecklessness and brutality were encouraged and corruption and indiscipline endemic. Motivated by short-term and narrow considerations casual workers were poor material for sustained protest or trade union organization.[2]

The large numbers of clerks employed by shipping lines, banks, insurance companies and shipping factors were also poor candidates for organization. Ramsey Muir commented in 1907 that 'the conditions of the clerk's life usually render him conventional, respectable, timid and unadventurous ... and so in any period of stress or depression many of them will drift helplessly, especially if once their moorings of respectability are cut'.[3] They clung to genteel poverty largely indifferent to or afraid of union organization.

Other factors contributed to the narrow base of trade union organization. The tidal wave of immigrants from neighbouring agricultural districts, North Wales and Ireland, especially from the 1840s, ensured an

[2]For a detailed analysis of the casual system and its effects, see G. Stedman Jones, *Outcast London. A Study in the Relationship between Classes in Victorian Society* (Oxford, 1971). For Liverpool see Eric Taplin, *The Dockers' Union. A Study of the National Union of Dock Labourers, 1889 - 1922* (Leicester, 1985), ch 2.

[3]Ramsey Muir, *A History of Liverpool* (1907), 307 - 8. See also B. G. Orchard *The Clerks of Liverpool* (Liverpool, 1871), who estimated there were 17,000 clerks in the city in 1871; and Gregory Anderson, *Victorian Clerks* (Manchester, 1976).

over-stocked labour market particularly in the unskilled sectors. Thus there was normally a plentiful supply of potential blacklegs to take the place of those who might be tempted to organize into trade unions and/or take militant action.

Problems of ethnic and sectarian bigotry, accentuated by immigration, buttressed the baleful influence of casualism that was characteristic of many occupations in Liverpool. These triple forces inhibited the development of a working class consciousness and collective action. It has also been suggested that the weakness of independent popular radicalism and of an independent working class Liberal tradition are factors that should be taken into account.[4]

In spite of these debilitating features some trade unions were established and there were spasmodic outbreaks of militancy. As might be expected organization was largely confined to craftsmen and, in the first half of the century, unions of shipwrights, ironfounders and coachmakers among others enjoyed considerable power. It was from this cadre of artisans that the Liverpool Trades Guardian Association was formed in 1848 that became the Liverpool and Vicinity United Trades Council in 1868. But during the second half of the century the influence of the artisan trades in Liverpool was declining.[5]

It is not surprising that collective action by workgroups among the unskilled was rare and spasmodic. To be sure sailors had struck work in 1775 and 1791[6] and some dock labourers had taken militant action in 1853 and 1866 which had raised the day rate of both quay labourers and stevedores. [7] Trade organizations were also found at the waterfront, but on a limited scale. There were a number of small clubs such as the Clarence Dock Club catering for those engaged in the coasting trade although they appear to have been no more than savings and burial clubs. Somewhat more important was the South End Dock Labourers Association formed in 1849 that existed until the early years of the twentieth century. Although not much is known of its activities it may have sought to negotiate with sailing ship employers but its primary function was probably as a sick and benefit club.[8]

---

[4]Joan Smith, 'Labour Tradition in Glasgow and Liverpool' *History Workshop Journal*, 17 (1984). See also John Belchem, 'Image, Myth and Implantation: the Peculiarities of Liverpool, 1800 - 1850', 32 - 56, unpublished paper delivered to the British-Dutch Labour History Conference, 1990.

[5]Eric Taplin, 'The Liverpool Trades Council 1880 - 1914', *Bulletin of the North West Group for the Study of Labour History*, 3 (1975), 12 - 16. See also W. Hamling, *A Short History of the Liverpool Trades Council*, 1848 - 1948 (Liverpool, n.d.).

[6]H. R. Hikins, 'Origins of Working Class Politics: Liverpool 1756 - 91' in H. R. Hikins (ed), *Building the Union. Studies on the growth of the Workers' Movement: Merseyside, 1756 - 1967* (Liverpool, 1973), 7 - 27.

[7]Eric Taplin, *Liverpool Dockers and Seamen, 1870 - 1890* (Hull, 1974), ch 2.

[8]*Ibid*, 17.

The impact of national movements such as Owenism and Chartism failed to establish deep roots in Liverpool. A cooperative society was founded by John Finch in 1829 but it had collapsed by 1832. His effort to form a Dock Labourers' Society in 1830 was 'strangled at birth by the employers' within a year; and in the 1840s his establishment of an Owenite socialist community at Harmony Hall 'dissolved in disreputable chaos'.[9]

By 1870 Liverpool labour had achieved very little. Many of the artisan societies which had exerted considerable industrial and political muscle in the first half of the century were now far less formidable. The increasing numbers of unskilled workers remained largely unorganised and passive.

II

It was events outside Liverpool that led to the unexpected explosion of militancy in 1872. At national and regional level there was an outburst of labour militancy in the boom of the early 1870s among semi-skilled workers and the labouring poor. This is well-documented and requires no more than a brief account here.[10] The most notable uprising was the 'Revolt in the Field' that led to the formation of a number of trade unions among agricultural labourers spearheaded by Joseph Arch's National Agricultural Labourers' Union formed in 1872. Their efforts secured widespread sympathetic publicity. Regional strikes took place some of which were successful leading to increased wages for the poverty-stricken labourers of central and eastern England.[11]

In London the activities of the radical Land and Labour League led to the formation of the Labour Protection League in 1871, a union supported principally by London dockers. Some successes were achieved and by the end of 1872 a more ambitious project had been launched, the Amalgamated Labour Union, a federation of all transport workers in London embracing the League, the Railway Servants' Association, the Carmen's Society and the Amalgamated Lightermen and Watermen's Association. The Federation, however, was short-lived but the League, after declining in the late 1870s,

---

[9]R. B. Rose, 'John Finch, 1784 - 1857; A Liverpool Disciple of Robert Owen', in Hikins (ed), 31 - 52.

[10]Eric Taplin, 'The Origins and Development of New Unionism, 1870 - 1910', unpublished MA Thesis, University of Liverpool, 1967, provides an account of these developments.

[11]There are many accounts of the 'Revolt in the Field'. A perceptive article is J. P. D. Dunbabin, 'The Revolt in the Field: the Agricultural Labourers' Movement in the 1870s', *Past and Present,* 26 (1963), 68 - 97.

was successfully transformed into a stevedores' union in the 1880s.[12] In the coalfields two national unions were established, Alexander Macdonald's National Miners' Union in 1863 and Thomas Halliday's Amalgamated Association of Miners in 1869, both of which enjoyed considerable success until 1875.[13] The Amalgamated Society of Railway Servants was formed in 1871[14] and in the same year the Telegraphists' Association was established in Manchester. In 1872 efforts were made to organise the gas stokers in London; and Patrick Kenney formed the General Amalgamated Labourers' Union primarily for builders' labourers.[15] In the same year postal workers organized on the initiative of William Booth into the United General Post Office and Telegraph Servants Benefit Society.[16]

Although most of these unions had collapsed or become moribund by the late 1870s it was clear that from the late 1860s unskilled workers were making unprecedented efforts to agitate and organize. Nevertheless the most important development in so far as Liverpool was concerned was initiated by the skilled engineers of the north east who had been seeking a nine hour day since 1866. By 1871 the Nine Hours League had been formed: its president, John Burnett of the Amalgamated Society of Engineers (ASE), encouraged all workers to join. Of the 7,000 men who struck work in support of the demand only about 800 were members of a trade union and of those only 500 belonged to the ASE. In effect the League was a general union embracing unionized artisans such as engineers, boilermakers, foundrymen and steam engine makers and unskilled and non-unionized labourers in the engineering workshops and shipyards of the north east. The League ultimately succeeded in securing its objective of a 54-hour week after a prolonged and bitter dispute that lasted five months.[17] This resounding victory reverberated across the country and led to the adoption of the nine hour day in many occupations.

---

[12]For the Land and Labour League see Royden Harrison, *Before the Socialists* (1965). For the Stevedores' Society see John Lovell, *Stevedores and Dockers. A Study of Trade Unionism in the Port of London, 1870 - 1914* (1969), ch 3.

[13]G. D. H. Cole, 'Some Notes on British Trade Unionism in the Third Quarter of the Nineteenth Century', *International Review of Social History,* ii (1937), reprinted in E. M. Carus-Wilson (ed), *Essays in Economic History*, iii (1962), 202 - 220.

[14]P. S. Bagwell, *The Railwaymen. The History of the National Union of Railwaymen* (1963), ch 2.

[15]For the gas stokers see G. Howell, *Labour Legislation, Labour Movements and Labour Leaders* (1905). For the builders' labourers see R. W. Postgate, *The Builders' History* (1923), 208.

[16]For postal workers and telegraphists see H. G. Swift, *The History of Postal Agitation* (1929).

[17]For the Nine Hours' Movement see J. Burnett, *A History of the Engineers' Strike in Newcastle and Gateshead* (1872); J. B. Jeffreys, *The Story of the Engineers* (1946); E. Allen et al, *The North East Engineers Strikes of 1871* (Newcastle, 1971).

It would have been surprising had Liverpool remained immune from these national and regional developments. From the autumn of 1871 to the spring of 1873 there was a sustained and substantial period of unrest. In October 1871 railwaymen and shop assistants held meetings over working hours but, more significantly, in the following month engineers employed by Messrs. T. & J. Vicars at the Wheatsheaf Foundry in Seel Street successfully petitioned their employers for a nine hour day from 1 December, the first group of workers in Liverpool to secure the concession. Their success was followed by a wave of petitions from engineering workers in workshops throughout the city and in Birkenhead. By the end of November employers without exception had conceded these claims. The impact of the successful nine hours movements in the north east in 1871 was the trigger for the general agitation in Liverpool. The success of local engineering workers encouraged other workers to try their luck in wringing concessions from their employers. The workgroups involved covered a wide spectrum of employments both skilled and unskilled. Appendix 6.1 lists the major workgroups involved, their claims and the result of the agitation where it is known.

Each agitation followed a broadly similar pattern. A meeting or series of meetings would be arranged by an individual or small group providing the opportunity for complaints to be voiced and demands formulated. Frequently outside help would be enlisted in the form of two local sympathetic businessmen, James Samuelson and William Simpson, but in any case a petition or memorial would be presented to the employers. The response of the employers varied. Some simply ignored or rejected the petition; some granted concessions immediately either in full or in part; some invited a deputation of workmen to discuss grievances. Further meetings of workers would follow to vote on the response of the employers. Those employers who proved obdurate faced strike action, the outcome of which depended upon the nerve and strength of purpose of the combatants. Strikes involving unskilled workers were short-lived but those involving artisans could be prolonged. Carpenters and joiners, for example, were on strike for six months before a compromise solution was reached.

The agitation of the omnibus workers though brief will serve as the first of two case studies to illustrate the general pattern. The horse-drawn omnibus and tramway system was in the hands of two firms, the Liverpool Road and Railway Omnibus Company and the Liverpool Tramways Company. Both were tyrannical employers even by the standards of those days. Men worked seven days a week with hours of up to seventeen a day. Their pay was low and they were subject to stringent company rules which if breached led at best to fines or at worst to prosecution in the courts and instant dismissal on the flimsiest of evidence. Nevertheless there was no shortage of applicants as men were permanently employed and there were promotion prospects, rare among unskilled occupations. Over one thousand men were employed by the two firms.

In April 1872 a petition was presented to the employers for a reduction in hours and a wage increase. This was ignored by the two companies and on 3 July a meeting of the men took place, chaired by William Simpson, at which grievances were expressed and a claim drawn up which was presented to the employers by Simpson. The Tramways Company proved to be conciliatory and concessions were granted under the threat of strike action. The Omnibus Company, however, was more stubborn, and on 22 July the men turned out for two days. By then the company was recruiting blacklegs to replace the strikers.[18] Simpson arranged for a delegation to meet the employers and they secured a written compromise offer which was sufficient to get the men back to work. Drivers' wages were increased from 28s (£1.40p) a week to 32s (£1.60p) a week with either one day off per month or two half-days instead of the 35s (£1.75p) a week claimed. Stablemen were to receive 2s (10p) a horse per day but a 10-stall stableman's pay of one guinea (£1.05p) a week was to remain unchanged in contrast to their claim for 28s (£1.40p) a week, with the undertaking that vacancies in a 12-stall stable would be filled by men from 10-stall stables. Guards received no increase and were to remain on 17s 6d (87½p) to 24s (£1.20p) a week according to grade instead of the claim for 21s (£1.05p) to 28s (£1.40p). A mass meeting of the men on 23 July agreed to accept the offer, the guards' representatives on the deputation to the employers recommending acceptance even though they received no increase so as not to jeopardize the advances secured by other workers. The major beneficiaries were the drivers, the most skilled of those employed. The only unusual feature of the episode was the 'ragged trousered philanthropy' of the guards.[19]

The nature of women's employment in Liverpool was worse than that endured by most male workers, and their experience provides the second case study. Kevin Moore has commented that 'the irregular, casual and unskilled nature of the work of thousands of men ... meant that the earnings of women played a vital role in a family's survival'.[20] Yet opportunities for regular work with reasonable earnings were minimal. Most women's work was 'spasmodic, casual and irregular' and 'sweating seems to have developed more rapidly in

[18]The poor quality of the blacklegs recruited created problems for the company. On 23 July 1871 the *Liverpool Mercury* reported that one conductor, having collected fares, quietly disappeared up a side street: 'anxious enquiries were made respecting him'.
[19]*Liverpool Mercury*, 29 June, and 4, 20, 23, and 24 July 1872.
[20]Kevin Moore, 'This Whig and Tory Ridden Town: Popular Politics in Liverpool, 1815 - 1850', unpublished M. Phil, University of Liverpool, 1987, 49.

Liverpool in trades such as tailoring than almost anywhere'.[21] As might be expected domestic service was the major source of women's employment but there were nearly 9,000 needlewomen in 1871.[22] The combination of long hours, low pay and poor conditions meant that women workers had little time or energy to express grievances, particularly as many were running a home and bringing up children. Liverpool working women were grossly exploited, more so than in other towns.

In spite of these debilitating circumstances some working women were involved in the militancy of 1872. Women cotton and rag pickers in the cotton waste warehouses struck work in July seeking a reduction in hours from twelve to ten a day and an increase in wages to 10s (50p) a week. After Simpson's intervention, the concession was granted by the employer.[23] The Cigarmakers' Association, a London based union, sought to extend its membership in the provinces and a recruiting drive was initiated in July 1872 among the 250 journeymen and 100 apprentices employed in Liverpool. To what extent it was successful is unknown as the local press failed to follow up progress after two meetings.[24]

Of greatest interest, however, was the needlewomen's agitation that received considerable public sympathy and support and led to the establishment of an ill-fated cooperative venture. In July 1872 letters from milliners, dressmakers and shirt makers appeared in the local press pleading for assistance. '... for God's sake do something for the poor needlewomen' one letter concluded. Requests for help were also sent direct to Simpson who attended a meeting of about 200 needlewomen, accompanied by his wife and daughter, held at the Wellington monument. At this meeting grievances over low pay, long hours and tyrannical forewomen were voiced. Some women worked up to twelve hours a day for wages of 9d (3.75p) to one shilling (5p) a day; some claimed they received no more than 3s 6d (17½p) a week while others earned 5s (25p). Fines were commonplace for trivial offences, for example 3d (1¼p) was deducted for a minute's lateness. There were no overtime payments and absence led to total loss of pay.[25]

The hardship endured by needlewomen received widespread publicity in the local press. Simpson pledged his support encouraging women not to be

---

[21]*Ibid*, 50.

[22]The Population Census of 1871 recorded 10,793 women aged 20 years or over employed as domestic servants. There were 6,599 milliners and 2,375 shirtmakers and seamstresses giving a total of 8,974 needlewomen. Source: *Census of England and Wales, 1871 (33 & 34 Vict.c.107). Population Abstracts*, Vol iii, C-872 (1873), Division viii, Table 15.

[23]*Liverpool Mercury*, 18, 19 and 26 July 1872.

[24]*Liverpool Mercury*, 24 and 31 July 1872.

[25]*Liverpool Mercury*, 12 July 1872.

frightened by threats or intimidation as 'the force of public opinion would protect them'.[26] He floated the idea of a cooperative provided there was public support. At subsequent meetings, attended by up to 400 workers and local dignatories, such support emerged. Henry Coffey and Sons of Manchester offered to send materials and buttons to be made up into shirts at 6d (2½p) a shirt (6s [30p] a dozen) in contrast to the local piece rate of 3s 6d (17½p) a dozen. Local clergymen and philanthropic dignatories promised money; sewing machine manufacturers agreed to supply machines on very easy terms. A management committee of six was appointed, rules were drawn up (see Appendix 6.2) and premises were opened in Myrtle Street in September 1872 offering employment initially for up to 150 women with an anticipated increase to 200 who could earn from 15s (75p) to £1 a week for a nine hour day.[27]

In spite of the wave of public sympathy and the good intentions of the organisers problems soon arose. By December allegations were made over the irregular appointment of supervisory staff and criticism of the lack of interest shown by Simpson.[28] In October 1873, just over a year after its foundation, the institute closed down. To be self-supporting the management committee required 200 workers earning 7s (35p) a week. Yet the average number of needlewomen enrolling over the year was no more than thirty. The enterprise had simply flopped.

There were many reasons for its failure. Simpson and the management committee had plunged into a business they did not understand on a wave of public sympathy. They had accepted all statements at their face value without evaluating the economic viability of the enterprise. Early complaints about Simpson's domineering paternalism were never resolved: in any case he soon lost interest in the venture. Moreover the needlewomen themselves remained in the shadows. There was no woman with practical experience on the management committee and to many the institute appeared to be little different from any other workplace. Why did so few women seek work at the institute? Some employers improved wages and conditions but pressure from the majority may well have deterred many workers from risking their livelihood by getting involved in the agitation or the institute. Indeed the management committee sourly commented that 'the distress amongst the so-called needlewomen is chiefly amongst the incompetent ... It seemed clear that the statements which led to the founding of the Institute were much exaggerated. The distress was amongst those who were incompetent or idle.'[29] It was a

---

[26]*Liverpool Mercury*, 19 July 1872.
[27]*Liverpool Mercury*, 19 and 26 July, and 16 Aug, 1872.
[28]*Liverpool Mercury*, 23 Dec 1872.
[29]*Liverpool Mercury*, 23 and 29 Oct 1873.

melancholy episode that confirmed the persistence of the exploitation of working women in nineteenth century Liverpool. Of course the needlewomen were not alone. Appendix 6.1 shows that shop assistants in spite of a long agitation secured little if anything from their efforts while others such as grain warehousemen, ship's painters and farriers struck work without success.

The factors that led to this period of unrest in Liverpool are not difficult to establish. Nationally there was a 'cyclical inflationary boom in the early 1870s'.[30] Most economic indicators rose sharply. Rates of unemployment are notoriously difficult to establish but, impressionistically, it appears likely that they fell to unusually low levels: even in Liverpool where unskilled occupations predominated there was probably work available for most people who sought it. Business confidence was high and the expectations of working people rose as work was more readily available and incomes more regular. Inflation encouraged demands for higher wages which were less likely to be opposed by employers in a period of expansion and rising profits.

Thus at both national and local levels the economic context was favourable for claims for advances by working people. It was further encouraged in Liverpool by sympathetic public opinion. In this respect the role of the local press was important. Liverpool possessed three daily newspapers, the *Courier,* the *Mercury*, and the *Post*. All gave extensive coverage of the agitations and the *Post* and *Mercury*, in particular, offered sympathetic support. As suggested above, it was the success of the Nine Hours' movement in the north-east that triggered the agitation in Liverpool. Appendix 6.1 illustrates that after some hesitancy demands proliferated in the summer of 1872, falling away by the autumn of that year.

III

A number of features emerge from an examination of this period of unrest. The majority of the agitations were by unskilled workers, unorganized and lacking an indigenous leadership. Their efforts were primitive and their resistance fragile. Sustained opposition from an employer usually led to the collapse of the movement. To most, if not all, experience of protest was lacking and in the circumstances it is not surprising that they were eager to secure outside sympathetic assistance. Hence the importance of William Simpson and James Samuelson. In most of the disputes involving unorganized workers one of these two, notably Simpson, played an important role. Simpson emerged during the year as the champion of the unskilled workers of the city.

---

[30]R. A. Church *The Great Victorian Boom, 1850 - 1873* (1975), 77.

William Simpson (1829 - 1883) came from humble origins and had experienced a chequered business career but by the late 1850s he had established a successful catering business on the Prince's landing stage at the Pier Head. During the 1860s he became well-known for his philanthropy and concern for the labouring poor. He had political ambitions, initially as a Conservative, but his egocentricity, flamboyant dress and manner, and outspoken criticism of political corruption and social abuses earned him the enmity of the political establishment. He could not, however, be ignored and his assistance to those who he felt had a genuine grievance was a major factor in the successes achieved. His strategy was to accept an invitation to attend or chair a meeting of workers and listen to the grievances expressed. If he felt they had a just case he would write or lead a delegation to the employer(s) and seek an acceptable compromise if the workers' demands were not fully conceded. If this failed he recommended arbitration. Although he enjoyed the publicity there is no doubting his sincerity. His faults were, however, considerable. He was antipathetic towards trade unionism and strikes in the belief that 'moral force could obtain that which was just and fair without resorting to the painful step of a strike'.[31] His mercurial temperament led him to abandon projects when a new challenge presented itself, as the needlewomen discovered to their cost. His egocentricity demanded unequivocal acceptance of his views. He was a difficult man to work with. He had no more than a paternalistic attitude towards the labouring poor and although he was an important catalyst in 1872 he had no interest in assisting the emergence of a Liverpool working class leadership or movement. His influence was short-term only.[32]

James Samuelson (1829 - 1918), less flamboyant than Simpson, was a well-known Liberal with 'advanced' views who owned a seed crushing and oil cake manufacturing firm in Birkenhead with an office in Liverpool,. He also held a paternalistic attitude towards the working classes but, unlike Simpson, strongly favoured the development of trade unions along 'New Model' lines, believing that strong organisations, responsibly led, would benefit society. Organizations with friendly society benefits would improve the welfare of members; conciliation and compromise in industrial relations would reduce the incidence of strikes, a prescription which may have been suitable for skilled workers but was quite inappropriate for the less skilled. Hence Samuelson's long-term influence on the Liverpool trade union movement was marginal

---

[31]*Liverpool Mercury*, 9 July 1872.
[32]For a short biography see Eric Taplin, 'William Shaw Simpson (1829 - 83), Radical' in J. Bellamy and J. Saville (eds), *Dictionary of Labour Biography* (1974), ii, 342 - 44.

though his genuine support for working class causes should not be discounted.[33]

It was, perhaps, inevitable that sectionalism was a characteristic of the unrest. Each workgroup acted independently, no effort being made to coordinate activity even among cognate workers. This is best illustrated by reference to events at the waterfront. Dock gatemen, cotton porters, provision porters, grain warehousemen, carters and some north end dock labourers were all involved in separate disputes without any perception of a common cause. One of the unusual features of the unrest was the lack of action exhibited by the mass of dock workers. There must have been over 20,000 dockers seeking work at the waterfront yet only a few thousand were involved in any show of militancy. The explanation is to be found partly in sectionalism. Men were divided by status and spatial factors into a 'caste system quite as powerful as India's' as James Sexton later commented.[34] Job specialisms abounded at the docks and men tended to look upon their particular skill as superior to those of their fellow workers. Moreover most men owed their allegiance to firms operating within a narrow range of docks where they customarily sought work. These factors buttressed by the casual system, sectarian differences and the blackmailing attitude of many foremen encouraged individualism or at best gang loyalties.[35] General wage rates did, of course, change over time through primitive negotiations with individual employers. The process normally began within a few docks where particular groups of workers squeezed a wage increase which would lead to others securing a similar increase to maintain customary differentials. Thus an increase would spread slowly along the line of the docks until a new going rate was established. In 1870 it appears that the dockers' wage rates had risen in this fashion from 4s (20p) to 4s 6d (22½p) a day for quay porters and from 4s 6d (22½) to 5s (25p) a day for stevedores' labourers (shipmen). The efforts of the cotton and provision porters in 1872 might be looked upon as the completion of that process covering a time lag of two years.

By the early 1870s a new feature was disturbing traditional practices at the waterfront, namely the rapid expansion of steamships that tended to berth at the north end of the docks. In the summer of 1872 the Liverpool North End Steamship Dock Labourers' Friendly Burial Society was formed. Its title suggests its major purpose was the provision of welfare benefits for members but its rules included matters of pay and conditions. In particular it

---

[33]For a short biography see Eric Taplin, 'James Samuelson (1829 - 1918), Liberal and Working Class Sympathiser' in *ibid*, 328 - 31.

[34]James Sexton, *Sir James Sexton, Agitator. The Life Story of the Dockers' MP. An Autobiography* (1936), 111.

[35]For a more expanded analysis of sectionalism at the Liverpool waterfront see Taplin, *Dockers' Union*, ch 2.

demanded that all foremen join the society otherwise members would cease to work for them, provisions that were bound to incur the opposition of employers. Once that opposition emerged the union climbed down over foremen membership but it was clear that the employers sought the destruction of the fledgling organization that appeared to threaten managerial prerogatives. A brief strike involving some 5,000 men proved unsuccessful. The union leaders were now out of their depth in knowing what to do next and sought Simpson's assistance. He advised the men to return to work stating that he would approach the employers over their grievances, recommending arbitration if his efforts failed to resolve matters. No more was reported in the local press of the society or the results of Simpson's endeavours. There is little doubt that the union collapsed. It had failed to capture the interest of the mass of north end dockers, its leadership was inadequate and Simpson, characteristically, did nothing to encourage the organization.[36]

Finally it should be remembered that in spite of the widespread nature of the agitations of 1872 and the excitement they generated in the city, the numbers affected by the disputes represented a minority of Liverpool's labouring population and the successes achieved were in most cases no more than marginal. By the spring of 1873 the unrest had run its course and with the end of the cyclical boom by 1874 - 5 the economic context was no longer favourable for widespread militancy.

IV

Labour historians have long agreed that industrial conflict in nineteenth century Britain proceeded by brief but spectacular explosions of activity. In particular interest has concentrated upon the three strike waves of 1871 - 1873, 1889 - 1890 and 1911 - 1913. In a perceptive article James Cronin has suggested that 'the early 1870s probably were the years when strikes became the dominant form of workers' collective activity'.[37] There is much to be said in support of this view but in relation to the experience of Liverpool there are reservations. As stated previously, Liverpool workers had struck work well before the explosion of the early 1870s but activity had been confined largely to skilled artisans. The early 1870s witnessed militancy on a considerable scale among unskilled workers for the first time, establishing a

---

[36]For a more extended analysis of the waterfront dispute of 1872 see Taplin, *Liverpool Dockers and Seamen, 1870 - 1890,* ch 2.

[37]James E. Cronin, 'Strikes and Power in Britain 1870 - 1920', *International Review of Social History,* xxxii (1987), 147.

precedent that was to be repeated and developed thereafter. But it has to be appreciated that in most cases strikes took place only after memorials, petitions and deputations to employers had failed. Workers were driven to strike only when employers refused to grant concession of any kind. Strikes were, in any case, of short duration. To be sure this was a new feature, particularly as Simpson and Samuelson persistently advised against strike action whatever the circumstances but it is not to be compared with the blazing militancy that was to occur in later waves of protest. Although strike activity fell away during the depression of the mid and late 1870s there was a major eruption in 1879 when the seamen turned out partly over low pay and poor conditions but also over abuses of the advance note and allotment note system.[38] More seriously the first port-wide strike of dock labourers occurred lasting for three weeks. Although the strike was lost, discontent persisted and the threat of a further strike in the following year led employers to restore the wage cut they had imposed that had precipitated the militancy.[39] A decade later the next surge of militancy exploded with the onset of new unionism which swept across Liverpool with considerable force. Thus the view that 'the strike truly came into its own as the workers' preferred form of action in the 1870s'[40] can only be accepted if it is understood that peaceful methods to secure redress of grievances had been exhausted and the strike was the only means left to protest. It should also be appreciated that militancy by the unskilled was not always linked to the three strike waves. The waterfront conflict of 1879/80 was on a far greater scale than anything witnessed in the early 1870s and occurred when the economy was in the depths of depression.

Cronin also suggests that the strike wave of the early 1870s witnessed a shift towards union organization among the unskilled not dissimilar from that of succeeding waves of militancy.[41] Events in Liverpool scarcely support this view. Of the unskilled occupational groups that were involved in disputes only six formed associations most of which had limited, non-belligerent aims and

---

[38]Advance notes were granted to seamen by employers to purchase goods before the voyage, i.e. wages paid in advance. But they were subject to large discounts at stores and their face value was never enjoyed by seamen. Allotment notes permitted a proportion of wages to be drawn by families of seamen while they were away at sea. But they carried high rates of interest so the employer benefitted greatly particularly on long voyages. Sums paid out in advance and allotment notes plus interest charges were deducted from the seaman's earnings when he was paid off at the end of the voyage.

[39]Taplin, *Liverpool Dockers and Seamen,* ch 3

[40]Cronin, 150.

[41]*Ibid,* 147. 'Like the later waves of 1889 - 90, 1911 - 1913 and 1919 - 1920, it (the early 1870s) represented not merely an escalation of overt conflict between workers and employers, but also a shift towards the more inclusive organization of less skilled workers, together with an upsurge of rank-and-file activism, a rejection of the cautious advice of established officials, and a renewed emphasis upon the efficacy of strike activity'.

were, in any case, short-lived. The Liverpool Shop Assistants' Association derived from a movement originating in Birmingham but under the influence of Samuelson it was no more than a weak pressure group seeking principally the earlier closing of local shops and securing few successes. The Cotton Porters' Registration Society was formed on the suggestion of Simpson to recruit the most efficient and reliable men for employment by the brokers. It had no industrial pretensions and soon faded away. The local seamen's union was favoured by the employers as a means of securing more efficient and trustworthy labour but it soon disappeared as did the plasterers' labourers union. The agitation by railwaymen led ultimately to the foundation of a Liverpool branch of the Amalgamated Society of Railway Servants which had been formed in 1872. Only the ill-fated North End Steamship Dock Labourers Friendly Benefit Society had objectives of a more radical nature in seeking to exercise control over foremen and hence influence the work process. Thus the influence of unions among the less skilled can virtually be discounted. It was a false dawn for workers' organisations in Liverpool and indeed for most the objective was not to organise at all on a permanent basis.

One of the major contrasts between the agitation of 1871 - 1873 and the later waves of protest was the temper of the working class. In the early 1870s, Liverpool unskilled workers accepted their lowly position in the economic and social order. They sought limited gains in wage rates and conditions but had no pretensions to radical change in work practices or job control. Their petitions to employers were expressed in respectful terms to superiors and if concessions were granted employers were often thanked for their courtesy and understanding. No working class leadership emerged. Indeed, by turning to Simpson and Samuelson for advice and leadership they emphasized their servility and acceptance of their position in society. It was to take another twenty years to galvanize the workers of Liverpool towards mass union organization and major confrontations with employers.

The agitations of the early 1870s should not, however, be lightly regarded or dismissed. In seeking to discover the origins of new unionism in Liverpool a strong case can be made for the labour unrest of these years. It was a false dawn in the sense that organization failed to develop and the aspirations of the less-skilled were limited. But many of the workers involved were from the lowest and most exploited sectors of the workforce who, hitherto, had been perceived as incapable of protest. They now emerged from the shadows and although their efforts were hesitant and primitive precedents had been set.

What was lacking in Liverpool was a radical working class leadership to develop and harness aspirations within a structure of trade unionism that looked beyond the confines of the city. It was to take further time and experience to lift horizons and promote a more belligerent temper than was evident in the early 1870s. Perhaps a further period of depression was necessary to sharpen the appetite for protest and, perhaps, an ideology to rouse a minority who could emerge as a cadre of working class leaders.

The impact of technological change was also a factor that was to affect working-class attitudes. This was particularly evident at the waterfront with the increasing dominance of steamships over sailing vessels and the emergence of impersonal joint stock shipping companies. In 1872 relationships between employers and workers were still largely on a face to face basis; by 1889 that had diminished significantly. Grievances had to be channelled through foremen to paid managers who were often less sympathetic than owners. The development of the liner traffic led to adherence to strict timetables and increased pressure for a quick turn round in port. This, coupled with intensifying international competition in shipping that cut profits to the bone, greatly increased the intensity of work discipline at the waterfront. James Sexton, a dock worker in 1879 who became general secretary of the National Union of Dock Labourers in 1893, recalled in his autobiography that 'Gradually the old methods which, if slow, were comparatively safe, gave way before the cut-throat competition for freights and the clamour for quick dispatch and with the change there came into the business a new type of boss'.[42] The accumulation of these factors transformed the Liverpool waterfront worker into a more pugnacious frame of mind to the extent that sectional divisiveness was sufficiently reduced for a measure of unified and unionised militancy to take place when economic conditions in the late 1880s were favourable.

Many of the occupational groups who had agitated in the early 1870s renewed their protest at this time in a more formidable fashion. Dock workers and seamen flocked into newly-formed regional and national unions, and local unions were established for carters, flatmen and tramwaymen. In the new unionism not all, of course, were successful in securing their objectives but, unlike the few associatons formed in the early 1870s, some of them survived unsuccessful strikes, the return of unfavourable economic conditions in the 1890s and the counter-attack of the employers although it was not until the Liverpool General Transport Strike of 1911 that fundamental change in industrial relations was secured.

It is highly unlikely that the events of 1872 in Liverpool were unique. More research is needed to discover what, if anything, was taking place in other urban provincial cities with a different economic structure such as Manchester, Bradford, Glasgow, Bristol and Birmingham. It would appear that beneath the well-known national and regional examples of militancy such as the agricultural labourers and the coal miners there was a sub-stratum of

---

[42]Sexton, 67 - 8.

labour agitation taking place at local levels that illustrates that the less skilled, though unable to develop or sustain permanent organisation, were sufficiently roused to demand limited advances by agitation and, if need be, by strike action.

Appendix 6.1:

Table 6.1: List of Agitations by Liverpool Workers 1871 - 1873

Date	Occupation	Action Involved	Results
Oct 71 - Aug 72	Railwaymen	Meetings; petitions to employers for reduction in hours and increase in wages. involved brief strikes. (Samuelson).	Some concessions over hours and wages.
Oct 71 - Mar 73	Shop Assistants	Formation of Liverpool Shop Assistants' Association to press for shops to close at 7 pm on five days a week. (Samuelson).	Some minor successes, e.g. drapers and some grocers agreed to close at 7.30 pm but probably short-lived.
Nov 71 - ?	Plasterers' Labourers	Formed association and on strike over wage reduction.	Unknown.
8 - 15 Dec 71	Telegraphists	Liverpool branch of Telegraphists Association on strike over classification scheme.	Some concessions granted.

Date	Occupation	Action Involved	Results
Feb 72	Workers employed by Liverpool Rubber Company	Strike to secure nine hour day. Firm recruits blacklegs.	Unknown.
Apr - May 72	Liverpool Carters	Agitation for shorter hours and increased pay. Up to 8,000 carters on strike 29 April to 4 May. (Simpson).	Referred to Mayor as arbitrator who awarded in favour of men. Wages increased from 27s (£1.35p) to 29s (£1.45p) per week for thirteen hour day.
May 72	Seamen	Agitation for wage increase. Petitions to Shipowners' Association. Liverpool Seamen's Union formed.	Unknown.
May - June 72	Mersey Docks and Harbour Board Dockgatemen	Agitation for higher pay. (Simpson).	Increase granted.
May - July 72	Cotton Porters	Agitation for wage increase. Liverpool Cotton Porters' Registration Society formed. (Simpson).	Wage increase granted from 4s (20p) to 4s 6d (22½p) per day.

Popular Politics

Date	Occupation	Action Involved	Results
June 72	Operative Bakers	Reduction in hours and pay increase demanded. (Simpson).	Master Bakers concede claim.
June 72	Cunard Dockers	Men on strike to secure equality of wage rates with other firms.	Wages increased but men cease to be permanent - to be employed as casuals.
June 72	Provision Porters	Agitation for wage increase and employment for full day instead of half day. Offer by employers rejected and men strike.	Unknown.
June - July 72	Grain Warehousemen employed by Mersey Docks and Harbour Board	Agitation and strike for increased wages. (Simpson).	Employers refuse to concede claim. Strike lost.
June - July 72	Birkenhead Unskilled Workers	Labourers' Association formed among engineers' labourers, shipwrights labourers, sawmill labourers, dock labourers, gas workers. (Simpson).	Wage increase granted to engineers' labourers by some firms. Patchy impact among other occupations.

6: False Dawn

Date	Occupation	Action Involved	Results
June - July 72	Omnibus and Tramway Workers	Agitation for reduction in hours and wage increase. Strike by some workers. (Simpson).	Concessions agreed by Liverpool Tramways Co. Following strike Liverpool Road and Railway Omnibus Co. grant concessions.
July 72	Journeymen Coopers	Journeymen Coopers' Association claim for higher wages rejected by masters; men go on strike.	Unknown.
July 72 - Oct 73	Needlewomen (Milliners, Dressmakers, Shirtmakers)	Long agitation for better pay and conditions. (Simpson).	Formation of Liverpool Needlewomen's Institute, September 1872; closed down October 1873.
July 72	Women Cotton and Rag Pickers	Agitation and strike for shorter hours and higher pay.	Concessions granted by employers.

Popular Politics

Date	Occupation	Action Involved	Results
July 72	Women Cigarmakers	Recruiting drive by London Cigarmakers Association.	Unknown.
July 72	Skilled Ironworkers of Birkenhead and Liverpool skilled Engineers	Demand for wage increase rejected and men locked out.	Unknown.
Aug 72	Liverpool Clerks	Employers petitioned to raise wages.	Unknown.
Sept 72	Liverpool Tobacco Pipe Makers	Agitation for increase in piece rates and strike threatened.	Concessions granted by employers.
Oct 72	Dock Labourers	Formation of Liverpool North End Steamship Dock Labourers' Friendly Burial Society. Society rules demand that foremen join; rejected by employers and strike of 5,000 men.	Strike lost. Society probably collapsed.

6: False Dawn

Date	Occupation	Action Involved	Results
Apr - May 72	Operative Farriers	Demand wage increase; rejected by employers and men go on strike.	Strike lost.
Apr - Sept 73	Carpenters and Joiners	Demand for increased wages rejected by employers; men go on strike.	Compromise solution.
May 73	Ships' Painters	Demand for wage increase rejected by employers; men go on strike.	Strike lost.
May 73	Marble Masons	Demand for wage increase rejected by employers: men go on strike. (Nine firms employing 80 men).	Unknown - men still on strike 31 July 1873.

Notes: 1. This list excludes demands for the nine hour day by engineers Oct - Nov 1871. All such claims were conceded by employers.
2. The names 'Simpson' and 'Samuelson' are appended in the column 'Action Involved' when they played a role in advising the work group listed.
Source: Liverpool local press

Appendix 6.2

Rules of the Liverpool Needlewomen's Institute

1. NAME
    The name to be 'The Liverpool Needlewomen's Institute.'
2. OBJECT
    To assist respectable needlewomen, often strangers without connections or influence, to earn their own living by their own work, at fair prices and during reasonable hours. In carrying the foregoing into effect it shall be the aim of the promoters to make the institute self supporting.
3. MANAGEMENT By two committees. A gentlemen's committee, with treasurer and secretary, to look after the business and working department, assisted by a ladies' committee, with such officer or officers as they may appoint, to examine into the characters of the women, and generally to promote their moral and social well being. No interference to be attempted with their distinctive religious opinions. A report to be published annually with a statement of the accounts; new committees to be elected by the donors, any or all of the previous committees to be eligible for re-election. The working plant or stock of the institute to be the property of the gentlemen's committee, as trustees for the donors. Three to be a quorum. All officers of the committee to be honorary.
4. PAID OFFICERS OF THE INSTITUTE
    1. A well qualified matron, acquainted with the various kinds of sewing and shop work.
    2. An assistant matron, also acquainted with the various kinds of sewing and shop work, and capable of acting as registrar in the registration department.
    3. A messenger, to collect and deliver the goods and solicit orders.
5. PLAN
    1. A registration office for needlewomen and domestic servants, for the mutual benefit of ladies wanting sempstresses and servants, and of sempstresses and servants wanting work. This to be under the care of the assistant matron.
    2. Sewing of the finer and more common kinds for families and shops, upon such terms as shall hereafter be agreed upon.
6. A SUITABLE HOUSE to be taken, rented for a period not exceeding two years, in a clean, healthy, and central situation, to be fitted up with

sewing machines and such other appliances, at a moderate cost, as may be found necessary for the effective working of the institution.

7. GENERAL RULES FOR THE INTERNAL MANAGEMENT

1. The character and antecedents of the women to be carefully inquired into.

2. The women to come clean and tidy.

3. To conduct themselves in and orderly and sisterly manner, under the government of the matron and subject to such rules as may hereafter be adopted by the committee.

4. Arrangements to be made to enable the women to have the use of the lavatory and cooking apparatus without charge.

5. The hours of work to be from eight a.m to six p.m., with an interval of one hour for dinner, the women to receive all they earn for the first twelve months, deducting twelve per cent afterwards for working expenses. To be paid weekly on Friday evenings when leaving work.

6. A statement of accounts, with complaints, etc., to be made weekly

7. A list of prices, and all details as to the collecting and delivery of work and the management of the institute to be decided upon after the appointment of the ladies' committee.

8. These and such other arrangements as may now be agreed upon, to be revised at the end of two years, or sooner if thought necessary.

Source: *Liverpool Mercury*, 18 Sept 1872.

7: From Militancy to Social Mission: The Salvation Army and Street Disturbances in Liverpool, 1879-1887

Norman H. Murdoch

In the 1880s the Salvation Army surrendered its 1840s American revivalist nature to become the hybrid revivalist-social service agency it is today. What was the dynamic that nudged the Army to moderate its revivalist message in Anglo-American cities? Our concern is not with the social gospel to which William Booth turned after he realized that he could no longer employ evangelist techniques to save the urban 'heathen'. Rather, we are interested in the roadblock - the urban Irish Roman Catholic resistance to Salvationist revivalism - that forced Booth, the Army's founder, to adopt a form of social gospel which he termed 'wholesale salvation'. This Irish Catholic resistance halted Salvation Army growth as an evangelical mission in the cities by 1887. While the Army continued to expand in small towns, implacable resistance from urban ghetto neighbourhoods revolutionized it in both British and overseas cities.

Liverpool[1] offers a classic case study of how the Irish turned the Salvation Army away from militant evangelism when it failed to win the 'heathen' (Irish) to its evangelical gospel. One Salvationist looked back from 1907, the twenty-seventh anniversary of the Liverpool 1 Corps (the Army's term for a mission branch), and recalled that in spite of its role as the 'mother of fourteen corps there has rarely been a period when the element of hardness has been lacking'.[2] In plain words, since 1865 the Salvation Army had expanded beyond east London to other metropolitan areas, but it had failed in

---

[1]This essay is a revised and shortened version of an article in the *Journal of Social History*. Although Liverpool is the case study for this essay, I have also studied east London, Cincinnati, Montreal, and Quebec City to substantiate these findings. I was assisted by grants from the Wesleyan/Holiness Study Group, the Pew Charitable Trust, and the University of Cincinnati Research Council and Humanities Department.

[2]'Faithful Veterans', *All the World*, Apr 1907, 207 - 210. With a picture of the Army's first Liverpool convert, Brother Ralph, the text states: 'It is a comparatively easy thing to serve a Corps with a roll mounting up to four figures; ... it is quite another thing where the fighting force grows less and less ... and the inhabitants are either passively indifferent or actively hostile to the Army's propaganda. Decreasing numbers does not necessarily imply failure'.

its mission to convert urban 'heathen masses' to its Wesleyan evangelical gospel.

After William Booth renamed his Christian Mission 'a salvation army' in 1878, its growth beyond London's East End slums became more institutionalized.[3] His mission had prospered in the early 1870s as laymen and women moved to new neighbourhoods to open branches in areas in which they lived and worked. Most of those Booth now sent to open corps were not bred in urban slum environments. After 1878, he assigned officers (clergy) to 'invade' hostile areas, often by invitation of evangelical mission or temperance advocates. But Salvationists soon found that criticizing neighbourhood residents for the way they lived had limitations as a recruiting device. The Salvationists' religion was *for* but not *of* the people, and slum-dwellers rejected it.[4]

The Salvation Army's Liverpool invasion came in the military fashion it had adopted in 1878. In 1879, Henry Cottle, a Liverpool baker and Wesleyan lay-revivalist with his own rented chapel, invited General William Booth to take over his work in the hope that the Army's aggressive soul-saving would succeed in his Irish Roman Catholic neighbourhood.[5] Composing a quarter of Liverpool's population in 1861, the Irish formed a 'Catholic workers' culture', centered in slum parishes, which called the faithful to affirm religious and national shibboleths by returning to the church. As a result the Irish developed a devout nationalist piety which joined the sacred with the secular, the spiritual with the political, and allowed them to avoid assimilation into the English working class. Priests found that they could make pre-Christian Irish folk beliefs compatible with Christian devotion.[6] Hence, when an outside agent like Cottle, who wanted to alter the Irish life-style, issued the invitation to the Army, the neighbourhood could be expected to resist the intrusion.

---

[3]Norman H. Murdoch, *The Salvation Army: An Anglo-American Revivalist Social Mission* (Ann Arbor: University Microfilm, 1985), 224-266.

[4]Donald M. Lewis, *Lighten Their Darkness: The Evangelical Mission in Working-Class London, 1828 - 1860* (Westport, 1986).

[5]*Gore's Liverpool City Directory, 1880,* lists Henry Cottle at 21, Wawdar St. S., as a baker/flour dealer, along with James Cottle. They had shops at 4, 32, 68, and 418 Mill St. S., and at 52 Oldham St. W. Edward, Peter, James and William I. Cottle are also listed as bakers/flour dealers. By 1887, the *Directory* lists Henry Cottle, baker, at 26 Victoria Rd., New Brighton.

[6]Lynn Hollen Lees, *Exiles of Erin: Irish Migrants in Victorian London* (Ithaca, 1979), 164 - 169. Kerby A. Miller, *Emigrants and Exiles: Ireland and the Irish Exodus to North America* (New York: 1985), 306ff., discusses Irish hatred of English protestants as a basis of their homogeneity and of their unwillingness to merge their culture into the home culture of England or America. He holds that the Irish sentiment that they were 'exiles' covered their failure to progress in areas of increasing affluence. They soon forgot their motherland when their economic circumstances improved.

Before it invaded Liverpool, the Salvation Army had already failed in east London with its large Irish Catholic population.[7] Ethnic enclaves with alien cultures were not fertile ground for planting the seed of evangelical Christianity. The Army's continued failure in the 1880s gradually drove it away from militant evangelism in urban areas, while it retained its revivalist creed and continued impressive growth in smaller Anglo-American towns.

Types of Salvation Army Disturbances

David Jones lists Salvationists as the fourth 'highest number of persons taken into custody on a charge of riot' in the nineteenth century.[8] Historians have focused on the most publicized resistance to Salvation Army invasions, when their street processions, a noisy disrupter of community order, attracted increasing police intervention.[9] Notable attempts to silence Salvationists in small towns occurred in Torquay in 1886, and Eastbourne in 1890, resort towns concerned lest the Army's noisy bands and ranting preachers would shatter a holiday atmosphere. Salvationists blamed pub owners and brewers for bringing charges against them of disturbing the peace. Victor Bailey, assessing small town disturbances, argues that they were 'not merely over the abstract legal rights of processioning and meeting', but represented intentional resistances by 'integrated social communities' to outsiders.[10] This analysis can be extended to cities, where urban neighbourhoods were in themselves

---

[7]See Norman H. Murdoch and Howard F. McMains, 'The Salvation Army Disturbances of 1885', *Queen City Heritage: Journal of the Cincinnati Historical Society*, 45 (Summer 1987), 31 - 39, for an analysis of the Army's invasion of Cincinnati.

[8]David Jones, *Crime, Protest, Community and Police in Nineteenth Century Britain* (1982), 123. Jones' categories are: 1) political and economic agitation; 2) anti-police riots of the 1830s and 1840s; 3) pro-Sunday trading demonstrations, 1855 and 1870s; and 4) Salvation Army riots, 1880s.

[9]Salvation Army literature chronicles disturbances in 51 towns and villages in England. For United States riots see: Edward Carey, 'Persecuted for Righteousness Sake', *War Cry*, 4 October 1980, 5: Herbert A. Wisbey Jr., *Soldiers Without Swords* (New York, 1955), 37ff.; and Edward H. McKinely, *Marching to Glory* (San Francisco, 1980), 62 - 65, who cites 'Roman Catholics and Jews' as categories of those involved. For Canada, see R. G. Moyles, *The Blood and Fire in Canada* (Toronto, 1977), 44ff. Cyril R. Bridwell, *Fight the Good Fight: The Story of the Salvation Army in New Zealand, 1883 - 1983* (Wellington, New Zealand, 1983), 31ff., refers to street roughs in Australasian slang as 'larrikins', who, he says, were probably connected with publicans and were a result of the high rate of immigration of Britain's lowest class.

[10]Victor Bailey, 'Salvation Army Riots, the "Skeleton Army" and Legal Authority in the Provincial Town', in A. P. Donajgrodzki (ed), *Social Control in Nineteenth Century Britain* (1977), 231 - 253, sees three reasons for the riots: conduct of brewers; popular disapproval of the Salvationists' 'moral imperialism' and community resistance to organizations from outside.

integrated social communities. Here, however, the instigating populations in anti-Salvation Army disturbances were socially radical and ethnically unEnglish.

David Williams cites the important influence Salvation Army disturbances have had on Anglo-American common law. He reviews charges the authorities made against Salvationists, including disturbing the peace and obstructing public thoroughfares, and argues that the effect of court cases dealing with the riots has been to clarify the need to permit free speech while maintaining public order. In most cases courts sided with Salvationists, who, according to Williams, did not intentionally produce turmoil. The Army soon achieved the right to preach, sing and procession through the streets, but this was only a partial victory.[11]

Our concern, unlike the legal or strictly social foci of these historians of small town Salvation Army riots, is with less chronicled, but more institutionally transforming repercussions of Salvationist invasions of ethnically diverse urban neighbourhoods.[12] When England first registered church attendance in 1851's Religious Census it became aware of urban heathenism. Among the thirty-six areas with low church and chapel attendance were eight London boroughs, and the four largest provincial cities, including Liverpool. Many of these were areas of Irish migration. In the case of the Army's clash with the Irish, it lost its singular evangelical mission, but found a new identity in social services.

In London's East End slums in 1865, William Booth had hoped to 'win the masses' to the gospel, masses with whom his missioners did not sympathize. He wanted to save those to whom he referred as 'mobs', or 'rabble',[13] no matter how offensive he found their life-style or habitat. Loving

---

[11]David Williams, *Keeping the Peace: The Police and Public Order* (1967) focuses on the *Beaty v. Gillbanks* case from an 1882 Weston-super-Mare incident. After a riot, Salvationists refused to obey a peace-keeping ban against assembly. The appeals court finally ruled in the Salvationists' favour, rejecting the notion 'that a man may be punished for acting lawfully because he knows that his so doing may induce another man to act unlawfully'; that is, the Salvationists' lawful activities should not be prohibited because of the unlawful attack upon them by the Skeleton Army.

[12]Primary sources abound concerning urban clashes between Salvationist invaders and ethnic neighbourhoods: see *War Cry*, 17 Apr 1880, 2 - 3; George Scott Railton, 'The American Campaign', *War Cry*, 8 Oct 1887, 3. Even a town could display ethnically diverse features of large cities. Gordon Watkinson, 'The Broughton Riots, 1882', Salvation Army Archives, London, states 'So it was into this strongly Roman Catholic, lawless part of the town that the leaders of the Army decided to go. It didn't need much to inflame these inhabitants, who didn't like the English anyway. The Salvation Army's decision to invade "was taken against police advice"'.

[13]Here I place in quotation marks pejorative names Salvationists gave to crowds who attacked them. Bramwell Booth, William's eldest son and successor as general, discusses the Army's early East London difficulties with 'roughs and rowdies', the Skeleton Army,

outcasts, hoping to become one with them by living in their midst as settlement workers would soon do, Salvationists found themselves in a world they could not fathom - of Irish, Italian and French Catholics, Jews, Blacks and Germans - a world which saw itself as besieged by an antagonistic home culture. Booth's English, provincial, youthful recruits of Wesleyan Methodist heritage led these invasions. Quiet Sabbatarians, abstinence advocates, non-smokers, anti-feathers and fashion, they represented a pietistic tradition at considerable odds with those they came to save.[14]

Urban disturbances, more than small town riots dominated by a homogeneous working class, represented the Salvation Army's failure to convert the masses to its Wesleyan religion and forced it to reverse course in its salvation methodology by 1885. By 1890 Booth devised his 'Darkest England' social reform programme to end urban unemployment. Since 1890, this new strategy for saving slum-dwellers has become the urban logo of Salvation Army operations.

The 1879 Invasion of Liverpool

The Salvation Army's Liverpool invasion illustrates how it planted an urban slum corps in 1879 and how Irish Catholics resisted its revivalist message, thus turning the Army in a new direction.[15] The invasion included these elements: an invitation to Liverpool from a Wesleyan revivalist; reconnaissance of the area by General Booth; support of local churches, evangelical associations, and newspapers; and assistance from the police. Liverpoool's Irish neighbourhoods into which the Army marched resisted what they saw as a threat to their life-style and institutions, particularly their religion. The Army's attempt to save slum-dwellers' souls proved to be its most notable failure and had the effect of turning it in directions of which Booth had not conceived when he launched his work in London's slums in 1865. The Army persisted in urban mission work after 1885, but thereafter its primary concern was with social services.

'the rabble', 'mobs', who congregated in public houses after harassing the Army, in *These Fifty Years* (1929), 120ff. Neither here, nor in his biography, *Echoes and Memories* (1935), 28ff, does he provide a more specific description of the Army's enemies, who were 'marshalled from the beerhouses, and generally led by well-known men of evil repute'.

[14]The 1882 *War Cry* (the Salvationists' official organ) ran at least 500 officer biographies. Analysis of these indicates that officers came primarily from provincial, nonconformist, Wesleyan backgrounds.

[15]F. Neal, *Sectarian Violence: The Liverpool Experience 1819 - 1914* (Manchester, 1988), documents a long history of Liverpool's sectarian violence within the larger scheme of Anglo-Irish history. I have drawn on this work for the 1879 - 1887 period.

Of all the slums which the Salvation Army invaded, none was more alien to its evangelical protestant culture than Liverpool's dockside Irish ghetto. Furthermore, Liverpool was a rank urban sectarian battleground. Religion, more than economic and social issues, defined Liverpool's ethnic animosities at a time when states were defined by their state churches and writers were reworking the tradition of the Reformation (Foxe's *Book of Martyrs* was republished in 1875). E. R. Norman argues that 'in such circumstances, mob violence could often be provoked by the wandering band of 'No Popery' preachers'.[16]

On Tuesday 22 July 1879, William Booth visited Liverpool after Henry Cottle had pressed him to 'send a detachment'. Having read about the Salvation Army, Cottle begged Booth to take over his rented Ebenezer Chapel at 41 Beaufort Street at Bertha Lane, South Toxteth Park, an area near the docks, with a 1,400 seat capacity.[17] When Booth walked through the city he found it as appropriate for the Army as any he could imagine, but could not resolve whether to 'attack'. Undecided, he spent the night at Runcorn, whose workingmen made it 'just the sort of a town for the Army'. On Wednesday he returned to Liverpool and received 'approbation from Jehovah' to make arrangements for an 'attack'.[18]

Booth appointed a newly married couple, Captain Isaac and Lieutenant Hannah Skidmore[19] to 'open' Liverpool. The Skidmores had joined the Christian Mission, the Salvation Army's name before 1878, at Middlesbrough. Isaac was a labourer before he became an evangelist in January 1878. Workmates called him 'Moody-Sankey' because he was a lifelong teetaller and Sabbath-keeper, alien attributes to his Liverpudlian parish. In a year and a half he had served five mission stations. Now at the mature age of twenty-one, he and Hannah would launch the Liverpool corps and reside at 60, Ponsonby Street, several blocks away from the docks.[20] The *Liberal Review* described Isaac as 'an ordinary looking "sort of working chap"' with 'a habit of half-closing his eyes when he speaks'. Hannah (née Atkinson), had served at eight stations, was youngish, thin and pale, according to the

---

[16]E. R. Norman, *Anti-Catholicism in Victorian England* (1967), 16 -17.

[17]*Gore's Liverpool Directory*, 1880. Cottle contributed songs to the Salvation Army's *War Cry* for at least ten years after the Liverpool opening.

[18]'Jottings from the Journal of the General', *The Salvationist*, Sept 1879, 226 -229.

[19]'The Army of Fiddlers', *Liberal Review*, x (9 Aug 1879), reported that sometimes wives outranked their husbands.

[20]*Gore's Liverpool City Directory*, 1880, lists Skidmore as a Scripture reader and evangelist. The Ponsonby St. residence was ten blocks west of the Liverpool corps, which was situated in the south dock district. In 1992 this area is being rehabilitated; the Ponsonby St. area is the home of poor Asian, African and West Indian immigrants. The Salvation Army no longer has a corps in the area.

reporter, with eyes that remind one of a 'female spirit medium just going off into a trance'. They arrived at Liverpool without benefit of honeymoon. A converted pugilist, Brother Pargeter, came to assist them.[21] They opened Liverpool's first corps on Sunday 3 August at Ebenezer Chapel, in an Irish Catholic neighbourhood near the docks.[22] Cottle reported the first day's meetings to Booth - 'a splendid victory for your army in Liverpool'. Booth had expected trouble from neighbourhood roughs, but Cottle had not asked the police superintendent for a detachment, sensing they would need none. He was pleased with the captain and wife - Skidmore's 'hallelujah fiddle' was a great attraction; he also played the cornet. Cottle noted a shortage of 'outside workers', evangelical church members on whom the Army depended for financial and moral support, but was hopeful that they would soon come to assist. Skidmore's report of the opening was in a terse telegram to Booth: 'Good day. Rough open air [at St. George's Place]. Five hundred indoors afternoon. One thousand night. One soul. Send real good lass'. Women opened most Army corps as the number of its female ministers burgeoned after 1879, an innovation that made the Salvation Army the fastest growing foreign and home mission in the world by the mid-1880s. [23] Soon things were looking up in Liverpool, with large bands of evangelical supporters and many sinners 'under deep conviction'.

As local protestants began to support the Salvationists, Skidmore noted that 'Roman Catholics follow us and pelt us by the hundreds'. Twelve souls had come to Jesus, and 'the police are extra kind, indeed they take care of us'. In an embellished autobiographical sketch in 1887, Skidmore reported that 'ten thousand Roman Catholics rose en masse' to stop the work as 'night after night the new recruits spoke in the open air staggering like drunken men shoved, pushed, pelted with sticks, stones and pokers'. Battle lines formed: Salvationists, evangelical friends, and police on one side; the neighbourhood's Irish Catholics on the other. The *Liverpool Protestant Standard* threw its support to the Army, not endorsing the way it conducted its services, but acknowledging 'its usefulness in the saving of souls'. The Army's members [surely not the Skidmores] were evidence of God's grace to lift those 'beyond

---

[21]'Captain and Mrs. Skidmore', *War Cry*, 3 Sept 1887, 6 - 7; 'Skidmore File', the Salvation Army Archives, London; 'The Army of Fiddlers', *Liberal Review*, x (9 Aug 1879), reported that the Salvation Army had been threatening invasion for some time.

[22]'Opening Liverpool', *The Salvationist*, 1 Sept 1879, 233 - 234; 'Salvationist Screams', *Liberal Review*, x (23 Aug 1879), 10 - 11; 'The Salvation Shriekers', *Liberal Review*, x (6 Sept 1879), 11 - 12; also see *Liberal Review* reports for 25 Oct, 1 Nov, and 20 Dec 1879.

[23]Norman H. Murdoch, 'Female Ministry in the Thought and Work of Catherine Booth', *Church History*, 53 (Sept 1984), 363 - 378; and 'The Salvation Army's U. S. Arrival', *Organisation of American Historians' Newsletter* (15 May 1987), 12 - 13.

the pale of human hope' from 'the very depths' and make them 'useful members of society'. It deserved support since 'the quarry in which they labour is composed of adamantine hardness'. On 23 August, the secularist *Liberal Review* quoted Booth as aiming to overcome 'Popery, publicanism, infidelity, and devilish' influences in the 'godless town of Liverpool'.[24] Meanwhile, Booth sent the Skidmores a 'real good lass' - Mary Bullis from Sheffield.

The 1879 Disturbances

On Sunday afternoon, 24 August, the worst violence occurred. Salvationists identified for the police an earlier stone thrower, a girl of about eighteen. Skidmore and another Salvationist turned her over to police and then followed to the station to give their statement. The girl 'danced along' between two policemen 'in high glee'. So fierce was the quickly-gathering crowd that Skidmore requested protection to take him back to the chapel. On the way another offender threw a stone. This drew a larger crowd and more commotion; the police arrested another girl. Skidmore suggested that it was not safe to take the second girl to Bridewell jail and invited the police to bring her to the Army's chapel. The mob spread the news that the Salvation Army was '"locking up the Roman Catholics,"' and this increased its size. The crowd threatened to storm the chapel unless the police released the girl, but they refused. As one gentleman fell on his knees to beg Skidmore for the girl's release, the 'mob' broke windows and pushed the doors in on top of men guarding them. Mrs. Skidmore, through the din, carried on with the meeting. '"I thought most were like to be killed"' she said, '"And I wanted to get as many saved as possible"'.

The Chief of Police arrived with reinforcements, but was unable to cope with the 'mob'. At last the police released the girls, which brought a cheer from the crowd. There is no further record of legal action against the offenders. The police then cleared the street and made plans to take the Skidmores home to tea. But the Skidmores had other plans. They were to spend the afternoon at the home of a 'friendly policeman'.

On every street corner the crowd increased. Women lashed out at Hannah through the police cordon. Isaac's 1887 analysis was that '"the insanity which any like mob seems to contract in a few hours was upon them"'. Finally, the police inspector and Skidmore drew up a strategy. The police would hold off the 'mob' while the Skidmores scurried down

---

[24]'Captain and Mrs. Skidmore', *War Cry*, 3 Sept 1887, 6 - 7; 'The Army Fiddlers', *Liberal Review*, x (9, 16 and 23 Aug, 6 and 27 Sept 1879) provides some detail, but no significant interpretation of the disturbances.

side-streets to their destination. But the 'maddened crowd' outwitted the police and beat them to the hiding place. Before, the police arrived the crowd had filled the street in front of the house and forced in the door. The first man through the door threatened, '"I'll have your blood"'. Fearing the worst, Isaac clutched his bride, '"Give us a kiss my dear. The grace of our Lord Jesus Christ be with you"'. At that moment the police arrived and dispersed the 'mob'. The Skidmores returned to the chapel for their Sunday evening meeting where souls were saved.

The lack of evidence of arrests or court cases may be due to the fact that neither the Army nor the police wanted to stir up unnecessary trouble in this volatile neighourhood. In 1878, the year before the Salvation Army arrived, the Watch Committee had ordered Head Constable W. Nott Bower to assign a special group of officers to a public-house inspection detail. Police gradually attempted to drive open vice from the streets, amid considerable criticism, until the 1880 elections removed the temperance majority. It was in this volatile two-year span that the Salvation Army invaded Liverpool. And the Toxteth area adjacent to the South Docks into which the Army marched was the centre of criminal activity.[25]

After the 1879 altercations General Booth immediately transferred the Skidmores to Bradford, near their Yorkshire homes, where they spent ten months which 'seemed to be quiet to them' after Liverpool. By the time they had composed their 1887 biographical account they had served fourteen stations since Liverpool.[26] With the arrival of Captain James Dowdle, the Skidmores' mentor in the 1870s and a mission evangelist since 1867, attendance declined and an 'unruly mob of roughs' haunted Ebenezer Hall. [27] To attract roughs, just the sort he hoped to save, Dowdle held 'Salvation Free and Easies', a term borrowed from pub sing-alongs, but with little success.

The unsympathetic *Liberal Review* held that the Army correctly attributed opposition to the '"ire and indignation of the papal rabble which inhabit the neighbourhood,"' who are '"under the guidance and direction of the papal priesthood."' But Salvationists' attacks on Roman Catholics mean they have 'only themselves to thank for being molested as they are now very frequently'. In October a young lady named Connor, with others, attacked the Army as it marched up Beaufort Street. The 'Colonel' was hit in the face with a meat can, Cato was hit, Barrow kicked in the leg, and a young man was hit

---

[25]Michael Brogden, *The Police: Autonomy and Consent* (1982), vii, 51, 57, 67, 242; *Liverpool Mercury* (17 July 1835); R. Muir, *History of Liverpool* (Liverpool, 1907), 326.

[26]'Captain and Mrs. Skidmore', *War Cry*, 3 Sept 1887, 6 - 7.

[27]Robert Sandall, *The History of the Salvation Army, 1865-1878* (1947), 73, 95, 125, 128, 132, 164, 173, 198, 205, 210, 215, the Army's official historian, does not mention Dowdle's appointment in Liverpool in 1879.

in the head with a brick.[28] But again there is no evidence that the Army pressed charges. Disturbances continued through the 1880s, but without evidence of police arrests.

Several conclusions flow from these Salvation Army riots. First, after Cottle's initial failure to seek police protection, Salvationists requested police support against what Skidmore referred to as a 'mob'. Booth knew from east London experience that marching a protestant 'army' into a Catholic Irish neighbourhood would likely cause resistance. That the Skidmores had planned to spend Sunday afternoon with 'a friendly policeman' underscores the degree to which they were cordial with the police. But there is no evidence that police action led to indictments. Police support was ultimately aimed only at public order and not at protestant hegemony. Nor was it in the Salvationists' interest to be seen as cosy with policemen, the sworn enemies of the 'roughs' they came to save.

Second, Salvationists depended on evangelicals for support. The encouraging article in the *Liverpool Protestant Standard*, and Cottle's fear that such support was not forthcoming, reinforces this conclusion. The Army had come to do battle for souls; but Irish Catholics saw 'Orange' at such a threat and reacted with stone throwing at the invaders. There is no evidence that protestants attempted to intervene on the Army's side in these clashes. While they were willing to support the Army's right to worship and speak in public, most were unwilling to adopt its military tactics.

New Tactics and New Aims by 1887

By 1887, the Salvation Army's eighth Liverpool anniversary, it still hoped its imperial revivalist venture would succeed in a city that in its view only London could contest for 'vice, poverty and degradation', or 'superabundant rowdyism'. Salvationists had 'planted a colony' which, they claimed, 'had grown and was growing' in spite of 'doubt expressed of our real powers to hold the masses. After eight years we are more in touch than ever with the people'. Salvationists did not acknowledge failure to win the masses to the gospel, but they had begun to modify their militant revivalist tactics and to develop social schemes. While the Army still aimed at the salvation of

---

[28]'The Salvation Shriekers', *Liberal Review*, x (6 Sept 1879), 11 - 12. Also see *Liberal Review* reports for 25 Oct, 1 Nov, and 20 Dec 1879

souls, it was shifting toward a social salvation emphasis, or, as Booth put it, 'wholesale salvation'.[29]

Once again, if only to remind them of their failure, an eighth anniversary procession of Salvationists along narrow streets met 'threatening' crowds. A 'disgraceful disturbance' took place at the corner of Everton and West Derby Roads during the customary march prior to the Sunday afternoon meeting. Young men jeered as a crowd of several hundred jostled the Salvationists. A young man 'deliberately put his foot through the bass drum', a common object of the opposition.[30] A woman, 'evidently drunk, threw herself headlong in front of the procession' and bashed the leader, Major Rees, over the head with her market basket. After rolling in the gutter and throwing her boots at marchers, she was brought under control by the police, who made 'things safe and pleasant for us', according to the *War Cry*. On Sunday an old woman of at least sixty threw oyster shells at Rees as Salvationists marched the 'worst streets'. Captain Welshaw encouraged the crowd to avoid the gods of 'the multitudes', including 'Drink, the pipe, the fashions', and to 'imitate the Hebrew children, and make a stand for God'.[31]

The Irish persisted, resisting Salvation Army militant revivalist tactics. By 1887 the Army had been unable to increase its membership on alien soil. In 1884 the *Liverpool Review* claimed that Liverpool had largely escaped scenes of violence enacted against Salvationists in Birkenhead, Brighton, Worthing and other places, not due to 'any self restraint on the part of the Army, but to the fact that in Liverpool the organization only maintains of fitful and struggling existence ... let them plant the ragged and dirty handkerchief

---

[29]The Army continued to open corps in the 1880s. Captain Josiah Taylor opened no. 2 at Walton, a 'stronghold of Satan', on 20th Mar 1881. (One source credits Captain Emily Munns from Whitechapel, *War Cry*, 24 Mar, 7 Apr, and 19 May 1881, *All the World*, Oct 1916, 421 - 424.) Captain S. J. Wright opened Bootle on 2 Apr 1881, *War Cry*, 19 May 1881. Breckfield and Everton (Roscommon St) opened in 1882. See *All the World*, Jan 1927, 27 - 30. There were 15 corps when Ballington Booth spoke at Hope Hall (later Everyman Theatre) in 1882, where some 'rolled on the floor in agony while waiting for the blessing', *War Cry*, 8 June 1882. 'Liverpool', *All the World*, May 1909, 271 - 274, lists 17 corps and states that 'the Army is making drunken, shiftless, aimless individuals in Liverpool into sober, God-fearing citizens'. But new social services, led by Adjutant Vincent and 10 Slum Officers, included: The Hollies, home for 40 women and girls; Chesterfield House for 20 young mothers and infants; a Metropole for 100 women; a Slum Settlement; and a Shelter for men on Pitt St.

[30]'Attack on Liverpool Salvationists -- Disgraceful Scene', *Liverpool Echo*, 15 Aug 1887. The drum was a central feature of protestant and catholic marching units.

[31]'Eighth Anniversary of Liverpool I, The Lowest Strata of Liverpudlian Humanity', *War Cry*, 3 Sept 1887, 11 - 12. See Michael McGiffert, 'God's Controversy with Jacobean England', *American Historical Review*, 88 (1983), 1151 - 1174, which discusses early 17th century puritan militancy, observing that Englishmen embraced the Hebrew notion that they were a chosen nation, church, and people.

they call a flag where they like and bawl ... loafers will not follow them'. The writer asked, 'what blasphemy, too, can be more repulsive than for a woman, obviously suffering from hysteria, to engage publicly in what is called "prayer"'. They were the same as the Roman Catholics in their holy hierarchy - General Booth was Pope.[32]

But Booth had learned some lessons from the 1879 riot and had begun to alter his tactics. In 1880 he had ordered precautions in holding street services: 'we must improve our singing', use hymns everyone knows; and avoid 'provocation to disturbance'. He wanted no trouble with Catholics. Salvationists should not attack sabbath-breakers, and must 'keep off the Virgin Mary, for there are always some Roman Catholics about'.[33]   Booth also implored Salvationists to: 1) 'Remember that no good can ever be served by a conflict whether with the roughs or with the police' - good Salvationists 'attack the largest number of people with the least amount of disturbance'. 2) Be 'so disciplined and led as to outwit and overcome a mob anywhere'. 3) Keep on good terms with the police; they 'are never disposed to get into any sort of trouble'. 4) Remember, your enemy is 'the liquor traffic'. If it did not exist the Army would 'never be troubled with open opposition of any sort'. Unfortunately, seeking police aid put the Army 'in a pitiful position' by 'separating us from the people we want to get'.[34]

More important than his new caution in holding street meetings in Irish Catholic neighbourhoods was Booth's new strategy for saving the masses, commenced in earnest around 1885.[35] Booth had at least three options for reviving his failing mission in urban slums in the 1880s. He could have assumed the role of a protestant-Orange Order leader as George Wise and John Kensit were doing.[36] Or he could have followed other working-class denominations to the suburbs, leaving behind the masses he was committed to save. Instead Booth, like Cardinal Manning, turned to social services, largely because of the difficulty of winning the 'heathen masses' to the gospel by revivalist methods of spreading the Army's Wesleyan protestant gospel. To deter protestant advances, Manning had aimed at establishing a strong

[32]'Blasphemy and Black Mail', *The Liverpool Review*, xv (11 Oct 1884), 10 - 11.

[33]William Booth, 'How to Improve our Open Air Services, Part II', *War Cry*, 31 Jan 1880, 1 - 2.

[34]'Golden Rules for Open Air Work', *War Cry*, 7 Aug 1880, 2.

[35]Neal, *Sectarian Violence*, 207. Not everyone changed strategy by 1890. In 1902, John Kensit Sr. and Jr. came to Liverpool for an anti-ritualist campaign, aimed largely at Anglican high church clerics, but also indirectly at Roman Catholics. One leader of this movement was a former Salvation Army officer, G. Musgrave-Brown, vicar of St. Clements', Toxteth. Musgrave-Brown was one of three curates who had joined the Army earlier.

[36]Neal, *Sectarian Violence*, 200 - 09. See below, ch 8.

Catholic Church in England through social programmes: rescuing Catholic children from non-Catholic schools; teaching Catholics temperance; and improving diocesan priests.[37]

Always open to adaptation at points of failure, Booth began his social salvation programme modestly as Salvationist women opened shelters for 'fallen women' in 1883. By 1885 he and Catherine became involved in W. T. Stead's 'Maiden Tribute' crusade to raise the age of consent for prostitutes to sixteen, a crusade that had Manning's support as well. Finally, in 1890, with the help of Stead, Frank Smith, and Suzie Swift, he published a scheme to move unemployed workers out of urban ghettos to Britain's imperial wastelands overseas. These social schemes saved his Army from being just another failed urban revival mission and provided it with a world-wide mission of 'wholesale salvation' through social services.

The Irish Roman Catholics, whom he detested, had induced William Booth's new social reform vision to bring light to 'Darkest England', to place excess urban population 'back on the land', and to rid cities of vice and sin. Although Booth never acknowledged his lack of success with revivalism in cities - nor did he point to the Irish as the reason for his failure - there can be no doubt that the Roman Catholic Irish convinced General Booth that his revivalist methods could not succeed in cities. As clerics and journalists announced his 'unique failure' in cities by the late 1880s, Booth turned to a new 'wholesale salvation ' programme to save the 'heathen masses' who would not yield to his revivalist message of retail individual soul salvation.[38]

---

[37]In 1870 Cardinal Manning had organized the Total Abstinence League of the Cross. He even called for government intervention to prohibit the use of alcohol in 1871 and 1882.

[38]By 1968, the Salvation Army had 11 corps, 2 goodwill (social) centres, men's and women's shelters, homes and hostels, of which there were 4 corps and 1 goodwill centre in the 'inner areas of the city', according to Frances J. C. Amos, 'The Salvation Army', in *Places of Worship in Liverpool* (Liverpool, 1968), 34 - 36. The 1988 *Liverpool Phone Book*, listed 5 corps: Bootle, Clubmoor, Edge Hill, Kensington, Prescot; and two community centres: Childwall Valley and Mildenhall Road.

8: More than One Working Class: Protestant-Catholic Riots in Edwardian Liverpool[1]

John Bohstedt

'...Politics dissociated from religion would be a miserable thing not worth fighting about'. - Delegate to the Working Men's Association, 1898.

'But as the difference of tradition, temperament, and adherence which finds expression in these processions is not confined to those taking part in them it is difficult to prohibit any given procession without giving offence to a large section of the community...' - H. C. Dowdall, Lord Mayor of Liverpool, to Home Office, 2 July 1909.

In 1909 Liverpool was rocked by weeks of Protestant-Catholic violence. Religious pageantry touched off murderous assaults. Mounted police charged rioters up narrow streets. Women and children brawled outside schools, and men were attacked on their way home from work, one lethally. The authority of the city's police hung by a thread. These scenes of mayhem brought to a climax the fiery career of street-preacher George Wise, whose antics had already drawn a landmark King's Bench ruling on free speech. Yet even an exhaustive Home Office Inquiry failed to find a remedy, despite hopes for conciliation. For social calm depended upon political will rather than enlightenment. It was to take a further social earthquake before the town fathers would act to stop the sectarian rioting which had raged on and off for generations in Liverpool.

For a long time, the history of ethnic violence in Britain was underdeveloped perhaps because it did not seem to square with the history of

[1] I am very grateful to Andrew Charlesworth, Professor P. N. Davies and colleagues in the Department of Economic and Social History, University of Liverpool, for their hospitality while I was researching this essay, an early version of which was presented to the Centre for the History of Social Policies seminar organized by Professor E. P. Hennock. I am also very grateful to Kathleen E. Bohstedt, Todd Diacon and Robert K. Webb for their helpful comments.

the working class. The parameters of that classic story have been proletarianization, class consciousness, and the arduous building of working-class movements, with peaks in Chartism and the socialist revival rising above valleys of defeat and declension and a boggy 'culture of consolation.'[2] Ethnic conflict was left outside the mainstream of labour history, perhaps because it was not widely visible until after the Irish Famine, or perhaps because it seemed an embarrassing diversion from the 'real' story of working-class advance based upon identity grounded in work, class consciousness grounded in clear perceptions of material interests and power, and solidarities based upon those interests. Labour historians, perhaps fearing that sectarian hostility was a species of false consciousness, have seemed inclined to *reduce* ethnic tensions to economic competition.[3] By contrast, historians of the American and German working classes have certainly recognised that ethnicity provided important bases for solidarity. Martin Shefter has said it well: 'When workers did join with others in an effort to improve their lives, ethnicity was at least as likely as social class *per se* to be the basis of association. It will not do, however, to speak of ethnicity and class as competing principles of identification and organization..'.[4] Only recently, perhaps influenced by recurrent ethnic issues including immigration and Northern Ireland, have ethnic conflicts in Victorian and Edwardian Britain begun to receive their due attention.[5]

Protestant-Catholic violence was hardly unique to Liverpool in this period, but conditions in Liverpool made it more bitter and more chronic than

---

[2]Gareth Stedman Jones, 'Working-Class Culture and Working-Class Politics in London, 1870-1900: Notes on the Remaking of a Working Class,' in his *Languages of Class: Studies in English Working-Class History 1832 - 1982* (Cambridge, 1983), 237.

[3]See section III below.

[4]Martin Shefter, 'Trade Unions and Political Machines: The Organization and Disorganization of the American Working Class in the Late Nineteenth Century', in Ira Katznelson and Aristide R. Zolberg (eds), *Working-Class Formation: Nineteenth-Century Patterns in Western Europe and the United States*, (Princeton, 1986), 231; for Germany, see Mary Nolan, 'Economic Crisis, State Policy, and Working-Class Formation in Germany, 1879-1900' in *ibid*, 374.

[5]D. G. Paz, 'Popular Anti-Catholicism in England, 1850 - 51,' *Albion*, 11 (1979), 331 - 359, and *Popular Anti-Catholicism in Mid-Victorian England*, (Stanford, forthcoming); Kenneth Lunn, (ed.), *Hosts, Immigrants and Minorities: Historical Responses to Newcomers in British Society* (Folkestone, 1980); Colin Holmes (ed), *Immigrants and Minorities in British Society* (1978); Walter L. Arnstein, *Protestant versus Catholic in Mid-Victorian England: Mr. Newdegate and the Nuns* (Columbia, Mo., 1982); Neville Kirk, *The Growth of Working-Class Reformism in Mid-Victorian England* (1985); Roger Swift and Sheridan Gilley (eds), *The Irish in the Victorian City* (1985) and *The Irish in Britain, 1815 - 1939* (1989).

anywhere else except Belfast.[6] Liverpool's sectarianism has recently been the subject of a number of valuable studies, and this essay does not challenge their findings so much as it tries to carry their work further. P. J. Waller has highlighted the central importance of sectarian themes and rivalries in electoral politics. Frank Neal has connected that story to street violence in a study emphasizing the history of the Orange Order. More attention needs to be given to Catholic political advance which triggered Protestant aggression. Joan Smith and Andy Shallice have fully appreciated the significance of sectarianism in Liverpool and have explained how Liverpool did not fit the classic contours of the making of the labour movement.[7] In seeking to understand Protestant-Catholic violence from the viewpoints of the participants, I want to suggest that violence was not a sharp break from everyday beliefs and politics. For indeed it was just the *constructive* beliefs and organizations of Protestants and Catholics that gave the combatants the necessary solidarity to act collectively. Liverpool's sectarianism offers a case study in that twentieth-century phenomenon, the paradoxical mixture of progress and atavism in populist political mobilization.

The following analysis will test two propositions:

1) That the sectarian riots were deeply rooted in the structures and processes of Liverpool community politics. They resulted, not from spontaneous explosions, but from sustained campaigns and deliberate political choices, some of them unattractive but nonetheless intelligible.

2) That sectarian conflicts enlisted their thousands not simply by brutal hatreds but by sustaining values and organizations that served *progressive* functions in working-class life.

If class is a relationship formed through historical experience, in which one group of people come to feel and articulate their interests against others,[8] these riots remind us that more than one working class was made in Victorian England. In Liverpool, ethnic 'cocoons' of values and organizations

---

[6]For comparisons see, for instance, Neville Kirk, 'Ethnicity, Class and Popular Toryism, 1850 - 1870,' in Lunn (ed), *Hosts, Immigrants and Minorities,* 64 - 106; Tom Gallagher, 'A Tale of Two Cities: Communal Strife in Glasgow and Liverpool before 1914,' in Swift and Gilley, (eds), *Irish in the Victorian City,* 106 - 129.

[7]P. J. Waller, *Democracy and Sectarianism: A political and social history of Liverpool 1868 -1939* (Liverpool, 1981); Frank Neal, *Sectarian Violence: The Liverpool Experience, 1819 - 1914: An aspect of Anglo-Irish history* (Manchester, 1988); Joan Smith, 'Labour Tradition in Glasgow and Liverpool,' *History Workshop,* 17 (1984), 32 - 56, and 'Class, skill and sectarianism in Glasgow and Liverpool, 1880 - 1914,' in R. J. Morris (ed), *Class, Power and Social Structure in British Nineteenth-Century Towns* (Leicester, 1986), 158 - 215; and A. Shallice, 'Orange & Green and militancy; Sectarianism and Working Class politics in Liverpool, 1900 - 1914,' *Bulletin of the North West Labour History Society,* 6 (1979 - 80), 15 - 32.

[8]E. P. Thompson, *The Making of the English Working Class* (New York, 1963), 9.

comprehensively answered the needs of working-class life and created the mentalities and regiments for combat. Our task is no less than to rescue the Catholic docker, the Protestant carter, and the poor deluded follower of Pastor George Wise from the enormous condescension of labour history. In order to do that, I want to look first at the short-range pattern of events and choices made by the players; second at the main protagonists; third at the progressive features of sectarian ideologies; fourth at the structures of community politics that underpinned conflict; and fifth at the resolution of sectarian conflict.

I. The Pattern of Events

The pattern of events suggests that the riots resulted from deliberate decisions taken by Catholic and Protestant leaders in a pattern of political competition. They were the articulate and specific products of culture and politics, not simply outbreaks of spontaneous atavism. The ranks, rancour, and rituals of the combatants were of long standing and significant social utility.

A culture of sectarian violence became well-established in mid-Victorian Liverpool, as shown abundantly by Anne Bryson's essay in this volume and by Frank Neal's work. Occasional large riots arose out of a steady succession of smaller sectarian fights triggered by insults in streets and pubs, family disputes, or bar brawls. Even a marigold in a lapel might trigger attack. Marching on ethnic holidays like St. Patrick's Day or the Glorious 12th of July was an established folkway. Like the mass politics of platforms and demonstrations, marching was an elemental way of showing physical strength and making territorial claims. 'Where you could "walk", you were dominant, and the other things followed'.[9] Besides the visceral reaction to partisan orange and green, the battle hymns of Orange fife-and-drum bands had begun to rouse friends and foes by the 1880's at least.[10] Songs like 'The Boyne Water', 'Paddy was a Bastard', and 'The Boys of Wexford' became weapons to test the foes' mettle.

Ironically, political reform intensified sectarian conflict. On the heels of the Second Reform Act of 1867, riots touched off by William Murphy's tour of the Midlands and Lancashire showed that sectarian hatreds were a strong and cheap way to mobilize the newly enfranchised working class. Liverpool's Working Men's Conservative Association was founded in 1868 to link

---

[9]M. W. Dewar, J. Brown, and S. E. Long, *Orangeism: A new historical appreciation* (Belfast, 1967), 139, quoted in Sybil E. Baker, 'Orange and Green: Belfast, 1832 - 1912', in H. J. Dyos and Michael Wolff (eds), *Victorian City: Images and Reality*, ii, 790. Cf Shallice, 24.

[10]Neal, 166, 187

Orangemen to the party leaders. Over the decades its leaders would flirt with the social reform rhetoric of Tory Democracy while keeping one foot on the sure ground of sectarianism.[11] Given partisan legitimacy, ethnic hostilities achieved the festering permanency of old wounds.

From about 1850 sectarianism was focussed in local and national politics by the issue of Ritualism. Evangelical anti-ritualists attacked practices in Anglican parishes that resembled Roman Catholic usage, such as vestments, incense, and especially auricular confession which gave priests access to the innermost thoughts of 'their' women. Evangelicals hated Ritualists as closet Catholics and traitors. From 1898 anti-ritualists began to push for legislation to enforce orthodox church discipline, and for Liverpool M.P.'s, support for the Church Discipline Bill became a litmus test of Protestant solidarity.[12] It was flamboyant demonstrations against Ritualism that first won notoriety for George Wise and made him a political force to be reckoned with.

Yet if sectarian violence was well established in Victorian Liverpool, serious riots were neither inevitable nor incessant. Specific events had proximate causes. Indeed, Liverpool remained relatively quiet between 1905 and 1908. There were many large festive processions on both sides, including Catholic ones bearing images of the saints, without a general conflagration like that of 1909.[13] At the same time, the Catholic community of Edwardian Liverpool was on the move, reaping the gains of earlier struggles, growing in numbers, institutional and political strength, social staus and confidence. They were not simply passive victims. On St. Patrick's Day, 1906, perhaps emboldened by the Liberals' recent landslide victory, rowdy hangers-on following the Irish National Foresters left the parade to attack George Wise's church.[14] But if the equilibrium of Protestant dominance and Catholic

---

[11]Waller, *Democracy and Sectarianism*

[12]See G. I. T. Machin, 'The Last Victorian Anti-Ritualist Campaign, 1895 - 1906,' *Victorian Studies*, 25 (1982), 291ff; Neal, 191; Waller, 174 - 176.

[13]*Catholic Herald* [hereafter *CH*], 21 Mar, 30 May, 25 July 1908; Liverpool *Daily Post and Mercury* [hereafter *DPM*], 21 June 1909; *Police (Liverpool Inquiry) Act, 1909: Transcript of the Shorthand Notes of Proceedings* [hereafter *PAT*] Liverpool, 1910), 1468-9, 1515, 1585. This source includes barristers' examination of witnesses before the Commissioner appointed by the Home Office, Arthur J. Ashton, as well as his Report [hereafter *PAR*].

[14]Joan Smith, 'Commonsense Thought and Working-class Consciousness: Some Aspects of the Glasgow and Liverpool Labour Movements in the Early Years of the Twentieth Century,' unpublished Ph. D. thesis, University of Edinburgh, 1980, 355; *The Times*, 19 Mar 1906; Catholic ambitions are emphasized in Arnstein, *Protestant versus Catholic*, 3, 212, and passim.

inferiority no longer seemed so secure, such incidents remained isolated rather than triggering a chain reaction.[15]

As Liverpool's stability from 1905-8 suggests, it was not simply Irish or Catholic processions that touched off Protestant fury. Rather it was the Roman Catholics' Eucharistic Congress of 1908, a sort of religious World's Fair, which seemed to raise the antagonism to a whole new plateau by challenging English law. One hundred Catholic bishops and archbishops came to London from the six continents for 'the most triumphant demonstration of Catholic faith and unity seen in Britain for three centuries'. The purpose of the Congress was to celebrate the Eucharist, 'the sacrifice of the Mass, the real presence', 'the central mystery of our religion', in song, sermon and seminar.[16] The grand climax was to be a solemn ceremonial procession of the Host through the public streets of London - the Host, the consecrated wafer, the embodiment of the doctrine of transubstantiation, the key bone of doctrinal contention between Catholics and ultra-Protestants (I shall refer to them simply as Protestants). For the Protestant and Catholic faithful who took the spiritual world seriously, the Congress and its processions were religious 'aggression', not mere pageantry.[17] The Catholic press announced that, 'The Holy Father ... has been pleased to grant the faithful an Indulgence ... each time they spend five minutes before the Blessed Sacrament and pray for the success of the Congress and for *the conversion of England* ...' The President of the International Eucharistic Congress, the Bishop of Namur, added that all should pray 'to bring back Protestant England to the Worship of the Eucharist ... May these meetings be the signal, nay even the first stage of the triumph of the Holy Church in the great English nation'.[18]

The climax of the Eucharistic Congress, announced the Archbishop of Westminster, was to be the carrying of the Host by the prelates as a test of Catholic piety, English law, and public toleration.[19] The law in question was the Catholic Emancipation Act of 1829, which prohibited Catholic clergymen from conducting religious services or wearing the habits of their orders outside their churches. Quite reputable authorities, including the Head Constable of Liverpool, had assumed that the Catholic Emancipation Act was a dead letter,

---

[15]Allan Grimshaw's 'accommodation thesis' holds that ethnic violence often results when a subordinate group rejects, or is perceived to reject, its previous 'accommodation' to a social pattern of domination and subordination. The now-insecure dominant party then acts violently to restore equilibrium. Allen D. Grimshaw (ed), *Racial Violence in the United States* (Chicago, 1969), 7.

[16]*CH*, 22 and 29 Aug 1908; Gordon Wheeler, 'The Archdiocese of Westminster,' in George Andrew Beck (ed), *The English Catholics, 1850 - 1950*, (1950), 174.

[17]*Protestant Standard* [hereafter *PS*], 5 and 12 Sept 1908.

[18]*CH*, 18 July (my italics), 15 Aug 1908.

[19]*Ibid*, 5 Sept 1908.

for it had not been enforced for eighty years.[20] But now that test was stopped in its tracks by Protestant outcry, spearheaded by a large rally led by Pastor George Wise in the centre of Liverpool. The *Protestant Standard* called for the 'millions of London' to rise up and 'scatter the procession in all directions'. The Prime Minister intervened and the Host was dropped from the procession. Protestants chalked up a double victory and lesson: they had foreseen concrete Catholic aggression and had defeated it by vigilance and political muscle. Not surprisingly they declared that God himself had given them the victory, thus consecrating it above criticism.[21] Henceforth aroused Protestants would be on guard.

In the spring of 1909 the challenge seemed to be renewed, as Catholics paraded the Host through the streets in Manchester (14 March), Reading (4 April), and London, (Walworth, 13 June). Even the Roman Catholic Bishop of Liverpool conceded that these episodes seemed to be trying to suggest that the Catholic Emancipation Act was no longer in force.[22] That amounted to Catholic aggression in Protestant eyes, which justified, even demanded, preventive aggression on their part. The *Protestant Standard* said that Protestants had been brought 'into the Valley of Decision ... They must either submit themselves to the yoke of Rome, or fight - to the death if necessary to maintain their freedom'.[23] At the same time Catholics were pushing legislation in Parliament to alter the Accession Declaration, in which new monarchs denounced transubstantiation in harsh language unnecessarily insulting to Catholics.[24] Ultra-Protestants had long clung to that Declaration as their chief protection against the return of James II! The parallel Catholic moves, on the streets and in the legislature, gave Protestants ammunition for the outdoor campaign season of 1909. The *Protestant Standard* proclaimed

---

[20]Head Constable's Report to Watch Committee, 17 May 1909, reprinted in *PAR*, 16.

[21]*PS*, 5 and 12 Sept 1908; Cf Neal, 227. *The Times*, 14 Sept 1908; British Library, Herbert Gladstone papers, Add. Mss. 45989, ff 182 - 196; 46096, ff 191 - 231; 45994, 141, 144, 151, 159, 164; *CH*, 19 Sept 1908.

[22]Manchester, *CH*, 20 Mar 1909, and *Protestant Observer*, Apr 1909; Reading, *PS*, 1 May 1909, and *CH*, 19 June and 3 July 1909. Thomas Whiteside, Lord Bishop of Liverpool, to L. Dunning, 18 May 1909, in *PAR*, 19, copy in HO45/11138/186474.

[23]*PS*, 19 Sept 1908.

[24]*PS*, 23 Jan 1909; *CH*, 8, 15, 22 May 1909. Liverpool's Protestant M.P., Charles M'Arthur, having received a protest petition of hundreds of thousands of signatures, tried to warn Parliament of the danger to the Protestant succession, but he was interrupted by laughter, (*DPM*, 12, 15 May 1909). Liverpool's Head Constable Dunning believed that 'the introduction of the Catholic Disabilities Removal Bill, the defeat of their champion M'Arthur, was the defeat for which the Orangemen wanted to get something back.' PRO, HO45/11138/186474/6 L. Dunning, private note, to H. B. Simpson, Under-Secretary of State at the Home Office, 27 June 1909.

'WAR AGAINST THE CHURCH OF ROME', which aimed at nothing less than 'universal sway over both religion and politics'.[25]

The Liverpool riots of 1909, then, sprang not simply from 'spontaneous' fury, but from Catholic assertiveness, Protestant vigilance, and, as we shall see, police impotence. The first phase of the violence grew out of a series of sectarian marches. Protestants recalled that Bishop Whiteside had closed the outdoor marching season of 1908 with the hope that 'before long ... a magnificent Catholic procession would be seen in Liverpool, the like of which had never yet been witnessed in any other part of the country'.[26] That hope seemed destined to be fulfilled in May 1909 by the celebration of the sixtieth anniversary of the Holy Cross 'famine church'. Excitement from the Eucharistic Congress fed anticipations of both Protestants and Catholics. Head Constable Leonard Dunning planned adequate police protection for the procession through the parish streets. But in the preceding weeks, letters from feisty Orange leaders and Pastor George Wise sounded the alarm: the Host was about to be carried in Liverpool, and that breach of the law might provoke a breach of the peace.[27] Instead of going directly to the parish authorities, Dunning consulted an old-boy intermediary, Roman Catholic City Councillor Thomas Burke, whom he mistakenly assumed to be privy to the parish plans, and he then assured the Protestants that '...there is no intention whatever of carrying the Host or *any other religious emblem* through the streets or in any way contravening the law. The procession without such circumstances would be perfectly legal'.[28] Unfortunately, Burke failed to confirm critical details of his forecast. Nor did Dunning know about an 'altar' to be erected in the street, for the Catholic planners had asked permission of the borough Health Committee, which had not informed him.

With his diabolical instinct for publicity, Pastor Wise sent his exchange of letters with Dunning to the Orange *Evening Express* and other newspapers, thus both maximising public attention, and claiming a victory for vigilance in his reply to Dunning: 'Your timely action has averted what might have been a very serious breach of the peace'.[29] By converting his exchange of information into a 'repression' of the Host, he was trying, consciously or not, to conjure up an encore of the Protestant victory over the Eucharistic Congress in 1908. Wise had attached 'tremendous importance' to the

[25]*PS*, 27 Mar 1909.
[26]*CH*, 25 July 1908. Cf. George Wise, *DPM*, 13 Sep 1909.
[27]PAT, 185, 1597; *CH*, 15 May 1909. Orange letters in PAR, 4-5.
[28]L. Dunning to George Wise, 5 May 1909, in PAR, 6 (my italics). Burke testified he was not on the parish organizing committee, but the *Catholic Herald* said he was, perhaps because he was their City Councillor. The point bears on how much reliance Dunning could place on Burke's opinion. (PAT, 1595-1603; *CH*, 15 May 1909.)
[29]PAR, 7. The *Evening Express* was sometimes printed on orange paper.

Congress, and when the procession of the Host had been prevented, he had gained the impression from the *Catholic Times* that indignant priests were going to take the Host round all the parishes. He seemed to project aggressive intentions onto Catholics in order to justify his own aggressive inclinations. The letters implied that his party would punish any 'irregularities' and that the Catholics had been blocked from such irregularities, and so their publication stirred 'excitement' and deep resentment among the Young Men's Societies of the Holy Cross Church.[30] The Protestants focussed the tension still further. On Friday, 7 May, Orangeman Colter advertised a rally for Saturday night at St George's Hall Plateau, Liverpool's equivalent of Trafalgar Square, to protest against John Redmond's bill to alter the King's coronation declaration. He added that in view of the Head Constable's assurance that no religious emblems would be carried, an Orange counter-demonstration on Sunday had been called off.[31] Wise and his fellow lecturers busily discussed the prospect of 'images' in the Holy Cross procession at outdoor meetings at the St. Domingo Pit in the week leading up to it. Two issues had been set up for testing by rigid Protestant standards: the legality of the procession itself and the honour of the Head Constable.

Curiosity and suspicion brought thousands of spectators to the Holy Cross procession. Friendly Protestants had contributed to the festive preparation of the parish. The *Catholic Herald* described the procession with customary exuberance. The neighbourhood streets were extravagantly decorated. Small wayside shrines were improvised from kitchen tables set in crowded slum courts. Police escorted some 4,500 marchers: brass bands, a cross bearer, acolytes, and choir boys in surplices; guilds, confraternities of men; Sunday School children; the Irish National Foresters in uniform; three hundred lay brothers costumed as monks; two priests in cassocks; the rest in morning dress, and the Bishop of Liverpool in an open carriage. Carried by the marchers were banners depicting the Stations of the Cross and statues, the most striking of which was a life-sized statue of the Madonna borne by members of the Italian community, who seem to have come spontaneously from a different parish. The *Catholic Herald* commented that this display 'eclipsed' even the St. Joseph's parish fete of the previous year, and that 'these jubilee celebrations offer striking evidence of the progress of Catholicity in Liverpool in the last half century'.[32]

---

[30]PAT, 773, 1598-99 and cf 822.

[31]PAR, 9. In the logic of ritual aggression, by calling off their counter demonstration, the Orange leaders had put their prestige on the line and let down their vigilance, so they felt richly entitled to feel betrayed by the Catholic statues and the Head Constable.

[32]*CH*, 15 May 1909; PAT, 1132, 1143, 1605 - 6. Catholic progress and community acceptance was the theme of the Bishop's speech. *Liverpool Courier* [hereafter *Lp Courier*], 10 May 1909.

The day passed peacefully except when the procession came briefly out of the Catholic neighbourhood onto the main thoroughfares at Dale Street and Byrom Street, within a good stone's throw of St. George's Hall, the ceremonial centre of the city. There some Protestant rowdies struck up their version of 'Dare to be a Daniel!', the Protestant fighting song: 'Dare to be a Wiseite!/Dare to stand alone./Dare to be a Protestant,/And to Hell with the Pope of Rome'. When the Madonna passed, they made a rush for it, crying out, 'This is illegal', and 'We had the promise of the Head Constable ...', and 'We won't let the bloody thing pass, we'll break it up!' The Catholic processionists tried to fight back. The mounted police escort, however, interposed their horses to prevent a riotous brawl.[33]

In the following days, Orange and Wiseite leaders protested furiously to the Head Constable and the Watch Committee over two issues: the illegality of 'this idolatrous procession in which men and women bowed themselves to a piece of chalk image in a Protestant city', and the breach of the Head Constable's promise that no images would be carried. If 'these aliens are allowed to break the law', Protestants threatened to use their own power to enforce it.[34] The law was rhetorically crucial to the Protestant position. It was at once the palpable rock of their established religious privilege over Catholics and the licence for their aggression in its defence. Hence they were outraged by Catholic 'encroachments' on the law. But they were only barrack-room lawyers, and so their long clamorous campaign was not legally well-founded. They complained of the clerics and laymen marching in religious costumes, but those were not the genuine religious 'habits' prohibited by the Act. The 'images' were provocative but not illegal. Dunning responded coolly and formally to their protests. He reported fully to the Home Office and to the City Council's Watch Committee (which supervised the police) that merely technical violations of the law had occurred, that the only disturbance had been 'caused by a small number of the extreme Protestant party, fathered for the purpose', and that there must have been some misunderstanding between Councillor Burke and himself about the images, though he did not see it as cause for alarm. In the following weeks and months, Orange and Conservative City Councillors allowed the Protestants to smear the Head Constable as partial to Catholics, instead of refuting such claims by making public the information the Head Constable had furnished them. It was not until 22 October that the Chairman of the Watch Committee revealed that the Health Committee, not the Head Constable, had approved the erection of the 'altar' (replica) on the neighbourhood fountain.[35]

---

[33]Waller, 208; PAT, 1155.
[34]PAR, 12, 14; PAT, 57, 220, 259 - 60.
[35]PAR, 15; PAT, 1075 - 76, 1157; *Lp Courier*, 22 and 23 Oct 1909.

The next events were mostly significant for what did not happen. The Catholic Young Men's Societies, parish social clubs, planned to celebrate their sixtieth anniversary on Sunday 23 May, by marching to St. George's Hall Plateau, where they would receive the bishop's blessing. The Orange lodges planned a parade to attend church en masse nearby on the morning of the same day. Anticipating a physical clash, the Head Constable asked leaders of both sides to call off their parades. Both declined. The Catholic Bishop replied that the Catholic procession was neither aggressive nor wholly novel, and that he would not yield to the objections of 'a few noisy bigots'. The previous year's celebration had mustered 5,000 marchers from 26 parishes, and had been hailed as an unprecedented demonstration of 'concentrated strength'.[36] But then the marchers had marched from the pierhead to four churches. Now they were assembling on the ceremonial civic centre itself! When the day came, the Catholic rally passed off with no trouble at all: apparently the less overtly religious demonstration (with no images or vestments) did not offend Protestant sensitivities - or possibly it was more dangerous to attack. The Orange paraders, however, had to push their way through crowds of hostile Catholics.[37] Accordingly, the Protestants protested that police protection was inadequate by contrast with the large police escort of the Holy Cross procession.

Two weeks later, on 6 June, Pastor Wise led his Men's Bible Class, 1,500 strong, through a mixed Protestant and Catholic neighbourhood in the North End, accompanied by Orange brass bands. On Fountains Road an Irish Catholic woman stepped out of her house to wave a green flag at them, and several of the Orange bands stopped and circled in the street while Protestants attacked two Catholic homes before the police moved in to make arrests. Two Protestants and the woman were brought before the police court. It was a minor, stereotypical skirmish, but assumed key legal significance later when Wise was arrested.[38]

The climax of the first phase of the 1909 disturbances occurred two weeks later on Sunday 20 June. Another large Catholic procession was planned by another parish deep in the North End slums, St. Joseph's on Grosvenor Street. Yet although the Host had just been reported carried in London, the Head Constable took no real precautions and went on his planned holiday to Ireland the Monday before the scheduled procession, leaving arrangements and authority in the hands of his capable deputy, H. P. Lane. In that Friday's *Evening Express*, the Grand Lodge of the Orange Institution summoned 'male members' to attend a 'Monstre [sic] Demonstration ...[along

---

[36]PAR, 20; *CH,* 30 May 1908.
[37]PAT, 312, 1166.
[38]PAR, 48. They had previously paraded without incident on 11 April.

the Catholics' chosen route] for the purpose of preventing any illegal processions taking place in the city of Liverpool. Wake up Protestant England! We must have no compromise and no surrender. N.B. The procession [counter-demonstration] to be led by the [Orange] provincial officers, etc. ... God Save the King'. At the Thursday meeting of the Grand Lodge, Pastor Wise had opposed the demonstration; indeed, he later sniffed that they had only planned a 'very stupid passive protest' to watch the Catholics, though hair-trigger vigilance was not exactly passive. In his Friday night speech at the St. Domingo Pit, Wise said, somewhat ambiguously, 'The Orangemen proposed to hold a counter-demonstration in Juvenal Street, and that if the Orangemen did so, there would be bloodshed. He also said he would go a step further, and there would be murder'. The Liberal *Daily Post and Mercury* referred to the Orangemen's advertisement in its report of the day's events, concluding 'There can be little doubt the opposition was an organized one'.[39]

Curiously, it was only on the Saturday morning after seeing that Orange advertisement, that the Acting Head Constable sent for the St. Joseph's priest, Father Rigby, to warn him not to allow images to be carried in the procession. The Acting Head Constable tried to get the Orange leaders to call off their demonstration, but by this time it was Saturday noon, and their actions were too little and too late. That night at a meeting at Edge Hill, Pastor Wise told the crowd not to go to Juvenal Street, but if they did go, to obey their leaders. Witnesses for the Catholics at the Inquiry testified that Wise had said '...if there were no images there would be no onslaught. [Otherwise] We will spare no one, men women or children!' He said he could not be there because of a prior engagement, 'but I am not a coward', evidently anticipating physical battle. After Wise left, the Orange chairman announced that all Orangemen should go to Juvenal Street and obey their leaders.[40]

On the Sunday, crowds massed at midday in the neighbourhood, at the border between the Catholic Scotland Ward and Protestant Netherfield, coming down from the artisan districts on the rising heights of Everton. An hour before the procession was scheduled to begin, the powder keg ignited. The Orange leaders were unable to get through the crowd to exercise any control. A woman came out of a public house and threw beer on an old man. That touched off fighting in the packed street. Bricks and bottles began to fly, sticks and swords were brandished. Nineteen mounted police, held ready in a covered market hall at that very spot, were ordered out to clear Juvenal Street, backed up by several hundred foot policemen. The fighting between crowd and police became fierce a couple of hundred yards up the road on Prince Edwin Street. Stones and brickbats hailed down on the police. Their

---

[39]PAR 27; PAT, 722, 1171; *DPM*, 21 June 1909.
[40]PAR, 28; PAT, 941, 942, 977 - 996, 1019 - 1031.

commanders ordered two main mounted charges up the street and another cross charge. Protestants cried police brutality. Eye-witnesses disagreed about the force and speed of the police charges. On the insistence of the Acting Head Constable, the Catholic procession was curtailed to a sally down the street a hundred yards and back. Fierce rioting continued in the back streets of the neighbourhood until midnight. Much of it consisted of violence against the police though several Catholic houses in mostly Protestant Beresford Street were badly smashed up with stones, and their decorations set afire. Fifty were arrested, and twenty taken to hospital including eight constables.[41]

That violent clash brought the simmering tension to a rolling boil. The second (summer) phase of the riots of 1909 now began - a chain reaction of physical violence and reprisal. George Wise generated the heat for that chain reaction in the St. Domingo Pit, the Protestants' outdoor meeting place, in a series of nightly meetings attended by thousands.[42] For four months, Pastor Wise and other speakers assailed Catholic treachery and police favouritism, posing as martyrs for law and freedom in the face of police tyranny. Though Wise had not been present, he declared that '...on Sunday, June 20th,... there would have been no disturbance only for the police charging and battering the Orangemen about in a dastardly and cruel manner... Why should the police arrest respectable and orderly young men of excellent character and lead them to the Bridewell with a smile on their faces whilst a howling half-drunken mob applauded them and cheered them on'. The police, he cried, protected the Catholics in their illegal procession but interfered with his Bible Class parades. He repeated the abusive invective against Catholics he had used regularly before. His followers marched away from those meetings with fire in their bellies. In some cases, led by Orange bands of fife and drum, they marched off to attack the nearby cluster of Catholic institutions, including the Everton Valley convent, the Beacon Lane orphanage, the Bishop's house, the college, and the St. Alphonsus Church, as well as Catholics' shops and homes. Priests and nuns were abused and assaulted as they went their rounds. Such attacks flickered in isolated incidents through the summer, but they were especially concentrated around the weeks of 10 - 14 August, when George Wise went to gaol after refusing to be bound over to keep the peace, and 10 - 24 October, when Wise's appeal was heard and rejected and he returned to gaol. Both weeks were also the twin climaxes of Protestant rallies and petitions demanding an inquiry into the behaviour of the police and calling for the

---

[41]PAT, passim; *DPM*, 21 June 1909, and *Lp Courier*, 21 June 1909.
[42]Wise's responsibility was emphasized by both the Police Superintendent in charge of the district and the Home Office Commissioner. PAT, 1487, and PAR, 68.

resignation of the Head Constable. So collective violence marched in step with more orderly protest, legal contest, and high feelings of martyrdom.[43]

Catholics were not prepared simply to turn the other cheek, even though their priests preached pacifism. The day after the procession, a Catholic crowd scuffled with police in Juvenal Street, and Catholic crowds attacked Protestant churches and mission halls in the predominantly Catholic North End. The priests complained that the violence was the work of those who rarely came to mass. In Gordon Street a conflict between the pupils of opposing schools led to a large punch-up among the women of the neighbourhood, who 'fought like vixens', with loud and heated language, and 'much tearing of hair, and flinging of mud, stones and brickbats'. Protestant and Catholic elementary schools were closed amidst parent panics over rumours that the enemy was about the attack the children. Protestant carters were assaulted on their way home from stables in the North End; one died of his injuries. Predominantly Protestant or Catholic workplaces and neighbourhoods were purged of their minorities of dozens of workers and hundreds of residents. At the Palatine Oil Cake Mills, Mary Catherine Flynn attacked Orangeman William S. Daniels with a pair of tongs; he had rather ostentatiously sharpened a sword at work, and then brandished it at the St. Joseph's procession. Shops were attacked. Two more riots were touched off by Protestant parades, while on 5 September a riot was touched off by a Catholic priest's complaint to the police that he had been assaulted.[44]

Besides the street violence, the other interwoven strand of that summer of conflict was the legal and political battle over the arrest and imprisonment of Pastor George Wise. Wise had scheduled another of his Bible Class parades for Sunday 27 June, despite the serious riot of 20 June. He agreed to alter his route, but Head Constable Dunning decided the parade must be called off or it would lead to a riot. Wise was still stirring crowds to fury at 'the Pit' against the Catholics, the police, and the police magistrate, saying for instance, 'There is a limit to our human endurance, and it might possibly come to a bloody riot in our midst'. In the Friday night newspaper the notice for his Sunday parade was juxtaposed with George Wise Crusade themes that seemed to foreordain violence:

---

[43]PAT, 167-170, 1409-14, 1416, 1427, 1440-48, 1467-92, esp. 1487-8, and 1495-1508. Fr. John Fitzgerald to Town Council, Nov 1909, in P.R.O. HO 144/704/107039/96.

[44]PAT, 78 - 81, 435, 470 - 472, 608 - 609, 1427, 1449, 1465, 1490 -92, 1547 -50, 1564, 1566, 1583. *DPM*, 23 June, 6, 9 Sept, and 8 Oct 1909; a comprehensive statement of Protestants' injuries was laid before the Watch Committee and published in *Lp Courier*, 30 Oct 1909.

Protestant Reformers' Church, Netherfield Road, Sunday next,
the 27th instant. Pastor George Wise... Bible class at three.
Subject, 'Our Solemn Covenant.' Important. Every member must
attend Bible class parade. Be in the ranks. Obey orders. Several
bands will take part in the parade, 2-15 prompt. Don't fail to be
present.

'GEORGE WISE CRUSADE'

St. Domingo Pit.

Tonight, 8. Assemble in your thousands and
defend your rights.
Saturday, 8. Stand firm in defence of your liberty.
Sunday, 8. No Compromise and no surrender.
Speakers: Pastor George Wise...and others. Should
Rome kill heretics? St. Thomas Aquinas says
'Murder heretics.'[45]

When Wise refused to cancel his march, Dunning had him arrested and
brought before the police magistrate to be bound over to keep the peace.
Besides the current tension, Dunning based his case on Wise's long record and
on the disturbance triggered by the Bible Class parade of 6 June. Wise was
put in gaol, to be bailed on 26 June only upon agreeing to give up the parade.
After several postponements of a hearing, Wise still refused to be bound over,
preferring the martyr's alternative of going to gaol on 10 August.[46] He was
soon released (18 August) pending appeal, and after months of legal appeals,
he went to gaol in October, escorted by 100,000 sympathizers in a great
procession of state.

During the whole summer, the Wiseites mounted a loud campaign of
demonstrations demanding that the Head Constable resign, on account of his
breach of promise, police favouritism towards Catholics, and the police
brutality towards Protestants on 20 June. Wise actually charged that the
mounted police were 'almost all Roman Catholics'.[47] As the main vehicle for
their challenge to the Head Constable, the Wiseites demanded a public inquiry
into the conduct of the police. They played on the theme that George Wise
was a martyr for free speech and a victim of police tyranny. In August they
raised the question of the Marybone 'altar' at the Holy Cross procession. In
the eyes of Protestant vigilantes, when the police did not take action against
decorated kitchen tables they were being partial towards the Catholics and

---

[45]PAR, 30 - 32.
[46]*DPM,* 28 June 1909; PAR, 31.
[47]*Lp Courier,* 27 Sep 1909.

aiding their subversive advance.[48] In November, Parliament authorized the inquiry, and as part of the package to promote conciliation, Wise was simultaneously released from prison. Disturbances had died away for the winter. The inquiry was postponed until after the January general election, and sat for most of February in St. George's Hall.

This narrative of events suggests that, so far from being elemental fury, the riots of 1909 were sustained by deliberate campaigns chosen by the participants. Indeed one of the saner Orange leaders, S. G. Thomas, declared at the Battle of Boyne Day (12th July) Celebration that 'if ever the Orange Institution justified its existence it did so when it took action on June 20th'.[49] The violence was not a bolt from the blue. Catholics claimed a place in the sun - they were unwilling to accept permanent inferiority. As long ago as 1903, Alderman Purcell had declared in City Council that there were '40,000 men of might and muscle belonging to the Roman Catholic religion in Liverpool' who were not willing to be 'sat upon'.[50] Yet Protestants interpreted every Catholic advance as a threat to their liberty which must be resisted. The police seemed flat-footed, planning reactively for physical control of the streets but taking no effective steps to prevent clashes. The elected leaders of the City Council were culpably silent.

II. The Characters

The principal characters provided essential ingredients of the disturbances. Pastor George Wise was a short, stumpy, bespectacled, bachelor bear of a man, a monumental egotist, saint, demon rabble-rouser, crafty politician - an elemental force uncontrollable even by himself. Like other charismatic politicians of the twentieth century, he did not create the conflict on which he built, but he was a master at accentuating and twisting existing themes to arouse friends and foes to fury. He mobilized Liverpool's historic materials for both salvation and destruction.

Wise was born in 1855 of humble parentage in Bermondsey in London's dockland. A book-worm as a youth, he had little formal education and went to work in Peek Frean's biscuit factory. He converted to evangelical Christianity and became a boys' Sunday School teacher and urban missionary in London's dockland, working in the Metropolitan Tabernacle and the Dockland Mission Hall. At 26, his debating skills developing, he became a paid theological public lecturer for the Christian Evidence Society, attracting huge audiences in London parks and streets. He also attended University extension

---

[48]PAR, 38, 40.
[49]PAT, 302.
[50]Quoted in *Liverpool Daily Post*, 14 May 1903.

and adult education courses, in philosophy, physiology, and history, and toured America and British Columbia, lecturing in New York and Chicago. In 1888 he came to Liverpool and found his milieu.[51]

In the competitive world of street evangelicalism he discovered that confrontation and martyrdom paid off in the crucial coin of notoriety. Already in the 1890s he began to make his name as a militant Protestant lecturer, mentored by the Evangelical Bishop of Liverpool, J. C. Ryle, and sponsored materially by the local merchant, J. A. Bramley-Moore. The *Protestant Standard* prophesied for him a 'very brilliant future'. From 1897 onwards he began to attack Ritualism in the Church of England, leading demonstrations at the 'offending churches' during and after services, provoking uproar and police intervention. That notoriety cost Wise the lectureships he held with the Christian Evidence Society and the Y.M.C.A., and so, with his sponsors' backing, he set up on his own, creating a mission hall for his British Protestant Union, dedicated to the fight against 'a trinity of evils - Romanism, Ritualism, and infidelity'.[52]

By 1900, Wise had become a political force to be taken seriously sometimes an ally of, and sometimes an insurgent against, Tory boss Archibald Salvidge's Orange-flavoured Working Men's Conservative Association. In the municipal elections of that year, Wise won an astonishing 107,000 votes as a Protestant School board candidate, twice the number of the next candidate. Independent Protestant political strength soon re-entered the Conservative fold, but right through the Police Inquiry of 1910, Protestant spokesmen warned that something like 100,000 Liverpudlians looked to Wise as a political and spiritual leader, and so he must be treated with fitting respect.[53]

From 1901 to 1904, Wise conducted a virulent campaign against Catholic beliefs and doctrines which created indelible hostility on the part of Roman Catholics and the police authorities. In May 1901 he chose Islington Square, where Jesuit and Presbyterian institutions faced each other, to launch a campaign of outrageous mockery, dancing about with 'rosary' beads around his neck, waving a crucifix, and denouncing the Jesuits as liars and murderers.

---

[51]Ronald F. Henderson, *George Wise of Liverpool: Protestant Stalwart Twice Imprisoned for the Gospel's Sake* (Liverpool, 1967); *Protestant Search-Light* (Liverpool, 1 Dec 1903), 62-64; *Protestant Observer* (Oct 1909); The Wise Scrapbook, compiled by Richard Briggs, J.P., Liverpool Library, E Q 330, col. 35 (1917), obituaries; *Liverpool Post*, 30 Nov, 3 Dec 1917, *Lp Courier*, 30 Nov and 5, 12 Dec 1917; *PS* 14 Dec 1917; PAT, 718 - 945; Waller, passim.

[52]*Ibid*, 117 - 18, 175.

[53]*Ibid*, chs 11-13; 209; PAT, 43. Joan Smith points out that the 107,000 votes of 1900 could have been cast by some 7,000 plumpers who cast all their votes for him ('Class, skill', 198)

It provoked Catholic onlookers to violent protest. Having got the battle brewing, Wise agreed not to meet again at Islington Square, but then chose nearby St. George's Hall Plateau, with a march past the Square just for good measure. Tricks like that made the police distrust him. They were barely able to prevent a major riot. He was summoned by the police and bound over to keep the peace. Wise converted the issue from anti-Catholicism to free speech, a more respectable issue for his Conservative would-be allies. In what was to become a favourite inflammatory tactic, he attacked the police magistrate as partial to the Catholics. When he appealed, the Court of King's Bench issued a landmark decision on the rights of free speech, in the case of *Wise v. Dunning* (then assistant Head Constable), that outdoor speakers could be bound over to keep the peace if the 'natural consequences' of their actions would be a breach of the peace.[54]

His very success attracted competitors who raised the stakes of martyrdom. The established anti-Ritualist Kensit preachers came from London in the summer of 1902 to deliver a series of lectures against 'besotted Romanists' that provoked violence. John Kensit, junior, declined to be bound over and was jailed. That created a monstrous outcry, and the next two weeks were filled with Protestant marches and Catholic countermarches that the police were only just able to contain from violent collision, as Wise sought to regain centre stage and the Catholics began to react more aggressively. Dunning had Wise bound over for six months. In 1903, Wise petitioned to use St. Domingo Pit for outdoor meetings, but Dunning had him summonsed to be bound over again. This time Wise declined and went to gaol for two months, revelling in the celebrity of martyrdom for free speech, which he converted into a City Council seat for Kirkdale. Though he had to retire after one term upon becoming a full-time minister, he was busy, effective, and popular, visiting constitutents and criticizing municipal extravagance. His George Wise Crusade organization had begun to hold regular outdoor demonstrations in the St. Domingo Pit within pointing, shouting, and attacking distance of Catholic schools, churches, and a convent.The Pit was a railed recreation ground adjoining a slightly enlarged street intersection at the end of Mere Lane, where a slope created a small amphitheatre. At Christmas 1903, Wise opened his ultra-Protestant Reformers' (Memorial) Church, whose working-class congregation soon came to boast the largest Sunday attendance in Liverpool. While Wise was in prison, stand-in demagogue Albert Stones began to create his own base in the South End, and violence flickered through 1904 and 1905. The Head Constable condemned the rituals of street religion which shunned positive affirmation in favour of 'throwing dirt at the opposite creed and breaking the heads or windows of those who profess it'. He also criticized

---

[54]*Law Reports* (1902), 1 K. B. 167 - 180; Neal, 205.

Protestant professionalism: 'the exploiting of sectarian bigotry for private objects, direct or indirect pecuniary gain, or the satisfaction of personal vanity'. When 1906 was relatively peaceful he hoped that 'common sense will continue to prevail, especially with those who by financial support have in former years made the aggravation of sectarian dissension a means of living'.[55]

From 1906 to 1908, Wise kept relatively quiet, refraining from outdoor attacks on Catholicism and focussing on more esoteric targets. In 1908, it was evidently the Eucharistic Congress that prompted him to re-create the old battle lines of Protestant-Catholic enmity. Catholics later testified they could live in peace and harmony with Orangemen and other Protestants, but they found Wise's particular artistry with insults intolerable as it kept alive bitter sectarian feuding.[56] Here are a few samples of Wise:

If the present Jack the Ripper is a Roman Catholic, and which I believe he is, [and he] was to go to Father Fitzgerald and [confess] he had murdered two or three women, and the police were to call on him (Fitzgerald) and ask him if he had seen Jack the Ripper, he would say, 'No.'

[He said] that the Roman Catholic Church had power to kill outlaws, and heretics were classed as outlaws, and it was lawful to kill and burn them; and he himself was liable to be killed at any time.

[He described] Roman Catholic priests as crafty, lying, tyrannical, and murderous, and said that the Church had murdered more Jews than any other religion.

Jesus said, 'Feed my sheep;' but the revised version ought to read. 'Fleece my sheep',

We detest the mass in your Church; that mass which you swallow, and you think you are taking God in your stomach.

---

[55]*Ibid*, 207 - 20, 225 - 26; Waller, *Democracy and Sectarianism*, 201; Head Constable's *Annual Report on the Police Establishment...*, to the Watch Committee for the years 1905 - 1906, Picton Library, Liverpool. Wise's Church issued its own *Protestant Reformers Monthly Magazine* which said in January 1910 that the church 'consists solely of working people' (xi).

[56]PAT, 1495, 1527, 1535, 1539.

They waste their lives with harlots; they rob the poor to feed their own children; they are incarnate devils... your mass is gambled away. They live upon you, and you know it. No man likes whiskey more than they. The Monks in monasteries were living lives of devils. The Monks and Nuns live together in impurity...

Though the priest should outrage your daughter, no secular power must punish him....[57]

In his heroic/demonic role at the centre of the storm, how far did Pastor Wise intend to trigger violence? The Commissioner of the Home Office Inquiry concluded, 'I think Mr. Wise is responsible to a far greater degree than he himself appreciates for the disturbances which happened last year ... but I doubt whether he fully apprehends the effect which his language produces upon his followers and upon his opponents'.[58] Wise egotistically enjoyed the power he generated when his heroism and simplistic dogmas satisfied popular appetites. He gloated 'I... have never in my life seen people more indignant against the action of the authorities, particularly Mr. Dunning, and more in sympathy with myself'. He anticipated martyrdom from Catholic attack, 'because I have the credit of putting a stop to the Eucharistic Procession in London', and because 'I also have the credit of taking off the glory of the Holy Cross procession. If I did I am very pleased...' As he continued to stoke the fires of conflict in 1910, he complained that the editors of the *Daily Post and Mercury* were trying 'to crush my power in this city'.[59]

Wise's breathtaking mental gymnastics enabled him to be logically unreasonable. In 1903, for instance, having refused to be bound over to keep the peace, he chose to go to gaol to show Dunning 'that he was not going to consent to be bound over perennially; and the result of my action was that for a time prosecutions ceased. And this is a significant fact - all the time the police refrained from annoying us there was no disturbance'. In November 1909, Wise was freed from prison after promising not to speak outdoors, but he immediately addressed his followers at the Pit and planned another Bible

---

[57]PAT, 768, 847, 859 - 61. The third statement was reported by a police witness but denied by Wise (*DPM,* 28 June 1909). The last four were reported by the Head Constable in his *Report to the Watch Committee on the Protestant Demonstration* (23 Mar 1903) in Liverpool Archives, H 352 COU, Council of Liverpool Proceedings 1902 - 3. Wise used them all repeatedly.

[58]PAR, 69. The police magistrate had observed in 1909 after disposing of many rioters' cases, '...at times Mr. Wise indulges in language the meaning of which he does not fully appreciate, and without intending it to have the consequences or the effects which it does have.' Quoted in PAT, 1051.

[59]PAT, 729, 822 - 23, and *DPM,* 12 Aug 1910.

Class parade. He conceded 'that technically there might have been [a violation of his pledge] but morally, no'. On 26 June 1909, he was released from gaol only after agreeing to give up his Bible Class parade. But once free, he refused to admit that he had submitted to authority, telling his followers he gave the promise because 'had he been kept in prison there would have been a shocking riot'. But if that statement implied menace, Wise's congregation then passed a unanimous resolution to prevent disturbances. And Head Constable Dunning testified that Wise had cooperated with him in the past on many occasions, had taken his advice, and that, 'If there is going to be a row, I would sooner Mr. Wise would be there, because I am sure he would help to quell it'. Wise did not directly tell his followers to go out and attack Catholics, though neither did he restrain them. Rather he acted as though his religious crusade, which required tilting at Catholics, must not be contaminated by any earthly considerations such as order. The advancement of The Kingdom, i.e. his precise brand of Protestantism, would both recompense his 'martyrdom' and expiate any violence that might occur along the way. If his attacks excited Catholics to anger 'It... always has done, and sometimes has a very important effect I think', because some of them might reconsider his 'evidence' and convert. He rejected the moderation urged by the Home Office Commissioner: 'He believed the peace of the city should be maintained', he told his congregations, 'but not at the expense of truth, or of right..'. and so he would continue to 'expose' the Jesuits.[60]

Wise's chief protagonist was the Head Constable of Liverpool, Leonard Dunning, a man who by temperament and experience contributed to the unrest of 1909 by a narrow and rigid view of his duties and by an understandable contempt for George Wise. Born in 1860, the son of a London solicitor from Devonshire, Dunning had enjoyed an Eton and Oxford education, the latter in Jurisprudence in preparation for the Bar. Instead, however, he went into police work, spending his formative years significantly as District Inspector in the Royal Irish Constabulary from 1882-1895. In 1895 he beat 79 other applicants to become Assistant Head Constable of Liveprool. After seven years he became Head Constable of Liverpool. The press noted then that Dunning had a record of helping the poor and using the police to help the community.[61]

[60]Quotations; Interview, *DPM*, 23 Oct 1909; PAT, 928 - 29; *DPM*, 28 June 1909; PAT 1129; *Ibid*, 914, 755; *Lp Courier*, 28 Apr 1910.

[61]For Dunning, see PAT 1049; and *The Police Review and Parade Gossip*, 18 Apr 1902, 186, and 29 Dec 1911, 618. I am grateful to Dr. Clive Emsley for these references. Dunning's obituary in *The Times* (10 Feb 1941) was published in a Late City Edition, and could not be located in the British Library and other libraries.

Dunning was quite prepared to compare Liverpool to Belfast on the score of 'sectarian bigotry',[62] and Ireland seems to have formed his attitude toward sectarian conflict, which appeared to him to be purely atavistic, beyond reasoning. His attitude implied, 'A plague on both your houses!' He wrote of 'the perversity of the Irish', saying it was best to be plain, 'especially when you are dealing with Irishmen and you may take it that the bulk of the trouble is Irish here. The difficulty with Orangemen and Roman Catholic factions is to get them into a position where neither can claim a victory over the other'. 'I have some experience in Ireland with people obsessed with the yellow fever and the green fever'.[63]

A Home Office official said later that Dunning was a man of 'efficiency, courage, and discipline, and above all, uprightness, truth, and inflexible impartiality'.[64] That 'inflexible impartiality' was both a strength and a weakness. The Home Office Inquiry of 1910 completely demolished the Protestant charge of police partiality. But Dunning contributed to the conflict of 1909 by his unbending, almost obtuse, political insensitivity. In the first place he was restricted by the law and contemporary police practice which permitted predominantly reactive rather than preventive action. Dunning had asked advice from the Home Office about the 20 June procession, anticipating trouble especially since 14 June newspapers carried reports of the Host being carried in London. The Home Office suggested only that Dunning warn the Catholics to eliminate 'any clearly illegal features', leaving aside the grey area of provocative displays. Dunning wrote 'I am trying to talk to both sides', only after the riot of 20 June. When the Lord Mayor of Liverpool inquired of the Home Office for a legal opinion, the Home Office replied the law did not permit magistrates to ban lawful processions just because a breach of the peace might ensue.[65]

Second, Dunning's detachment led him to view sectarian conflict simply in terms of formal legal and peace-keeping considerations. He did not read the Catholic and Protestant press, he said. He had only once seen an issue of the *Catholic Herald* and that went straight into the wastebasket; he got his information from the Liverpool newspapers and *The Times*.[66] He presented Wise with a martyr's choice - cease parading or go to gaol - instead of offering

---

[62]Leonard Dunning to Home Office, 24 May 1909, HO 45/11138/186474, copy in PAR.

[63]Dunning to Mr. Simpson, 27 June 1909, HO 45/11138/186474/6; PAT, 1120

[64]A. L. Dixon, Assistant Under-Secretary of State in *The Times*, 22 Feb 1941.

[65]Dunning to HO, 14 June 1909, and HO reply, 17 June 1909, HO 45/11138/186474/3; Dunning to Mr. Simpson, 27 June 1909, HO 45/11138/186474/6; H. C. Dowdall to H. J. Gladstone, Home Secretary, 2 July 1909; and HO reply, 13 July 1909, HO 45/11138/186474

[66]PAT, 1130

restricted alternatives of time or space or trying to isolate him by negotiating with slightly more reasonable Orange leaders. Probably correctly, Wise felt that Dunning had despised him since 1901, even though as we have seen, Wise was occasionally cooperative.[67] He handled the Protestants with icy disdain, while he dealt with Catholics mainly through Councillor Burke. He regretted his misunderstanding with Burke over the images in the first procession, but did not see it as cause for either alarm or extensive repair of public trust. Dunning regarded the Orangemen as calculating troublemakers rather than offended perfectionists. He told the Home Office that the first disturbance had been 'caused by a small number of the extreme Protestant party, gathered for the purpose'. He coldly brushed off Protestant complaints rather than allaying them with better information, restrained by a code that such revelations must come from his (Conservative) political superiors. Perhaps he had a bit of martyr in him too. When the Protestants' barrister said that Protestants should have confidence in him, Dunning replied with liberal intolerance, 'They could have had if it had not been for their own stupidity'. He later conceded, 'I own that I was not able to put myself into the mental attitude of people who are offended by something of that sort... I quite see now, Mr. Rees, it would have been better if I had realized more fully the feelings of your clients but I did not... Although as I say, I have had some experience of people holding similar feelings in Belfast'. The clash between his logic and sectarian conflict took its toll on him. The months of personal attacks on his conduct, he declared, were 'living in a hell on earth...'[68] Photographs show a vigorous man in his prime taking charge in 1902 and a gaunt prematurely-aged official retiring in 1911. To *blame* Dunning for not succeeding at sophisticated community conciliation, not always possible even today, is probably anachronistic.[69] Perhaps sectarian hostilities were essentially unappeasable. But even if characteristic of his era, Dunning's restraints did contribute to the explosions. That a different approach was feasible is shown by the energetic intervention of his Deputy, H. P. Lane, on the Saturday before the riot of 20 June, when he consulted the leaders of both parties and might have won their preventive cooperation, if not for his late start.

III.Ideologies

The ideological commitments of the Protestant and Catholic sides mingled religious enthusiasms and antagonisms with progressive social and

---

[67]Interview, *DPM*, 23 Oct 1909.
[68]PAT, 1119, 1132, 1157; PAR, 15.
[69]This point was suggested by Professor Robert K. Webb.

political values. That seems to account for the loyalty of the tens of thousands of ordinary people who applauded militant sectarianism, even if their leaders seem unusually obsessed.

Anti-Catholicism was deeply rooted in English culture. In the thousands of pages of evidence discussing the disturbances, no one attributes Orange aggression to Ulstermen.[70] In the history of riots it is one of the rare instances in which the trouble was not blamed on 'outside agitators'. Rather, English no-Popery went back at least to Elizabethan times, and was aggravated by the mass migration from Ireland after the Famine and the re-establishment of the Catholic hierarchy in 1850. Guy Fawkes Day annually celebrated the abortion of the Gunpowder Plot, while the Glorious Twelfth of July commemorated the Battle of the Boyne, the repulse of James II's attempt to reinstate Catholic 'tyranny' over England after the Glorious Revolution of 1688. The Liberal editor of the Liverpool *Daily Post* commented, that the 'good, hard-headed fellows [of one working-class parish] don't care twopence about religion at all; but they to a man hate 'Popery' intensely...'[71]

Catholic conspiracy and aggression required vigilance and justified counter-aggression in the paranoid vision nurtured by Protestant sentries, who transformed real Catholic political advances, church growth, and limited social mobility into a design for Romish conquest. The standing ordinances of the Orange Institution said that Protestants were to 'resist the power, ascendancy, encroachments, and extensions of the Church [of Rome]'. The West Toxteth (Liverpool) M.P. warned his constituents in June 1909 that the Jesuits were plotting to recover England by subverting the Church and throne, and that the best remedy for 'Popery and poverty' was the 'British constitution of Protestantism and patriotism'. The secretary of Wise's church, Richard Briggs, testified that the George Wise Crusade, host sponsor at the Pit, was organized in 1903 'to oppose the aggression of the Church of Rome...We believe it is an aggressive church...(Q. And were the aggressive Protestants banded together to counteract the aggression of the Church of Rome in Liverpool?)...A. I should say yes'. The Protestant case in the Inquiry was that latent sectarian feeling had been galvanized to action by 'Roman Catholic aggression in the city of Liverpool' from the Eucharistic Congress to the processions, altars, and decorations of 1909 which attempted to mark out a district as definitely Catholic.[72] A representative lament was that 'England

---

[70]Cf Gallagher, 111. A Mr. Pollock from Belfast spoke at the St. Domingo Pit in 1909, but only after October.

[71]Quoted in Waller, 184.

[72]PAT, 44, 237, 680, 1662.

was sinking under the heel of priestcraft'.[73] The growth of the Catholic menace meant that Protestants must never rest but must be tirelessly active.

But the mass campaigns were not based simply on negative hatreds or paranoia. Parts of the Orange and the Wiseite ideology had progressive implications that help to explain the adherence, or at least neutrality, of many middle and upper-class Liverpudlians, and of thousands of working-class supporters who did not take part physically in bashing Catholics.[74] Foremost was the Protestant idea of the freedom of conscience. 'Free speech', more respectable than sectarianism, won Wise elite support.[75] The Protestants' barrister told Wise's congregation, 'That the teaching of that [Roman Catholic] church took from off the individual shoulders all responsibility, and obedience was enforced as against freedom, blind acceptance as against discussion and examination'. Wise preached that the Church had 'done her best to strangle truth, to crush science, and to annihilate free enquiry', while Protestants insisted upon *absolute* freedom of conscience and speech, regardless of the consequences. Moreover, said the *Protestant Standard*, in order to guarantee 'the civil and religious liberties of the nation... it is absolutely necessary that Orangemen should contend with a system which is opposed to freedom, and therefore between Orangeism and the Church of Rome there can [never] be, nor should there be, any peace or compromise whatever'.[76] Hence Protestants were virtually as hostile to secular authority, for peacekeepers were bound to insist on moderation in the interests of peace. 'No compromise and no surrender' was the formula of the Protestants, for whom grey was only a shade of black. They fled from reasonableness to a truth higher than the imperfections of earthly order and authority. Their notion of a higher law was a recognizable, even radical, caricature of the nonconformist conscience since the Reformation. Even the press joined in. The Head Constable threatened to prosecute the editor of the Orange *Evening Express* as an accessory if he published an advertisement for a Wise demonstration that resulted in a disturbance. The *Courier* condemned Dunning's attempt to curb free meetings ('important since Peterloo') and the freedom of the press. Working class Orange lodges could now gleefully condemn the Head Constable for interfering

---

[73]Speaker at the Pit, quoted in *Lp Courier*, 23 Oct 1909.

[74]Cf Shallice, 19. In 1899 Sir William Harcourt claimed that anti-ritualism 'expressed the growing freedom and power symptomatic of Liberal progress'. Machin, 'Anti-ritualist movement', 292.

[75]Waller, 200. See Marianne Elliott's persuasive study of the Protestant mind, *Watchman in Sion: The Protestant Idea of Liberty*, (Derry, 1985).

[76]G. C. Rees, *DPM*, 9 June 1910; Wise, in *Protestant Search-Light* (Liverpool) 1 July 1902, 21; *PS*, 10 July 1909.

with 'the liberty of the people and the press' as well as persecuting 'Brother George Wise'.[77]

Less progressively, the Protestant emphasis on liberty was connected with an obsession with nuns who 'escaped' from their 'imprisonment' in convents and the 'tyranny' of the superiors. Themes of enslavement and sexual perversity appealed to a characteristically Victorian prurience.[78] Wise recommended a pamphlet which promised the 'thrilling story of an escaped Nun'. He shrilled that priests lived with harlots and declared that Catholicism was 'a most immoral religion' as could be seen by reading the lives of the Popes and the 'confessions of Maria Monk'. As they attacked a convent, one man said, 'It is a pity the bloody bitches have escaped; they are nothing better than prostitutes'.[79] As in other cases of ethnic conflict, the projection of sexual perversities onto an adversary served to 'justify' aggression and seemed to reflect the aggressor's own sexual tensions.

Second, Wise's message also contained insurgent populist overtones - like the followers of John Wilkes a century before, the plebeian Wiseites loved it when their champion poked the Establishment in the eye. There were occasional elements of liberté, egalité and fraternité in Wise's oratory: it was no accident that he was able to say, 'any man who advocated revolution was a fool ... Yet the French Revolution did much good'. The absolute freedom of the nonconformist conscience had egalitarian implications. Political Protestants in Liverpool had equated their ritualist enemies with 'aristocrats' and revelled in anti-deferential attacks on the official elites even within the Conservative Party. Wise transformed 'Tory Democracy' into 'Protestant Democracy'. Protestants' unyielding insistence on legal technicalities and on the Head Constable's 'promise' was a populist way of claiming moral superiority over authority. Wise's right hand man, Briggs, declared that if Wise went to prison,

---

[77]*Lp Courier*, 16 Aug, 6, 9 Sept 1909. The words freedom and vigilance recur in Protestant rhetoric, an ideological cousin to notions of popular sovereignty practised by American vigilantes. (Cf Richard Maxwell Brown, *Strain of Violence: Historical Studies of American Violence and Vigilantism* [New York, 1975], 56 - 63, 115 - 17, 152 - 53).

[78]PAT, 683. Cf Arnstein, *Protestant versus Catholic*. For a series of 'revolting discoveries' about 'the abomination of Popish nunneries' touched off by the latest 'nun escape', see *PS*, 27 Feb - 1 May 1909, *passim*: those 'legalized Sodoms' depended on the 'Popish institution ' of the auricular confession, a 'woman-trap' (17 Apr). For an example of Protestant pornography, see *PS*, 30 Oct 1909, for the first instalment of 'The Convent Horror', a story about the discovery in 1869 in a Carmelite convent in Cracow of 'Sister Barbara ... the naked wild creature that had once been a beautiful girl ... now a wild ... semi-human beast, her body entirely nude, bristling with long jagged hair, filth and vermin ...' The *Catholic Herald* replied that in any Catholic community there were former nuns; that to speak of 'escape' was nonsense; and that ex-nuns had found that the Protestant Alliance would only pay for filth! (*CH*, 30 Mar 1909).

[79]PAT, 1417, 1434 - 36, 1459, 1478, 1557.

there would be a riot, and that 'I would not give much for your Protestantism if we took that quietly'. He urged Wise's supporters to go to Wise's trial in large numbers to 'show the magistrate that Mr. Wise was a power in the North End of Liverpool'.[80]

Third, Wise, the politician, espoused social reform. He referred to himself as a worker's candidate, and even as a socialist of a type superior to merely atheistic socialism. In 1905 he declared 'every Protestant should be a labour man ...'. He served on the West Derby Board of Guardians, and had been a member of the Liverpool Distress Committee. He visited the sick in the Netherfield Road Hospital and the Fazakerley Infectious Hospital. As councillor, he supported cheaper transport and council housing. Wiseites also loved to criticize the projected new Liverpool Anglican Cathedral as 'the Bishop's church, the church of the rich' - the money would be better spent, he said, alleviating misery in the slums. Wise was a more convincing populist than the Tory paternalists for he lived very penuriously, always ready to give away his tram-fare or overcoat. He also bragged about it, saying if he died with more than £5 they should put 'impostor' on his grave. 'Where did all the money go?' he would ask. 'To charity and the poor!' shouted the people, and Wise contrasted that with the luxury in which Roman Catholic priests allegedly lived. Wise was not alone. Watson Rutherford, Conservative M.P., City Councillor and Orange leader, told the Fabian Society in 1908 that 'Tory Democracy' owed socialism a great debt for pointing out 'the way to corporate, municipal and state enterprise', and the 'gross disparity in the distribution of wealth and in many cases, undeserving hardships of the poor'.[81]

Fourth, Wise was adamant about temperance. He loved to jibe that Catholics were drunks, despite the Church's efforts on behalf of temperance. Besides police persecution, Wise's church 'Agenda for 1910' declared, 'We shall have to face the great drink question, the evils of betting and gambling, the shocking immorality of our streets, the looseness of public morals, the spread of religious indifference, the desecration of the Lord's Day, the spread of infidelity and the arrogant intimidation of the Roman priesthood if we justify our existence'.[82] More than any other thing, Wise's successful efforts to wean the working-class members of his Men's Bible Class from drink won him credit with Liverpool's political establishment, including the Liberal editor of the *Daily Post*, Sir Edward Russell. Wise and his followers felt that his Men's Bible Class parades were proud demonstrations of their achievement of

---

[80]PAT, 703, 706, 863, 962, 1440. Waller, 178, 188 -89.

[81]Quoted in Smith, 'Labour Tradition', 46, cf Smith; 'Class, skill', 181 -82; Waller, 189, 203, 213; *Lp Courier*, 30 Nov 1917; PAT, 1458.

[82]*Protestant Reformers Monthly Magazine*, Jan 1910.

respectability, sobriety, and self-discipline, and indeed that the regular parades helped keep them sober.[83] Such arduously won self-esteem may have contributed to their self-righteous aggressiveness, particularly as they projected a stereotype of Catholics as still enthralled by drink. Perhaps sectarianism was a substitute opiate of the people.

Finally, these religious impossibilists revelled in martyrdom, and the execution of the educational reformer Ferrer by 'Jesuit' authoritites in Spain in 1909 gave them a fresh case of clerical tyranny, for Latimer and Ridley were really a bit stale. Martyrdom provided feelings of exaltation, justification, and moral compensation when the authorities compelled Wise to yield. Wise declared 'that though he had been persecuted from all sides he had never been hurt, and by some strange means he had always been successful and victorious... He felt that the more he was persecuted... his power became more augmented in the city [sic]'.[84] Wise told his supporters at the St. Domingo Pit, 'a spot [he had tried] to make sacred for the Protestants', 'that before I give up the right to expose the teachings of Jesuits and to hold my Bible Class parade I would rather die upon the spot ... Mr. Duder [the police prosecutor] did everything he could to crush this aggressive Protestant work. He [Wise] would rather be treated like Señor Ferrer, the great Spanish martyr of the twentieth century, than yield...'. One protest meeting finally proclaimed Wise the champion martyr! 'Mr. Wise stood second to none in the cause of martyrdom for religion. He was now in Walton Goal, a victim ... of the power behind the throne, the Jesuits'.[85]

The taut positive and negative social ambitions in sectarianism provided plenty of meaning and motivation for aggressive Protestantism without reducing it to economic animosity.[86] Historians often seem inclined to *reduce* ethnic antagonisms to economics in an effort to make rational what seems irrational, and so to imply that sectarianism is 'false consciousness', a diversion from the workers' 'real' economic interests. In thousands of pages of evidence about the disturbances of 1909, there is no significant evidence of economic competition between Protestants and Catholics, and plenty of

---

[83]A Unitarian businessman of the nieghbourhood raised objections to Wise's abuse of Catholics at the meetings in St. Domingo Pit, but he also made it a point to testify at the Inquiry to the good work Wise had done in his district. (PAT, 1546, and cf 721.)

[84]*DPM*, 28 June 1909. Instead of debating openly, Wise wrote as late as 1911, 'Romanism['s] ... argument is Church authority, kill the heretic, gag and muzzle the Protestant lecturer ... as poor [William] Murphy was done ... as was done to poor Mr. [John] Kensit ...', thus grouping himself with recently killed Protestant 'martyrs.' (*Lp Courier*, 29 July 1911.)

[85]*DPM*, 18 Oct 1909; PAT, 1417.

[86]Gallagher argues that Irish and English workers competed for unskilled work, and that contributed to sectarian tensions, but he provides no evidence. ('Tale of Two Cities', 110, 123).

evidence of fully conscious commitment to sectarian loyalties. Catholics were called many things, but job-takers was not one of them. In a rare reference to economic frictions, an Orange leader claimed in 1857, not that Catholics undercut wages, but that they were employed on better terms than Protestants.[87] One can find impressionistic references to job patronage organized on sectarian lines, without much specific evidence,[88] but if some employers hired co-religionists, the market was too open to permit monopoly. Perhaps only the carters with their union and badges came near to an ethnic monopoly.[89] Eric Taplin concludes that workers kept their work identities and their neighbourhood and family ethnic identities in separate compartments.[90] Far more than the dockland economy, sectarian battle rewarded dogged commitment: with visible self-improvement, political recognition, and the palpable advance of one's tribe. The docks provided dull poverty - by contrast, the crusade offered a chance for heroism, replete with swords and brass bands.

Catholic spokesmen did not advocate physical attack, even if they were rhetorically aggressive. A *Catholic Herald* editorial explained that while Protestants claimed freedom of thought, but restricted freedom of actions, Catholic doctrine was the reverse: Catholics required ideological conformity, for errors of belief threatened the mistaken believer with eternal damnation. But they were muich more tolerant of human lapses in behaviour, while Protestants were quick to cry immorality.[91] Catholics too embraced self-help, temperance, and progress, both individual and corporate. Newspaper columns headed 'Catholic Successes' listed students who had passed University entrance exams. Catholics were as enthusiastic boosters of organizational growth and pious display as Protestants. At the Catholic Young Men's

---

[87]Neal, 177.

[88]*Ibid*, 32, though cf 181, and Shallice, 21 - 22; Joan Smith also mentions 'strong religious ... barriers' in the Liverpool labour market without providing instances ('Labour Tradition', 49). Docker's leader Jimmy Sexton did claim that a religious and political 'caste system' permeated dock work; J. Sexton, *Sir James Sexton, Agitator: The Story of the Dockers' M.P.* (1936), 109 - 10.

[89]Smith 'Commonsense Thought,' 353.

[90]Personal communication, 24 Oct 1985, and Eric Taplin, *The Dockers' Union: A Study of the National Union of Dock Labourers, 1889 - 1922* (Leicester, 1986), 24; Pauline Milward concludes there is 'little evidence' to support contemporary *middle-class* beliefs that economic competition contributed to the anti-Irish riots at Stockport, 'The Stockport Riots of 1852: A study of anti-catholic and anti-Irish Sentiment', in Swift and Gilley (eds), *The Irish in the Victorian City*, 215. Jeffrey Williamson has argued that despite contemporary beliefs, the Irish impact on English wages was slight, 'The Impact of the Irish on British labour markets during the Industrial Revolution', in Swift and Gilley (eds), *The Irish in Britain*, 134 - 162.

[91]*CH*, 16 Sept 1911.

Societies anniversary march in 1908, the *Catholic Herald* boasted, 'never, perhaps, in the history of Liverpool's public demonstrations was witnessed a more imposing display of concentrated strength', or as a 'remarkable ebullition of Catholicity'. Catholics wanted and deserved social recognition, said their barrister at the Inquiry: 'In every department of public life and private enterprise, the Catholics have stood with the rest of the community, and have been treated and rightly treated, with the rest of the community as being upon an equality and as being entitled to the respect which they have won for themselves, having regard to the way they have behaved in Liverpool'.[92] They too had martyrs to cherish - from 1535.[93] Catholics supported material progress: at the time of the transport strike of 1911, the *Catholic Times* insisted that workers must have better conditions and a living wage.[94] For two decades Irish Catholic City Councillors had cooperated with Tory councillors to sustain Liverpool's impressive housing programme. At the same time Catholics allowed themselves to fantasize about the spiritual reconquest of England, their hyperbole gratuitously confirming Protestant paranoia.

In sum, the ideologies of both sides were aggressive and activist. Both felt they had exclusive possession of the truth, and both felt threatened by the other. Both were committed to practical self-help, and so they could undergird working-class loyalty with pride and self-esteem, earthly cousins of spiritual salvation.

IV.Community Politics

The structure and nature of community politics provided necessary components for the disturbances of 1909. Motivations are necessary but not sufficient conditions for collective violence: they do not always find the arms and legs that enable legions to take the field, nor authorities that encourage or permit the battle. Liverpool's sectarian disturbances were far from unique between 1850 and 1920.[95] But observers seem to agree that Liverpool had

---

[92]Quotations: *CH*, 30 May and 6 June 1908; PAT, 1364. For 'Catholic Successes', see, for example, *CH*, 25 July 1908. Current political difficulties 'were as completely thrown aside as if the Catholics of Lancashire were confident in their power to assert the traditional independence of their ancestors ... they showed the city an example of self-reliance and self-respect which could not fail to impress those who differ from them, and to stimulate the Catholic body throughout the country to united action on behalf of Catholic interests', *Catholic Times,* 29 May 1908.

[93]*CH*, 8 Aug 1908; *Catholic Times*, 5 May 1911.

[94]*Catholic Times*, 18, 25 Aug 1911.

[95]See, for instance, Kirk, 'Ethnicity, Class and Popular Toryism'; Swift and Gilley (eds), *Irish in the Victorian City,* passim and bibliography; and Arnstein, *Protestant versus Catholic*, ch 7 and 107 - 110.

nastier and more enduring sectarian conflicts than any other city in the United Kingdom save Belfast. That was because sectarian antagonism permeated Liverpool society and politics - furthermore, Liverpool's community politics added to negative attitudes the positive assets of well-established ethnic organization and solidarity to create combat-ready regiments.

First, some material foundations: the work of Eric Taplin, Tony Lane, Andy Shallice, Joan Smith, and others has shown how Liverpool's economy as a port and commercial centre, rather than a manufacturing city, shaped the character and structure of working-class politics.[96] The predominant form of work in Liverpool was casual, unskilled work on the docks or in transport, together with clerical work and domestic service. That created important conditions for sectarian conflict. The low pay and casual work of the docks created a vacuum of 'traditional' labour organizations, and that vacuum was filled by sectarian organizations which provided both the social services and the emotionally satisfying solidarities found elsewhere in labour movements. What was missing from Liverpool was the independent skilled artisanate or factory-based proletariat characteristic of industrial cities like Glasgow, Sheffield, or Manchester. These latter cities were more likely to have Liberal political traditions, and hence a Liberal 'commonsense' that could naturally evolve into rationalist labourism and socialism.[97] The whole history of the nineteenth century labour movement suggests that the higher living standards, social status, and defensible skills of artisans and operatives enabled them to organize unions based on partial job control, and empowered them to take more control of their economic fortunes rather than being buffeted by economic adversity as were the dockers in the casualized Liverpool labour market. Relatively high and regular pay and stable workgroups and trades unions endowed such workers with the capacity for, and ethos of, effective self-help, including collective self-help, embodied in such institutions as friendly societies, co-ops, Mechanics Institutes, building societies, Volunteers, perhaps temperance societies, and even Free Methodist chapels. These were the constituents of the sturdy Victorian labour movemnent and 'labourism'. By contrast, in Liverpool, poverty and casual unskilled labour set up great obstacles to trade union organization, for workers could ill afford the dues or the strikes which might lead all too easily to their replacement. So Liverpool lacked a 'classical' working-class culture with its network of self-help institutions. Instead of the great national self-help friendly societies, such as the convivial fellowships of Oddfellows or Foresters, most Liverpool working

---

[96]Taplin, *Dockers' Union*; Shallice, Smith 'Labour Tradition'; and Tony Lane, 'Proletarians and Politics in Liverpool, c. 1900 - 1911', unpublished paper, Nov 1979.

[97]Smith, 'Commonsense Thought', especially chs 3 and 5; 'Labour Tradition,' and 'Class, skill', passim.

men insured themselves either through insurance companies, or local tontines attached to ethnic groups.[98] At the same time, Liberalism was weak and declining in Liverpool, whether one speaks of the Liberal party organization or of the nonconformist churches that were leaving the city centre.

Sectarianism filled this vacuum in Liverpool's political culture, politically, ideologically and socially. Frank Neal has pointed out three levels of sectarian conflict in Liverpool: electoral politics, organizational marching and mud-slinging, and street violence.[99] How did the first two relate to the street violence that is the subject of this essay? Liverpool's electoral politics were soaked in sectarianism as Phillip Waller has made abundantly clear. Sectarianism had permeated Liverpool's politics since the 1830s and the arrival of McNeile. By the 1890s and 1900s the populist Tory boss, Archibald Salvidge, had used the Orange card to build the Working Men's Conservative Association (WMCA) into an urban working-class machine to unhorse the town's old 'currant-jelly' Conservative elite. The WMCA had 24 branches by 1911, many with working men's clubs, typically temperance.[100] For their support of the dominant Conservative coalition, workers received housing and a fair wage clause in Corporation contracts, but no working-class city councillors before 1914.

Sectarianism was not simply elite manipulation of the masses. The elites did not create it. Plebeian Protestants used the Conservative bosses to advance their interests more than vice versa.[101] Protestant working-men regularly put religion above wage packets and social reform: the anti-ritualist Church Discipline Bill was the litmus test of right-thinking (Protestant) Conservatism.[102] One must remember that only about half of the men in Liverpool could vote. The values and rewards held out by grass-roots community leaders like Wise had stronger attractions than those of the slightly distant municipal bosses; and populist Protestants were only conditional allies, as the Protestant insurgency against the Tories in 1903 - 5 shows. The Protestant masses were hardly mesmerized by Conservative bosses; rather the bosses were attracted by Wise's charismatic power in the streets, despite his populism, like moths to a flame.

Did the Conservative and Protestant elites tolerate or even encourage sectarian violence? They tolerated it but their sins were more of omission than commission. Protestant leaders like Austin Taylor found Wise's open air tirades in 1903 offensive 'to all who value the cause of true religion'. The

---

[98]Smith, 'Labour Tradition', 47.
[99]Frank Neal, 'The roots of violence', *The Tablet*, 1 May 1982, 421.
[100]Waller, 177 - 206; Smith, 'Class, skill', 177.
[101]Shallice, 17.
[102]Waller, 166, 196.

Protestant Standard decried the violence of the Glorious Twelfth in 1903 as 'religion being trailed in the gutter by a rowdy godless element for whom Roman Catholicism and Protestantism are mere names'. The Anglican Archdeacon Madden condemned Wiseite violence as 'brickbats and rowdyism ... bastard Protestantism ...'. Salvidge deplored Wise's abuse of free speech, but as Wise was quick to retort, the criticism came mainly when Wise had captured Kirkdale at the crest of the independent Protestant revolt of 1903.[103] The ultra-Protestants were such a potent political force that the Conservative leaders dared not repudiate Wise and his works, and indeed sought to identify themselves with him in his scrapes with the law. From 1901 right through 1909 Conservative councillors and M.P.s represented Wise in the courts, posted bail, and visited him in prison. In August 1909 when Wise was in and out of gaol, and the Protestant drums were calling for the Head Constable's head, Alderman Rutherford denounced the 'badly commanded' police for their 'unnecessary brutality', and applauded the community service of his 'personal friend' George Wise. Toadyism did not keep Rutherford from being unseated by the Protestant Labour leader, John Walker, who had actually been bloodied in the violence of 20 June.[104] While the police and the stipendiary magistrate sought to restrain Wise's incendiary speeches, the Conservatives on the City Council embraced his principles and remained silent about Wiseite aggression in 1909. That gave a tacit legitimacy and undercut the Head Constable and the police magistrate's authority.

The chief political opposition to the Tory Protestants was the Irish Nationalist Party, potent electorally because of the concentration of the Liverpool Irish in Scotland and Vauxhall wards in the North End. That concentration produced among other things a Catholic middle class to provide leadership in the search for status, and Home Rule city councillors began to be elected in the 1870s.[105] There were more than a dozen Irish Nationalists on the Edwardian city council, so that the Liverpool Irish had a greater presence in city politics than their brothers anywhere in Britain. Councillor Burke had broken the Nationalists' apprenticeship to the declining Liberal Party in 1899.[106] Eight Liverpool Irishmen ultimately became Nationalist M.P.s for Irish constituencies; Liverpool was the only English constituency to return an Irish Nationalist M.P., the redoubtable T. P. O'Connor. O'Connor ran a formidable working-class machine himself, based on patronage,

---

[103]Waller, 201, 202, 230, 205 - 06.
[104]*Ibid*, 240 - 241; *DPM*, 25 Sept 1909.
[105]See Bernard O'Connell, 'Irish Nationalism in Liverpool, 1873 - 1923', *Eire/Ireland*, 10 (1975) 24 - 37; *idem*, 'The Irish Nationalist Party in Liverpool 1873 - 1927', unpublished M.A. thesis, University of Liverpool, 1971, 132; and L. W. Brady, *T. P. O'Connor and the Liverpool Irish* (London, 1983), 37.
[106]Waller, 181.

neighbourhood, and clan.[107] After 1898 - 99 his old guard had to divide political mastery with the 'insurgent' Harford brothers, Austin and Frank, who insisted on a more radical social programme, took over the local connections of the Irish party, and cooperated with the Tories to produce Liverpool's pioneering housing programme, with 90 per cent Irish tenancy. Austin Harford did yeoman service as deputy chair of the Corporation Housing Committee, working with the Conservative chair, Colonel George Kyffin-Taylor. Sectarian democracy in Liverpool was not simply barren circuses![108] T. P. O'Connor, ever the cosmopolitan, despised the sectarian violence of 1909 and did his quota of defensive hand-wringing in Parliament to demonstrate his Irish bona fides, just as the Conservative elites ritually distanced themselves from the Orangemen's crudities.[109] So while neither party's leaders directly fomented violence, ethnic politics brought the resources of press and party to sustain sectarian identities which could be regulary displayed and refurbished in elections.

But finally, since half of Liverpool's men did not vote in 1910, we must examine the more direct rewards that Wiseites and Catholics obtained from *informal* politics. Social networks underpinned the rival armies with positive assets for collective action. First, collective perception and action were grounded in ethnic neighbourhoods, urban villages with their face-to-face clannishness and petty patriotism. Protestants and Catholics lived, worked, and shopped side by side, not separated in absolute apartheid, but poverty, cheap housing, and the need to be near the dockland hiring stands packed the Irish Catholics into the Scotland and Vauxhall wards, while Protestant workers generally lived east of Great Homer Street, the more fortunate rising up the neighbouring heights of Everton.[110] Physical contiguity did not prevent social and cultural segregation. Liverpool-born John Denvir wrote that in Liverpool and Manchester, Irish Catholics 'rarely marry outside their own creed and nationality'.[111] Neighbourhood concentration created the critical mass to support a full range of ethnic organizations. Catholic neighbourhoods were especially closely linked to their parish church. Janina Klapas' work has shown that members of Catholic parish churches lived very close to their churches, while Protestant churches drew their congregations from wider networks,

---

[107]John Denvir,*The Irish in Britain* (1892), 434; Shallice, 19 - 20; Brady, 37; O'Connell, 'Irish Nationalism,' 26; and Smith, 'Labour Tradition,' 46.

[108]Waller, 186 - 87; O'Connell, 'Irish Nationalism', 31, 33; Smith, 'Labour Tradition', 46 and 'Class, skill', 178 - 79.

[109]Brady, 186; Neal, *Sectarian Violence*, 68 - 72.

[110]See Colin Pooley, 'Segregation or integration? The residential experience of the Irish in mid-Victorian Britain', *The Irish in Britain*, 60 - 83; Smith, 'Class, skill', 171 - 2.

[111]John Denvir, *The Irish in Britain from the Earliest Times to the Fall of Parnell* (1892) 415.

attracting adherents on the basis of voluntary social and theological differentiation rather than territorial proximity. Wise's Protestant Reformers' Church, however, did seem to be powerfully neighbourhood-based - at least it dominated its neighbourhood, even if members came from across the city. Sectarian neighbourhoods were both seedbeds and targets for mob action. The neighbourhood purges of 1909 may have targetted socially mobile newcomers, for Catholics had just begun to move to Everton and Kirkdale.[112]

But besides neighbourhood, whole networks of social organizations were attached to the rival churches. The social functions they served must have reinforced or even replaced religious belief as the cement of tribalism. George Wise's Protestant Reformers' Church had two Sunday services, morning and evening, each of which often overflowed with more than 1,000 worshippers. His Men's Bible Class, 1,500 strong, marched five times a year to display their pride in abstinence and respectability. A settlement house, the Kirkdale Social Institute, across the street from the church recruited from the slums, replacing gambling and drink with draughts (checkers) and cocoa. Other family needs were filled by Endeavour Societies, Temperance Societies, Open Air Gospel meetings, Bible Study Classes, Women's Bible Classes, and Women's Pleasant Wednesday Evenings, Sunday Schools, and a Boys' Guild. The George Wise Tontine Society provided sickness, unemployment, and death insurance for its thousand members. The George Wise Cycling Club - the largest in the city, he boasted, - and Athletic Leagues provided for non-violent physical recreation.[113]

Wise was the chaplain of the Liverpool Province of the Orange Institution, and overlapping his personal empire were some 50 Orange lodges, which provided their working-class/shopkeeper membership with fraternal meetings, organized aggression, and periodic pageantry. For thousands of men and women their thirty annual parades were crowned by celebrations of the Glorious 12th of July, which included a chartered mass outing to Upholland plus carnival in Kirkdale; buntings and burnings of effigies of the Romanists in hair-raising bonfires in the narrow streets, as well as brawls and marching bands. The Orange lodges were also social centres, and provided funeral and illness insurance benefits, as well as a hope of mixing with potential employers

---

[112]J. A. Klapas, 'Geographical Aspects of Religious Change in Victorian Liverool, 1837 - 1901', unpublished M.A. thesis, University of Liverpool, 1977, 92, 129 -133, 170, 181 - 4; and interview with R. F. Henderson, Oct 1985.

[113]PAT, 721; Henderson, *George Wise*, 27; Wise's obituary, *Lp Courier*, 30 Nov 1917.

among the petty bourgeoisie. The Orange Defence Association countered the Catholic Defence Association in 1909.[114]

Such political and social organizations provided working class people with experience in leadership as well as the political recognition that often seemed more important in this period than the political issues emphasized by conventional political history. They enjoyed seeing their champion, Pastor Wise, courted as a powerful political force, and their other leaders, men like Richard Briggs, a foreman printer, Wise's church secretary and later a Justice of the Peace, seriously consulted as community spokesmen, at a time when the WMCA had still not elected any working class city councillors.

Roman Catholics enjoyed a parallel web of social organizations. Concerned about leakage from the church, the Church took well-organized measures to retain members, as well as promulgating an uncompromising creed which imposed attendance at Mass as a binding obligation sanctioned by penance. Church attendance was up 24 per cent between 1891 and 1902, by contrast with Anglican and Nonconformist decline in the central city.[115] Perhaps even more important than the churches themselves were the schools. Certainly they took priority in building campaigns. The Catholic school network in Liverpool reached all the way from elementary parish schools to secondary colleges plus the convent of Notre Dame and the Jesuit seminary. Ranged alongside T. P. O'Connor's Irish Nationalist machine, with its United Irish League, and the Parnellite Irish National Association, were a host of social organizations. The Gaelic League promoted Irish culture; the Gaelic Athletic Association, Irish sports. The parishes themselves sustained the Young Men's Societies, devoted, some complained, too much to cards and billiards, but also providing cycling clubs, debating societies, teas, and parties. The Irish National Foresters answered the Orange marches, some Foresters appearing in Robert Emmet costumes with pikes and swords. But above all, the Foresters were a large and important friendly society providing insurance, together with the Order of Irish Foresters, the Parnell Tontine Society, and two other societies. The League of the Cross temperance society seemed to be smaller and less powerful. Other Irish social organisations included the Clan-na-Gael, the Liverpool Irish Literary Institute, the Sunday League, and perhaps the Ancient Order of Hibernians. Church processions would also include the Third Order of Saint Francis, a men's devotional group, guilds and confraternities like the

---

[114] *The Times*, 15 July 1910; Neal, 'Roots of Violence', 421, and *Sectarian Violence*, 171, 244, 250 and passim; Shallice, passim.

[115] R. B. Walker, 'Religious Changes in Liverpool in the nineteenth century', *Journal of Ecclesiastical History*, 19 (1968), 201. The Young Men's Catholic Societies attended Mass monthly in a body, Thomas Burke, *Catholic History of Liverpool*, (Liverpool, 1910), 124.

Boy's and Girls' Guilds, the Women's Branch of the League of the Sacred Heart, the Children of Mary for young women, or the St. Vincent de Paul relief society for the poor. Other organizations included St. Oswald's Literary and Debating Society and debate league, a Catholic young men's orchestra, a Catholic students' organization at Liverpool University, a Catholic Prisoners' Aid society, a host of assorted parish cycling clubs, harriers, football and cricket teams. Churches also sponsored special Forty Hours Devotions, social events, and even chartered holiday outings like the popular shrine at Holywell in North Wales, where the faithful might hope (unofficially) for miracles. For the well-to-do the Vatican sponsored trips and pilgrimages on the Continent. A strong newspaper with many local editions, the *Catholic Herald*, functioned as a sort of Catholic *Northern Star*, holding the Catholic movement together, displaying it, and inspiriting it in its columns.[116] Most of the parish organizations were led by priests rather than laymen, so the Church did not provide as much direct leadership opportuniy for laymen, though the priests might have provided kinship ties between homes and parish, and the Church certainly intended its hierarchy of schools and debating societies to prepare young men for leadership in public affairs. Catholics were probably more numerous and more persistent than the ultra-Protestants in offical governing bodies like the City Council, the School Board, and the Poor Law Boards of Guardians, though these representatives were usually not working men.

In short both Protestants and Catholic working people could live their whole social lives in sectarian cocoons in which most of their needs were created and fulfilled. Head Constable Dunning observed that the processions flaunted allegiances rather than beliefs. The solidarities and antagonisms of Protestant and Catholic mobs were nurtured and lived in over a lifetime. The geographical and social separation of their social worlds helped breed alienation and suspicion as a basis for aggression. Indeed that separation might lull the naive into overconfidence. Pat O'Mara, a Liverpoool Irish 'slummy', recalled seeing his first Orange parade in the 1930s: 'I had never known there were so many enthusiastic Protestants, I had always been brought up in the belief that Protestantism was a dying cult, and its adherents cowards, easily frightened'.[117] Conversely, a threat to one's religious tribe shook - and mobilized - one's whole socio-cultural network. Sectarian violence was not the spontaneous combustion of brute antagonism. Organizations, more the Wiseite and Orange than the Catholic, not only manufactured sectarian hatred, but also gave it arms and legs in organized crowds to act it out. Social networks underlay that emblem of 1909, the Orange fife and drum

---

[116]O'Connell, 'The Irish Nationalist Party', 101 - 103; Smith, 'Class, skill', 178. For organizations, see for instance *CH*, 20, 27 Mar, 3, 10 Apr 1909.

[117]P. O'Mara, *The Autobiography of a Liverpool Irish Slummy* (1934), 87.

band marching down the street, followed by a crowd singing 'Paddy was a bastard', and chucking rocks at the Notre Dame convent.

V.Denouement

Sectarian violence finally subsided in pre-war Liverpool, not because ethnic antagonisms changed, but because community politics changed. What banished sectarian rioting was not enlightenment but trauma; the near-anarchy of the great transport strike of 1911 convinced the town's leaders they could no longer afford to permit sectarian disturbances, and they acted promptly to shut them down.

The Home Office Inquiry into the riots and police conduct sat all through February 1910 and produced much light but little political will to change. The Commissioner exonerated the police, resolving all the disputed testimony in their favour, perhaps because he felt it would invite anarchy to do otherwise. Mainly he worked for conciliation, passing up chances to fix blame if he could win contrition and support for his pet project, a Conciliation Board. The Commissioner pointed out George Wise's anti-Catholic crusade as one of the causes of the riots. Wise had promised the Commissioner at the Inquiry to moderate his diatribes, but he found excuses not to do so. When the report appeared, Wise responded that the Commissioner had been biassed, that he would continue 'exposing the aggression of the Roman Catholic Church', and that a conciliation board was impossible.[118] Besides the Conciliation Board, the Commissioner also proposed official controls over outdoor religious processions and meetings. These proposals were not adopted by the political leadership of Liverpool and died still-born.

Politics in 1910 showed nothing had changed. Following the Inquiry report, the Catholic Bishop suspended Catholic processions for the rest of the year, and promised that future processions would avoid features irritating to Protestants. At the same time he petitioned the Lord Mayor against the continuation of Wise's anti-Catholic speeches at the Pit. A Catholic magistrate, seconding the Bishop, noted that Catholics had up to now exercised 'wonderful self-control' under the direction of the clergy, but that if Wiseite insults continued unabated, none 'would be able to control the just indignation of the people' for 'the Catholics of Liverpool ... were absolutely united in their determination ... to resist the bigoted attacks ... made upon them'. Two days later three hundred young men wearing the badges of the Catholic Defence League, allegedly led by a Nationalist ex-Councillor, broke up a Wiseite meeting at Edge Hill, marched around the neighbourhood singing

[118]Wise; PAT, 1650, *DPM,* 12 Apr, 11 June 1910; Commissioners findings: PAR, 63 - 70.

'Faith of our Fathers' in triumph, and then rallied at St. George's Plateau, where the ex-councillor declared, 'If the authorities won't stop them, we will', and the crowd replied 'Yes, we will'. In June the Catholic Bishop of Liverpool was stoned by a Protestant mob. In July a by-election for the Kirkdale seat coincided with literally incendiary festivities for the Glorious Twelfth. Effigies were burnt in both Catholic and Orange streets.[119] The arch-Protestant Colonel Kyffin-Taylor stood for the Conservatives, 'pealing his hatred of Catholicism and the "national importance" of maintaining the King's Declaration', while Salvidge declared, 'We stand on this platform to prevent the people of Ireland from ruling Kirkdale'. They were both grateful to Wise for the Conservative victory, while Wise added the benediction, or rather malediction: 'This is Liverpool's answer to the Commissioner's report'.[120] There were plenty of disturbances.

Though the General Election of December was relatively quiet, the spring of 1911 brought a by-election involving the new Conservative leader Bonar Law and more sectarian agitation. Protestant workmen were attacked, Catholics were purged from Netherfield Road neighbourhood, and June saw more rioting on the second anniversary of the 1909 riots. John Walker and George Wise warned Protestants of a Catholic campaign against their liberties. When Catholic Alderman Taggart petitioned against his speeches at the Pit, Wise refused to yield to 'the dictation of the Roman Catholic hooligans of the [City] Council.. or the tyrannical demands of the Church...'. When Orange leader S. G. Thomas proposed that Orange processions be curtailed, Wise charged that he was 'playing into the hands' of the police and the Catholics'.[121] Wise claimed to have cut down on the number of his processions, but he and his colleagues at the Pit kept on viciously attacking the Catholics in 1910 and 1911.

Up to the eve of the transport strike, the town fathers had still not concerted measures to prevent riots despite the continued violence. The Watch Committee drafted a Bill to regulate processions in the autumn of 1910, but the Liberal *Post and Mercury* charged that Conservative leaders had delayed action so as not to antagonize Protestant voters before the autumn elections. When it came before the City Council in December, various quibbles were raised, and the Conservative majority failed to take action.[122] The city's clergymen were no braver: they issued a public appeal for peace, but

---

[119]Quotations: *Lp Courier*, 27 May 1910, and *DPM*, 30 May and 11 June 1910. Election: *The Times*, 13, 15 and 19 July 1910. For further violence, see *DPM*, 15 June and 11 and 28 July 1910. The Catholic moratorium lasted through 1911.

[120]Waller, 244, 246.

[121]*Ibid*, 250, *DPM*, 1 May and 30 June 1911; *Lp Courier*, 1 Aug 1910.

[122]*DPM*, 21 Oct, 8 Dec 1910. Until August 1911, no bill was in the works: Liverpool Public Library, 352 MIN/WAT, 1/47 Watch Committee Meeting, 2 Aug 1911.

omitted their original reference to George Wise by name. Wise professed to see the hand of Dunning behind it, and proclaimed he was 'still triumphant in the cause of free speech and protestant propaganda'.[123]

It was the trauma of the massive transport strike of the summer of 1911, not any melting of sectarian animosities, that generated the political will for a resolution of this festering situation. Starting with the firemen and seamen and spreading to dockers, carters and railwaymen, the transport strike closed the docks. Food supplies could only be moved with armed escorts. The strike reached its climax on 'Bloody Sunday', 13 August, when 90,000 people rallying on St. George's Plateau were charged by the police. Two hundred were injured and one policeman died. Syndicalist Tom Mann claimed authority over the strike, and launched the myth that sectarian animosities had melted into class solidarity.[124] But although the unionized north-end Protestant carters had joined Catholic dockers to march hand-in-hand to the great rally, [125] sectarianism still had its innings. The rioting of that night included much sectarian violence off Great Homer Street and round Islington, smashing of backyard walls, looting of shops and pubs, and the wielding of bricks and railings in as fierce Orange-Catholic fighting as had been seen in the city's history, brought to an end only by the intervention of armed troops. In the week of general strike that followed, while strikers fought with police, the press carried coded references to mobs and looters attacking the shops and houses of religious opponents in the North end.[126] On the following Tuesday police fired on a crowd trying to liberate prisoners: the two men shot dead were both Catholics. Their funerals brought token measures of conciliation: John Sutcliffe's was attended by his 'fellow carters', while three hundred Protestants and Orangemen attended Michael Prendergast's. The services brought an end to a week of chaos and alarm, and Lord Derby relayed the

---

[123]Waller, 250, *DPM*, 27 Apr 1911 and *Lp Courier*, 28 Apr 1911.

[124]Bob Holton, *British Syndicalism 1900 - 1914: Myths and Realities* (1976), 100. The ad hoc Home Office commission of O'Connor, Kyffin-Taylor, and Shackleton also reported on 20 August that Orangemen and Catholics had held joint meetings after the funerals (below), brought together by common exasperation against the military and police, PRO HO 45/10656/212470/356. Cf similar report in *CH*, 26 Aug 1911.

[125]Holton, 99; George Milligan (Catholic labour leader) and Tom Mann in *Transport Worker*, vol I, no 1. (Aug 1911).

[126]*DPM*, 14, 15, 16 Aug 1911, *Lp Courier*, 14 Aug 1911; *CH*, 19 Aug 1911; Wire from Dunning to Home Office, 15 Aug 1911, HO 45/10654/212470, Item 35; Brian Harrison, 'The Sectarian Disturbance of 1909 and the Transport Strike of 1911: A Comparative Study of two instances of disorder', unpublished B.A. dissertation, University of Liverpool, 1985, v.

Lord Mayor's fear to the Home Office that 'a revolution was in progress'.[127] Salvidge later wrote to Lord Derby that 'for three weeks turmoil and almost anarchy prevailed'.[128]

The brush with anarchy and the spectre of working-class revolt finally galvanized the town fathers to give up sectarian conflict. At its peak, the Liberal Home Office appointed the two leading sectarian M.P.s, T. P. O'Connor and Colonel Kyffin-Taylor, to sit with the Home Office labour adviser, D. J. Shackleton, to investigate and try to settle the strike. They held a day of hearings on sectarian conflict, and once the strike was settled, they recruited Lord Derby, the city's most prestigious and impartial political leader, to chair a blue-chip conference of leaders, an evenly balanced spectrum of the community, unlike the city council or the magistrates' bench. Pastor Wise, ever the prima donna, egotistically held out for special treatment.[129] But the City Council was no longer inclined to tolerate Wise's provocations at the Pit. In early September they debated a measure to limit Wise's campaigns. A Catholic councillor declared, 'What had happened during the last three weeks showed something must be done to stop Liverpool's troubles', while a Protestant councillor agreed that if Wise 'were allowed to continue thus, they would have the troubles they had had in the past - which he for one believed had brought on the troubles of the last three weeks'.[130] Then Lord Derby committed his prestige to intervention, studing the Commissioner's report on 1909, and agreeing not only to chair the peace conference, but to accept the Lord Mayoralty for 1911-12 to see that its recommendations were enacted.[131] The upshot of the peace conference was first a resolution to give the Watch Committee control over the place of meetings, and then Council endorsement of a Special Act of Parliament, the Liverpool Corporation Act 1912, enabling the City Corporation to pass by-laws empowering the

---

[127]*CH*, 19, 26 Aug 1911; Waller, 255 - 56; *DPM,* 21 Aug 1911; *The Times*, 16 Aug 1911. According to local tradition, the two men killed were a Protestant and a Catholic, and that helped bring the two communities together. Harold Hikins, 'The Liverpool General Transport Strike 1911', *Transactions of the Historic Society of Lancashire and Cheshire*, 113 (1961), 191 n. 23.

[128]Picton Library, Liverpool, Derby Mss., 920 DER (17) 8/1, A. Salvidge to Lord Derby, 4 Sept 1911.

[129]*Lp Courier*, 23, 26 Aug 1911; *CH*, 16 Sept 1911; Wise said, 'I shall not attend unless I can make a complete and full statement of my case,' which implied hours of snores. (*DPM*, 13 Sept 1911.)

[130]*CH*, 9 Sept 1911.

[131]Picton Library, Liverpool, 352 MIN/WAT 1/47, 18 Sept 1911, and Derby MSS., 920 DER (17), 8/1 A. Salvidge to Derby, 12, 14 Sept 1911. Salvidge and Charles Petrie, the Liverpool Conservative leader, pressed Derby to lead, and Salvidge then accepted a spot on the sectarian commission, though 'from a party point of view' he had been inclined to stay out. Cf Randolph Churchill, *Lord Derby, King of Lancashire* (1959), 131 - 44.

Watch Committee to regulate meetings, processions, and emblems, music and weapons.[132] Pastor Wise tried to convert the delicately balanced consensus into partisan victory by emphasizing his meetings would now get police protection from Catholic attacks.[133] But there was now a weighty consensus against the continuation of his provocations. That consensus, given teeth in the official control of processions and meetings, finally reduced sectarian clashes from riots to small punch-ups. Lord Derby was able and willing to intervene on individual occasions, persuading Wise to cancel an anti-Home Rule meeting, and Salvidge to move a meeting to a less provocative place.[134] Head Constable Dunning had retired in December 1911, a prematurely aged man near nervous collapse.[135] Despite the gathering storm over Home Rule which included both massive counter-demonstrations in Liverpool, and the rumoured enlistment of thousands of Volunteers on both sides, Liverpool had done with sectarian rioting. The annual report of the Head Constable for 1912 observed:

> It is gratifying to be able to report that for the first time for many years the City was during the whole of the year entirely free from even the semblance of sectarian disorder. Several very large processions and demonstrations were held without a single regrettable incident occurring, and I am personally grateful to the leaders of all parties in the City for the most harmonious manner in which they worked with the police for the preservation of order on these occasions.[136]

VI.Conclusions

What conclusions can we draw from the Liverpool riots of 1909? First, that ethnic violence has its history, its sociology, its anthropology. We cannot understand it merely by reference to hatred or to psychology. If Protestant anger was exaggerated, even paranoid, it was politically cunning rather than blind and brutal. Just when Protestant working-men were achieving corporate political recognition and individual respectability, the social and political rise of Catholics challenged their social dominance, their string of successes, and their religious perfectionism. Two working-class 'Pilgrim's Progresses' were

---

[132]2 & 3 Geo 5, cap xiii. *DPM*, 7 Dec 1911.

[133]*DPM*, 15 Nov 1911.

[134]*DPM*, 26 Jan 1912: Churchill, 137.

[135]Picton Library, 352 MIN/WAT 1/47, 11 Sept, 27 Nov, and 4, and 18 Dec 1911.

[136]Head Constable to the Watch Committee, *Report on the Police Establishment ... for the Year Ending 31 December 1912* (Liverpool, 1913), 12

set on collision course. The clash might have been reduced if the Head Constable had used simple measures of communication, but it could probably not have been eliminated.

Second, what needs to be explained is not simply motivation but mobilization. Though personalities and ideologies were crucial, it is necessary to go beyond them to discover what social and political relationships gave them arms and legs, livery and leverage. The sectarian violence, irrational and expressive as it appears, was rooted in structures of community politics with their own intelligible goals and *raisons d'être*. Pastor Wise's empire was held together by a powerful mixture of irreducibly religious aspirations and solidarities and socially useful goals and ambitions, and the same was true of the Roman Catholic parishes. The denouement further suggests that the mechanics of mobilization were easier to change than attitudes rooted in formative experiences, long-lived patterns of daily life, tribal rewards, and lack of training or motivation for critical thinking. Rather than re-educating the rioters, the town fathers simply clamped down on them, once the threat of anarchy seemed to outweigh the political gains of further flirtation with sectarian violence.

Third, more than one working class was making itself in Edwardian Britain. The stage has long been dominated by the makers of the Labour Party, socialists and labourists exchanging mutual political recognition with a capitalist state, and we have latterly recognized the creatures of a defensive 'culture of consolation', part hedonism, part jingoism.[137] To these might be added an artefact of social engineering, the impoverished *objects* of early welfare state measures. Now Edwardian Liverpool sustained a Protestant and a Catholic working class who placed the advance of their own communal interest above the economic and political interests pointed out for them by conventional politicians and historians. In one political firmament Church Discipline outshone both Tariff Reform and the Osborne Judgment, while on the other side housing outweighed Irish nationalism. Might still more working classes be discovered in the mini-universes of other communities and other areas whose dynamics and trajectories also fell outside the classic parameters of labour history?

Fourth, the conjuncture of social, economic, political, and geographical conditions in Liverpool was nearly unique. Otherwise, George Wise's aggressive Protestantism, with its deep roots in British tradition, its mixture of atavism and progressive populism, and its totalitarian impulses, might have

---

[137]Stedman Jones, *passim*, a not altogether convincing attempt to bring these urban plebs aboard the ark of *the* working class.

become the harbinger of a home-grown British fascism.[138]

---

[138]Cf Gallagher, 116 and Norman Stone, *Europe Transformed 1878 - 1919* (Glasgow, 1983), p. 127. Finally, extreme late-Victorian revivalism became part of an 'anti-modernist, anti-materialist, anti-democratic, and often anti-intellectual movement which had secular as well as religious forms ... [Moody's preaching was] psychologically kin to the irrational and violent strains which are only one, but often a very powerful, element in right-wing attitudes.' John Kent, *Holding the Fort: Studies in Victorian Revivalism* (1978), 257 - 58.

9: Class, Religion and Gender: Liverpool Labour Party and Women, 1918 - 1939[1]

Sam Davies

On 1 April 1936, Liverpool City Council discussed a motion that the annual grant of £100 to the Mothers' Welfare Clinic in Clarence Street be renewed. The leader of the Labour Group, Luke Hogan, led the opposition to the grant being extended to one of the few institutions in the city where women could get advice on birth control. It was reported that:

> He fully acknowledged the difficulties which maternity involved. He paid tribute to the clean-minded women who endured them, but he questioned whether birth-control was the way of approaching those difficulties ... Hogan disagreed with birth control because it was the negation of socialism.

In a bitter debate, the main supporter of the grant was a leading member of the left of the Labour Party at that time, Bessie Braddock. She pointed out that in the previous year 87 women had died in the city because of childbirth, and argued that three-quarters of them would still have been alive if they had been able to avoid pregnancy. She added that the sale of drugs for abortion was growing enormously, and that the alternative was 'decent, clean, scientific advice such as was given at the Mothers' Welfare Clinic'. She was supported 'warmly' in the debate by another Labour woman, Mary Cumella, and also by the virulently anti-Catholic leader of the Protestant Party, the Rev Harry Longbottom.

In the end the vote was taken. For renewing the grant there were 15 Labour members, 4 Protestants, 5 Liberals and 48 Tories, while against were 34 Labour, 4 Independents and 3 Tories. The motion was carried by 72 votes to 41, and a curious alliance of the left and right had triumphed over the majority Catholic caucus in the Labour Group. In a final twist, the four Labour women in the Council were also divided over the issue, with Bessie Braddock and Mary Cumella finding themselves in opposition to Mary Hamilton and Agnes Milton.[2]

---

[1] I am grateful for comments and suggestions made about this essay at various stages of its preparation by John Belchem, Karen Hunt, Neville Kirk, Tony Lane and Marion Price.
[2] Liverpool City Council, *Minutes*, 1 Apr 1936; *Liverpool Daily Post*, 2 Apr 1936.

Nationally the Labour Party was often divided over the question of birth control in the inter-war period, with male hostility to the provision of advice and facilities usually outweighing the Women's Sections in Conference.[3] But what the division in Liverpool in 1936 graphically illustrated was the complex inter-connection of class, religion and gender in the politics of the local party. The relationship between class and religion has already been analyzed from a number of angles in studies of the Liverpool Labour Party,[4] but the significance of gender has been much less studied. In an important contribution to the debate on 'traditional' working class culture and 'the rise of Labour', Neville Kirk has recently highlighted 'the importance of issues of gender and neighbourhood to a full understanding of popular politics', and pointed to local studies of Labour in Preston and Nelson to illustrate the point.[5] It is in the context of that debate that this essay will suggest ways of approaching the question of the relationship between the Liverpool Labour Party and women between the wars.

I

One possible way of examining the impact of issues of gender on the local Party is to look at how women fared within the Party itself, and conversely at how much they were able to influence the Party from within, whether in terms of political practices or policies. The problems of examining these relationships are, however, extremely difficult, given the state of the existing records for the inter-war years. There are no surviving records of any Women's Section or any other constituent part of the Liverpool Labour Party specifically involving women. All that are available

---

[3]See Sheila Rowbotham, *A New World for Women. Stella Browne: Socialist Feminist* (1977), 43-59; Jane Lewis, *The Politics of Motherhood: Child and Maternal Welfare in England, 1900 - 1939* (1980), 197-8; Beatrix Campbell, *The Iron Ladies: Why do Women Vote Tory?* (1987), 63 - 64; Hilary Wainwright, *Labour, a Tale of Two Parties* (1987), 178 - 9.

[4]See, for instance, Andrew Shallice, 'Liverpool Labourism and Irish Nationalism in the 1920s and 1930s', *Bulletin of the North West Labour History Society*, No. 8 (1982); Joan Smith, 'Labour Tradition in Glasgow and Liverpool', *History Workshop Journal*, xvii (1984); P. J. Waller, *Democracy and Sectarianism: A Political and Social History of Liverpool, 1868 - 1939* (Liverpool, 1981).

[5]Neville Kirk, 'Traditional Working-Class Culture and "the Rise of Labour": Some Preliminary Questions and Observations', *Social History*, 16 (1991), 213; Michael Savage, *The Dynamics of Working-Class Politics: The Labour Movement in Preston, 1880 - 1940* (Cambridge, 1987); Jane Mark-Lawson, Michael Savage and Alan Warde, 'Gender and Local Politics; Struggles over Welfare Policies, 1918 - 1939', in Linda Murgatroyd *et al, Localities, Class and Gender* (1985).

are the records of the central institutions of the local Party.[6] Nevertheless, from these it is possible to piece together some picture of women's involvement.

From 1906 to 1918 women nationally had been organized separately in support of Labour through the Women's Labour League.[7] Under the new Constitution of February 1918 they were absorbed into the Party, and the formation of Women's Sections at a local level became a priority. In Liverpool, however, the development of women's organizations seems to have been a rather long-drawn out affair. By September 1918 there was a 'Women's Association' organizing public meetings over the issue of war pensions and allowances for soldiers' wives and dependents.[8] This body was organized well enough to have its secretary elected to the Executive Committee of the Party at its AGM in April 1919. Its candidate was nominated under the 'other affiliated organizations' section alongside the Independent Labour Party (ILP), Fabians and the Trades Council, so clearly it was perceived as a separate organization at this time. It also seems to have withered away fairly quickly after this, and does not appear to be represented at the 1920 AGM.[9]

In April 1921 local reorganization came with the merger of the Trades Council and Labour Party, and at its first Executive Committee meeting a Women's Sub-Committee was established. However, the title of this sub-committee seemed to be rather a misnomer, as it consisted of three men and only one woman, and it was unable to find a delegate to represent the local divisional parties, suggesting that organization of women in the city was not well-advanced at this stage. In fact the sub-committee seems to have collapsed fairly quickly, and did not reappear at the next AGM in April 1922.[10] Eventually in May 1922 a proposal came forward to form a Liverpool Women's Central Council, and it is from this date that women's organization within the Party began to take shape. The inaugural meeting of the Women's Council consisted of 30 delegates from ward and divisional parties, and the formation of separate Women's Sections in the local wards was much encouraged.[11] By August 1923 six wards and one parliamentary division were recorded as having a Women's Section. The subsequent development of Women's Sections in Liverpool

---

[6]The surviving records of Liverpool Labour Party are all kept in the Local History Library, Liverpool City Library.

[7]For the history of the Women's Labour League, see Margherita Rendel, 'The Contribution of the Women's Labour League to the Winning of the Franchise', in Lucy Middleton (ed), *Women in the Labour Movement* (1977); Christine Collette, *For Labour and for Women: The Women's Labour League, 1906 - 14* (Manchester, 1989).

[8]Executive Committee, Liverpool Labour Party, *Minutes*, 27 Sept 1918.

[9]Liverpool Labour Party, *Minutes*, 2 Apr 1919 and 7 Apr 1920.

[10]Executive Committee, Liverpool TC & LP, *Minutes*, 11 Apr 1921 and 12 Apr 1922.

[11]Liverpool TC & LP, *Minutes*, 3 May, 7 June and 2 Aug 1922.

can be seen in Tables 9.1 and 9.2 below and in the maps which accompany them.[12]

As the tables show, separate Women's Sections were certainly not established throughout the whole of the city at any time in the inter-war period. In fact at the height of their achievement in 1933 only 20 out of a total of 40 wards were organized, and close analysis shows that only about a dozen wards had Women's Sections operating for most of the period. There were some suburban wards like Aigburth, Allerton, Much and Little Woolton, and Warbreck, and also some city centre wards packed with business voters like Castle St. and St. Peter's, which were so solidly middle-class that it is no surprise that Labour had little organization there.

What is less predictable, however, is that in a number of working-class areas where Labour was extremely strong for most of this period, women's organization was non-existent. These consisted of a swathe of dockside wards extending from the northern boundary of the city down as far as the Brunswick Dock - Sandhills, North and South Scotland, Vauxhall, Gt. George and Brunswick. These were all predominantly Catholic, and all became safe Labour seats when the Irish Nationalist councillors who had dominated them from the late nineteenth century switched their allegiance to Labour in the mid to late 1920s. Councillors from these areas formed the caucus led by Luke Hogan that dominated the Labour Group on the Council in the 1930s. It is probable that the lack of women's organization in these areas was a reflection of a general organizational vacuum. By the early 1930s Labour usually won unopposed in these wards, and there was no necessity for any organized electioneering by Labour there. In fact ward parties, let alone Women's Sections, were a rarity, and a political machine based on close-knit neighbourhood ties dominated. Nevertheless, what is particularly significant here is that Catholic women were clearly not organized to any great extent within the Labour Party during this period. Women's organization in Liverpool was limited, then, mainly to one side only of the sectarian divide, and for that reason alone its impact on the local Party would have been lessened. But there are other factors which may be important in explaining the effect of Women's Sections on the Party.

II

Among feminists in socialist and labour politics, there were some who feared that absorption into separate sections within a male-dominated Labour Party would result in women being confined to a powerless ghetto, and at the same time isolated from a wider feminist movement. At a

---

[12]My thanks to Phil Cubbin of the Human Geography Cartographic Unit at Liverpool Polytechnic for his assistance in preparing the maps.

national level at least these fears were borne out to some extent. The fact that in the 1918 constitution the four women members of the National Executive Committee were to be elected by the party, and not the women's conference, was an early indication that women members were to be kept on a tight rein. It was significant also that the women's conference was only an advisory body with no direct access to shaping Party policy. The failure to win over the party conference on the issues of birth control and family allowances were important examples of the lack of power of the Women's Sections. By the late 1920s it was also clear that over a number of issues, such as equal pay and protective legislation for women workers, Labour women had diverged sharply from feminists in non-party organizations such as the National Union of Societies for Equal Citizenship (NUSEC).[13]

However, this analysis pitched at a national level may be too simplistic to explain the complex reality of women's involvement in the Labour Party. A number of writers associated with the Lancaster Regionalism Group have shown that at a local level the relationship of women to the Labour Party varied greatly. Thus Jane Mark-Lawson *et al* have demonstrated how differences in women's participation in the local labour market, and also the gender relations involved in their work, explain marked differences in women's impact on local Labour Parties in Lancaster, Preston and Nelson. In Lancaster the relatively low participation of women in paid employment was linked to a lack of female political activity, and a consequent lack of impact on Labour Party organization and policies. In Preston a much higher level of paid female employment nevertheless resulted again in a restricted women's impact on the local Party. The patriarchal structure of work relations in the local cotton-weaving industry meant that skilled male trade unionists saw female labour as a threat, and carried over these attitudes into Labour Party practices and policies. In Nelson, however, a similarly high level of female employment resulted in a quite different relationship to Labour. Here men and women were employed in the weaving industry on a more or less equal basis, and also participated in trade union and political life much more equally. Thus women had a significant impact on the Nelson Labour Party, being highly organized and influencing policy considerably, particularly pushing the Party towards local state intervention in various welfare services.[14]

---

[13]On these developments, see Wainwright, 177 - 9; Harold Smith, 'Sex vs Class: British Feminists and the Labour Movement, 1919 - 1929', *The Historian*, 47 (1984); and Martin Pugh, 'Domesticity and the Decline of Feminism, 1930 - 1950', in Harold Smith (ed), *British Feminism in the Twentieth Century* (Aldershot, 1990).

[14]Mark-Lawson *et al*, 209 - 13.

Table 9.1: Ward Women's Sections
August 1923 to June 1930

		Aug 1923 *	Jul 1925 *	Nov 1926	Aug 1927	Nov 1928	Nov 1929	June 1930
1	Abercromby							
2	Aigburth							
3	Allerton							
4	Anfield		✓					
5	Breckfield							✓
6	Brunswick							
7	Castle St							
8	Childwall		✓	✓	✓	✓	✓	
9	Croxteth**						✓	✓
10	Dingle			✓	✓	✓	✓	✓
11	Edge Hill		✓	✓	✓	✓	✓	✓
12	Everton	✓	✓	✓	✓	✓	✓	✓
13	Exchange					✓	✓	✓
14	Fairfield		✓	✓	✓	✓	✓	✓
15	Fazakerley		✓	✓				
16	Garston		✓	✓	✓			
17	Granby		✓	✓		✓	✓	✓
18	Gt George							
19	Kensington		✓					
20	Kirkdale		✓	✓	✓	✓	✓	✓
21	L. Woolton							
22	Low Hill		✓	✓	✓	✓	✓	✓

		Aug 1923 *	Jul 1925 *	Nov 1926	Aug 1927	Nov 1928	Nov 1929	June 1930
23	M. Woolton							
24	Netherfield	✓				✓	✓	✓
25	Old Swan	✓	✓					
26	Prince's Pk			✓	✓	✓	✓	✓
27	St Anne's							
28	St Domingo		✓	✓	✓	✓	✓	✓
29	St Peter's							
30	Sandhills							
31	Scotland N.							
32	Scotland S.							
33	Sefton Pk E.							
34	Sefton Pk W.					✓	✓	✓
35	Vauxhall							
36	Walton		✓	✓		✓	✓	✓
37	Warbreck							
38	Wavertree	✓	✓	✓	✓	✓	✓	✓
39	Wavertree W.	✓			✓	✓	✓	✓
40	W Derby	✓	✓				✓	✓
	Total	6	16	14	12	16	18	18

Notes: * In August 1923 and July 1925 a Women's Section is also listed for the combined Constituency Parties of East and West Toxteth.

** Croxteth Ward existed only from 1928.

Source: Liverpool Trades Council and Labour Party, *Minutes,* various dates, 1923 - 30.

Table 9.2: Ward Women's Sections
January 1931 to June 1939

		Jan 1931	Feb 1932 *	Mar 1933 *	Jan 1935 *	May 1937	Sep 1938	June 1939
1	Abercromby			✓	✓	✓	✓	✓
2	Aigburth							
3	Allerton							
4	Anfield						✓	✓
5	Breckfield	✓	✓	✓	✓			
6	Brunswick							
7	Castle St							
8	Childwall							
9	Croxteth	✓	✓	✓	✓	✓	✓	✓
10	Dingle	✓			✓	✓	✓	✓
11	Edge Hill	✓	✓	✓	✓	✓	✓	✓
12	Everton	✓	✓	✓	✓			
13	Exchange	✓						
14	Fairfield	✓	✓	✓	✓	✓	✓	✓
15	Fazakerley							
16	Garston							
17	Granby	✓	✓	✓	✓	✓	✓	✓
18	Gt George			✓	✓			
19	Kensington		✓	✓	✓			
20	Kirkdale	✓	✓	✓	✓		✓	
21	L. Woolton							
22	Low Hill	✓	✓	✓	✓	✓	✓	

		Jan 1931	Feb 1932 *	Mar 1933 *	Jan 1935 *	May 1937	Sep 1938	June 1939
23	M. Woolton							
24	Netherfield	✓	✓	✓				
25	Old Swan		✓	✓	✓			
26	Prince's Pk	✓						
27	St Anne's		✓	✓			✓	✓
28	St Domingo	✓	✓	✓				
29	St Peter's							
30	Sandhills							
31	Scotland N.							
32	Scotland S.							
33	Sefton Pk E							
34	Sefton Pk W	✓	✓	✓	✓	✓		
35	Vauxhall							
36	Walton	✓	✓	✓	✓	✓	✓	
37	Warbreck							
38	Wavertree	✓	✓	✓			✓	✓
39	Wavertree W		✓	✓	✓		✓	✓
40	W. Derby	✓	✓	✓	✓	✓	✓	✓
	Total	17	18	20	17	10	14	11

Notes: * In February 1932, March 1933 and January 1935 a Women's Section is also listed for W. Toxteth Constituency.

Source: Liverpool Trades Council and Labour Party, *Minutes,* various dates, 1931 - 33, 1937 - 39; *The Liverpool Official Red Book, 1935*, p. 328.

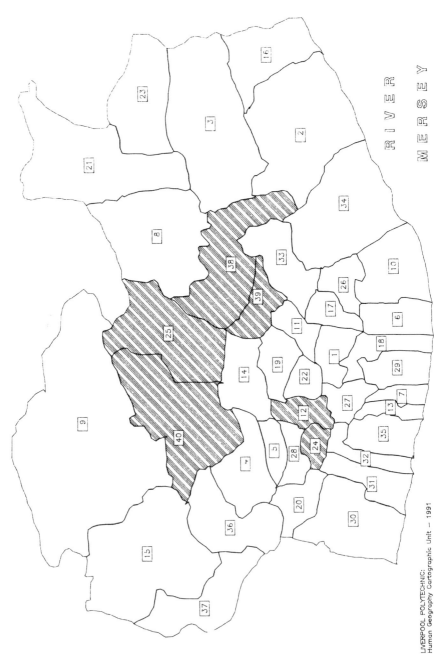

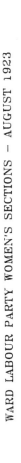

WARD LABOUR PARTY WOMEN'S SECTIONS – AUGUST 1923

LIVERPOOL POLYTECHNIC:
Human Geography Cartographic Unit – 1991

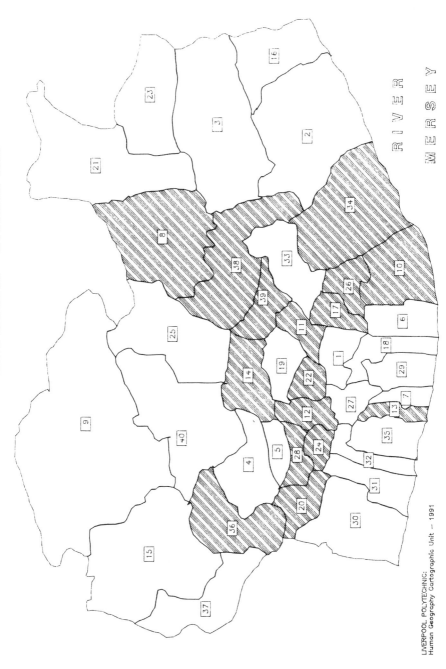

WARD LABOUR PARTY WOMEN'S SECTIONS – NOVEMBER 1928

RIVER MERSEY

LIVERPOOL POLYTECHNIC:
Human Geography Cartographic Unit – 1991

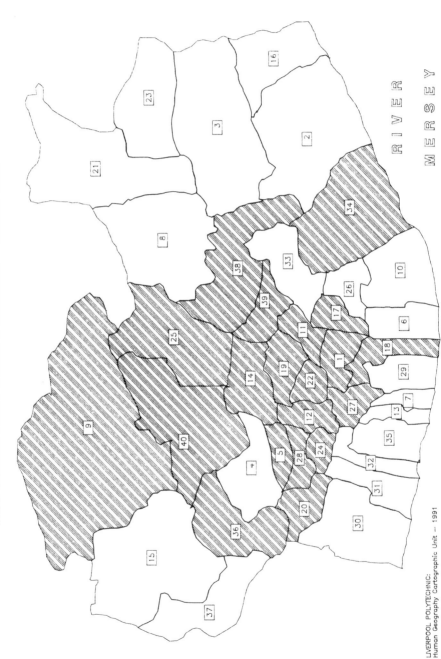

WARD LABOUR PARTY WOMEN'S SECTIONS – MARCH 1933

RIVER MERSEY

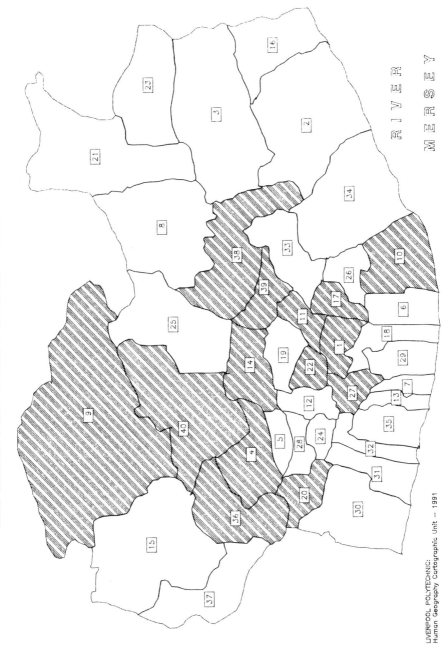

WARD LABOUR PARTY WOMEN'S SECTIONS – SEPTEMBER 1938

Michael Savage has also shown that changing economic circumstances can also affect the relationship between Labour and women. Thus in the mid-1920s, when employment in Preston was relatively high and therefore the perceived threat of female labour to skilled male workers was reduced, women were able to influence the Party considerably. This resulted in a development of neighbourhood-based politics which benefited the local Party electorally. When high unemployment returned in 1929, however, male attitudes to female labour reverted to their earlier hostility, partly explaining a decline in women's involvement in the Party and a shift in policy away from local state welfare initiatives.[15]

Members of the Manchester Women's History Group have developed a rather different perspective in looking at the impact of women on council housing provision in Manchester between the wars. They have shown that women in the Labour Party, and also in the closely linked Women's Co-operative Guild, were very active in attempting to influence the provision of public housing in the city. However, the effect of this campaigning is difficult to assess. The view that housing quality and design was a non-party issue, and therefore to be decided upon in the Council on a free vote, allowed male Councillors to ignore recommendations emanating from the Women's Advisory Council. This view also apparently affected votes concerned with education and maternity services. Labour Party women's opposition to flats in principle also seems to have been ineffectual. So despite the evidence of women being well organized and politically active within the Manchester party, over the issue of housing at least, their impact on policy was limited.[16]

More recently Pat Thane has argued that women in the party should not be viewed merely as 'puppets of male leaders or as traitors to a feminist movement', as such a view 'does less than justice to their organizational importance and independence of mind, to the coherence of their analysis of the role of women in society and of their strategies for change'. While she concedes that their overall achievement was 'minimal' compared with their ambitions, she also argues that in London at a municipal level women had an important influence on the Labour Party in the 1930s. They were elected in large numbers and had a considerable effect on policy, especially with regard to improved levels of health care.[17]

---

[15]Savage, 167 - 187.

[16]Manchester Women's History Group, 'Ideology in Bricks and Mortar; Women's Housing in Manchester between the Wars', *North West Labour History*, 12 (1987), especially 32 - 35. Linda Walker has been further developing this work on women and the Labour Party, and the results of her research are awaited with interest.

[17]Pat Thane, 'The Women of the British Labour Party and Feminism, 1906 - 1945', in Smith (ed), *British Feminism in the Twentieth Century*.

III

Turning back to the local experience in Liverpool, then, there are a number of inter-connected factors which need to be taken into account in examining women's impact on Labour. As far as the local labour market was concerned, women were in a particularly disadvantageous position. In the 1931 Census, 36 per cent of women aged over 14 in Liverpool were in paid employment or registered as unemployed.[18] Of course there were many unemployed married women excluded from this total due to the vagaries of the Unemployment Insurance system, and women's work has always tended to be underestimated in the Census,[19] but as a comparative measure the Census figure is instructive. By comparison, the national proportion was 35 per cent, and in Lancaster it was 33 per cent, in Preston 53 per cent and in Nelson 57 per cent.[20] Female participation in the paid labour force was low, then, but in the most detailed examination of women's work locally, Linda Grant has also shown that 'women workers remained concentrated in an extremely limited range of industries'.[21] Domestic service, the 'sweated trades' in the clothing industry, food, tobacco and paper production, sack making and mending, retail trades and clerical work were the only significant areas of paid women's work.

Linda Grant has also argued that the particularly strong dependence on work in dock-related jobs for men in Liverpool, coupled with the restricted areas of female employment, created a highly distinctive sexual division of labour. The distinction between 'men's work' and women's work' was sharply defined, 'producing and reproducing a model of masculinity which implicitly constructed a model of femininity'. In turn this sexual division of labour 'meshed perfectly with the assumptions of a society which drew sharp lines of distinction between the male and female worlds'.[22] She quotes the example of Liverpool dockers in 1916 resolutely refusing to work with women on the docks as indicative of the strength of this sexual division of labour.[23] On the face of it, then, the structural context of women's work seemed unfavourable for the prospects of women being able to influence the local Labour Party significantly.

---

[18]*1931 Census*, Tables of Occupation.
[19]Elizabeth Roberts, *Women's Work, 1840 - 1940* (1988), 18 - 20.
[20]Mark-Lawson *et al*, 210 - 11.
[21]Linda Grant, 'Women Workers and the Sexual Division of Labour: Liverpool, 1890 - 1939', unpublished PhD thesis, University of Liverpool, 1987, 102.
[22]*Ibid*, 85 - 97.
[23]*Ibid*, 86.

However, there were also distinctive features of the local Labour Party and its connections with the working class which have to be taken into account. As I have argued elsewhere, the Liverpool Labour Party was dominated up to at least the mid 1920s by trades and trade unions which hardly reflected the pattern of employment of male workers in the city as a whole.[24] Tracing its origins back to the Trades Council of the mid nineteenth century, and the socialist organizations like the ILP, Fabians and Social Democratic Federation (SDF) of the late nineteenth century, the Party which emerged in Liverpool was based mainly on the support of relatively small sections of skilled and semi-skilled workers generally unrepresentative of the working class as a whole. By contrast, the largest unions representing dockers and seafarers had only a spasmodic and often stormy relationship with Labour.[25] Indeed, the National Union of Dock Labourers, the National Sailors' and Firemen's Union, and other unions representing dockside workers formed a breakaway rival to the Trades Council in 1917,[26] and even after the war many of the dockside unions maintained only a distant link with Labour. The dominant sectors in the Party can be seen in the list of union delegates elected to the Executive Committee of the Trades Council and Labour Party throughout the 1920s. In 1927, for instance, delegates of distributive workers, clerks, postal workers, electricians, engineering workers, railwaymen, sheet metal workers, painters, insurance workers and the League of the Blind were elected.[27] One would hardly guess that this group represented the working class of the largest port in Britain.

The unrepresentative nature of the Labour Party up to the mid 1920s paradoxically meant that women had a better chance of influencing the Party overall. Skilled craft unions representing predominantly male workers might have seen female labour as a threat, especially as the very concept of 'skilled' work often had clear gender implications in its exclusivity.[28] On the other hand unions representing significant sectors of female employment were well represented in the Party. Most notable of these were the National Union of Distributive and Allied Workers (NUDAW) and the National Union of General and Municipal Workers (NUGMW), but dressmakers, shop assistants, clerical workers, tailors and garment workers were also well represented in the Party.

---

[24]Sam Davies, 'The Liverpool Labour Party and the Liverpool Working Class, 1900 - 1939', *Bulletin of the North West Labour History Society*, 6 (1979 - 80).

[26]See, for instance, Eric Taplin, *The Dockers' Union: A Study of the National Union of Dock Labourers, 1889 - 1922* (Leicester, 1986), 133 - 37.

[26]Taplin, 136.

[27]Liverpool TC & LP, *Minutes*, 8 Apr 1927

[28]See Ann Phillips and Barbara Taylor, 'Sex and skill: notes towards a feminist economics', *Feminist Review*, 6 (1980).

There are clear signs that the Party looked quite favourably on women's involvement, and women were able to win significant support and influence policy up to the mid 1920s. Even before the war, the Trades Council voted to support votes for women in July 1910, December 1911, and again in October 1912.[29] The then separate Labour Representation Committee (LRC) also supported the following motion in July 1913:

> This LRC strongly protests against the treatment of Mrs Pankhurst and other members of the Women's Social and Political Union by the Liberal Government. Considering the method of dragging them in and out of prison to be an inhuman form of torture and that no body of men suffering under the same indignities and oppression as women are suffering under would be treated in such a manner for rebelling.[30]

Again in January 1914 the LRC supported the National Union of Suffrage Societies in their campaign for votes for women, and agreed to send a delegate to their conference and demonstration in London.[31]

After the war women continued to influence policy to some extent. Labour's programme for the 1919 municipal elections for instance called for the development of municipal nursery schools, for more provision of playgrounds for children, more public wash-houses, and the establishment of municipal laundries.[32] In 1925 the manifesto again called for the child welfare services to be municipalized.[33] After the elections that year the Secretary of the TC & LP was minuted as saying that 'he desired to thank all the workers in the various wards for the fine work done by the various Women's Sections'.[34] Later that year the TC & LP even lifted its head from parochial concerns when it received a motion from one of the Women's Sections calling for the banning of submarines, which was passed unanimously.[35] Even on the issue of birth control the Women's Sections made progress within the Party. In 1927 the TC & LP were persuaded to invite a speaker to present the case for a Mothers' Welfare Clinic, the same clinic that was to split the Party nine years later. The speaker was listened to with interest and received the thanks of the meeting, and no dissent was recorded

---

[29]Liverpool Trades Council, *Minutes* 27 July 1910, 13 Dec 1911, 23 Oct 1912.
[30]Liverpool LRC, *Minutes*, 2 July 1913.
[31]Liverpool LRC, *Minutes*, 30 Jan 1914.
[32]Liverpool Labour Party, *Minutes*, 3 Sept 1919.
[33]Liverpool TC & LP, *Minutes,* 13 Sept 1925.
[34]Liverpool TC & LP, *Minutes*, 4 Nov 1925.
[35]Liverpool TC & LP, *Minutes*, 2 Dec 1925.

in the minutes.[36] One other sign of women's impact on policy can be seen in the influence of the Women's Co-operative Guild. They had mounted a major national campaign in the 1920s over the issue of food purity, improved hygiene in the preparation, packing and distribution of food, and especially the importance of a pure, healthy milk supply.[37] This campaign was taken up locally, and was eventually reflected in the 1928 municipal election programme. Two new demands were inserted in the programme, that a 'pure milk supply' be guaranteed for Liverpool, and 'that attention be called to for the need for hygienic conditions in all shops dealing with food supplies'.[38]

The clearest sign of women's impact within the Labour Party up to the mid 1920s, however, was the Party's willingness to campaign over women's working conditions and trade unionism. Over these issues before and after the first world war the key position of Mary Bamber (the mother of Bessie Braddock) in the Liverpool Labour movement was significant. As a NUDAW delegate Mary Bamber was one of the leading figures in the TC & LP for many years. She was re-elected onto the Executive Committee year after year, and continually worked for improvements in the working conditions of women and the unionization of women. Most of this activity was concerned with women in low-paid and poorly organized sectors of the local economy, but there is also evidence that the relatively small number of women in skilled trades were defended by the TC & LP in this period. Thus in 1923 a resolution from the Printing and Paper Workers' Union was passed unanimously condemning the fact that women workers who had served apprenticeships in a trade were being disallowed unemployment benefit if they refused to take work as domestic servants.[39]

The Labour Party took up the question of women's trade unionism most enthusiastically in June 1926, when the Industrial Committee of the TC & LP met to launch a major campaign to organize women workers. All affiliated unions were to be contacted, public speakers were to be made available for all meetings, an advert was to be placed in the *Liverpool Echo*, and a major conference was to be organized with other parties in the area. This was perhaps the highpoint of women's activity in the Labour Party between the wars, but it was also a turning point. The campaign ran until the conference in April 1927, but ultimately it petered out due to the poor response of affiliated unions. By December 1926 only 18 unions had taken up the offer of a speaker, and at the conference only 55 organizations were represented,

---

[36]Liverpool TC & LP, *Minutes*, 20 Apr, 19 May 1927.

[37]See for instance the Womens' Co-operative Guild pamphlets *The Milk we Want* (1925), *Food Purity* (1926), and *Food Values* (1926), in the Labour Archive at the University of Hull Library.

[38]Liverpool TC & LP, *Minutes*, 26 Sept 1928.

[39]Liverpool TC & LP, *Minutes*, 15 Aug 1923.

although 486 had been contacted. In the context of the defeat of the General Strike and the subsequent downturn in trade union fortunes, perhaps no more should have been expected.[40]

A new phase in the relationship between the Liverpool Labour Party and women came by the late 1920s. The Women's Sections seemed to become more marginal to the Party, and their impact on policy seemed to decline. Symbolic of the change perhaps was the special appeal made by the TC & LP to the Women's Sections to provide a decorative lorry or tableau for the May Day demonstration of 1927.[41] This stress on women's domestic skills within the Party was a pointer to the future.

IV

The politics of the Labour Party changed in the late 1920s. At a national level the Party, along with the TUC, became more inward-looking. Joint action with any organizations outside the Party, and particularly those that had any connection with the Communist Party, was frowned upon. The ending of joint work with the National Unemployed Workers Movement (NUWM) was the most notable sign of this trend. At the same time work with feminists outside the Party was also terminated.[42] Disagreement over protective legislation for women workers led to the 1927 decision to prohibit joint action with NUSEC, the leading non-party feminist organization of the time.[43] Labour women's isolation was only increased by the performance of their leaders in Parliament. Margaret Bondfield's acceptance of the 1927 Unemployment Insurance Act, which imposed a cut in benefit from 15s (75p) to 8s (40p) for women under 21, was a severe defeat for the Women's Sections. Even more damaging was the Anomalies Act introduced by Margaret Bondfield as Minister of Labour in 1931. This Act disallowed benefit to large numbers of married women, discounting their National Insurance contributions prior to marriage and also for any periods of temporary or seasonal work. By April 1933 half a million married women had had their benefit stopped under the terms of the Act.[44]

These national trends were reflected locally. Joint action with the NUWM was wound down from April 1926, and by March 1928 the TC & LP

---

[40]Liverpool TC & LP, *Minutes*, 23 June 1926 - 7 Apr 1927.

[41]Liverpool TC & LP, *Minutes*, 15 Nov 1926.

[42]See John Saville, 'May Day 1937', in Asa Briggs and John Saville (eds), *Essays in Labour History, 1918 - 39* (1977).

[43]Smith, 'Sex vs. Class', 32 - 3.

[44]On the full implications of the Anomalies Act, see Sam Davies *et al*, *Genuinely Seeking Work: Mass Unemployment on Merseyside in the 1930s* (Liverpool, forthcoming 1992), ch 5.

was setting up its own rival Unemployed Association.[45] Work with the Women's Co-operative Guild was also run down gradually. As early as October 1926 the Liverpool Co-operative Society was meeting increasing difficulties in coming to agreements with the Labour Party over standing mutually acceptable candidates in local elections. Labour began to insist that the Co-operative movement should simply be absorbed fully into the Party, and joint work was steadily eroded as relations between the two organizations worsened down to the late 1920s.[46] Labour women were at the same time increasingly isolated from local feminists in the Liverpool Women's Citizens Association (WCA), which was affiliated to NUSEC, over the issue of family allowances. The leading proponent of this measure, Eleanor Rathbone, was a Liverpool City Councillor with whom Labour women had worked in the early 1920s. By the late 1920s such cooperation had ceased. The WCA wrote to all local Parliamentary candidates prior to the 1929 General Election, asking them to support family allowances, but only four out of the ten Labour candidates agreed to do so.[47] At the 1930 Labour Women's Conference Bessie Braddock opposed family allowances, arguing that they would encourage employers to cut men's wages, and defended the trade union concept of the 'family wage'.[48] The impact of the Anomalies Act, which had caused 3,000 women in Liverpool to lose their benefit by November 1931,[49] further disheartened the Women's Sections in the Party.

There was another significant change locally in the late 1920s which adversely affected women's organization in the Party. The arrival of the group of Catholic councillors (as described earlier) had a profound impact on the Party. They brought with them few new ward organizations or new members, and therefore had little effect on the structure of the TC & LP. On the other hand most of them had little sympathy with socialist ideas, but they soon formed a majority in the Labour Group on the Council, and began to shape policy there. A conflict between the nominal determiners of policy, the TC & LP, and the real power brokers, the Catholic Caucus in the Council, was inevitable. It came in 1930 over the Catholic Cathedral, and resulted in the Labour Group being confirmed as the dominant force in the Party for the whole of the 1930s.[50] For women this meant that however effective they might have been within the TC & LP, their efforts could always be negated by the decision of the Labour Group. As in the case of Manchester mentioned

---

[45]Liverpool TC & LP, *Minutes*, 12 Apr 1926, 23 Mar 1928.

[46]Liverpool Co-operative Society Ltd, *Quarterly Report*, 25 Oct 1926, 12 - 13.

[47]*Liverpool Daily Post*, 28 May 1929.

[48]Pugh, 157.

[49]Davies *et al*, *Genuinely Seeking Work*, ch 5.

[50]Martyn Nightingale (ed), *Merseyside in Crisis* (Liverpool, 1980), 76 - 9; Tony Lane, *Liverpool: Gateway of Empire* (1987), 137 - 8.

earlier, many issues of importance to women were seen as non-party and were therefore left to a free vote by Labour Councillors, thereby serving to magnify this major political problem for women in the Party. The only way women could effectively influence the Party thereafter was by getting onto the Council, and with a few exceptions this proved difficult.

The other important effect of this change was to bring religion to the centre of Labour politics. Over a key issue for feminists in the 1930s, birth control, this was particularly damaging. At a national level, this divisive issue had been partially resolved by the Labour government in 1930 allowing Ministry of Health clinics to give free contraceptive advice 'in cases where further pregnancy would be detrimental to health'.[51] Birth control and Catholicism was an explosive mix in localities like West Yorkshire and Manchester, but less so in the 1930s than in the 1920s.[52] In Liverpool, as the events of 1936 evince, the religious complexion of the Labour Group kept the issue alive. This is not to suggest, of course, that religion alone accounts for opposition to birth control within the Labour Party. Opposition on the grounds that limitation of population would be forced on the working class to reduce or even eliminate the 'lower orders' had a history going back to the ideas of Malthus over a century earlier. The eugenicist idea of population control for the poor to eliminate 'social problems' was a significant early twentieth century variant, and many orthodox socialists opposed birth control on these grounds. Oswald Mosley's advocacy of birth control in the 1930s as part of the fascist plan to 'improve the race' and eliminate the 'unfit' revived fears of birth control among some socialists.[53] But in Liverpool it was religion that was the main factor in stirring up the controversy in the 1930s.

In Parliament as well, Liverpool's Labour MPs continued to oppose birth control. Davie Logan, who had been the first Nationalist councillor to defect to Labour in January 1923,[54] became the MP for Scotland Division in Liverpool in 1929. In his first speech to Parliament he stated his principles:

> I stand for the great things that go to make the family life and
> to help to make the manhood of the nation great and strong,
> because of deep religious convictions.[55]

---

[51]Thane, 137.

[52]J. Reynolds and K. Laybourn, *Labour Heartland: A History of the Labour Party in West Yorkshire during the Inter-war Years, 1918 - 1939* (Bradford, 1987), 42; S. Fielding,'The Irish Catholics of Manchester and Salford: Aspects of their Religious and Political History, 1890 - 1939, unpublished PhD thesis, University of Warwick, 1988.

[53]Sheila Rowbotham, *Hidden from History* (1973), 151 - 56.

[54]Liverpool TC & LP, *Minutes*, 3 Jan 1923.

[55]*Parliamentary Debates*, 5th Series, 234, 24 Jan 1930, 538-42.

In 1932 he defended the sanctity of marriage by arguing against divorce even in cases where a spouse was clinically diagnosed as 'incurably insane'.[56] In 1935 and 1936 he opposed any measures to allow contraceptive advice to be given to married women by the Ministry of Health.[57] A father of ten children, he argued in the 1935 debate:

> If the Ministry of Health wishes to encourage the welfare of the nation, it will not be by the scientific dispensation of the knowledge of Marie Stopes. The welfare of the nation will depend upon a healthy manhood and womanhood, not so much the knowledge of the prostitute as the knowledge that goes to make for human happiness and the welfare of the people. This nation was never made on the scientific dissemination of material. It is only fit for the gutter. It is not for decent homes to have any knowledge of ... I believe it is pernicious. I believe it is the worst kind of propaganda that was ever introduced ... The object of the speech that has been made tonight is that, without denying the pleasure of sexual delectation, there must be no children. I am against this doctrine.

Despite much barracking and several attempted interruptions by other members of the House, Logan continued in this vein for ten minutes. For some sections of the Liverpool Labour Party this was clearly still a contentious issue.

It is far less clear, though, to what extent Labour leaders like Logan and Hogan accurately reflected the views of Catholic voters, and particularly Catholic women, on this and other issues. In the 1936 Council debate on birth control, the Protestant leader Longbottom sniped away at his sectarian enemies by questioning their right as an all-male group to speak for Catholic women. He was quoted as saying that 'he did not believe the opposition [to birth control] was a layman's opposition. It certainly was not a laywoman's opposition. If this was a free issue there was no doubt the women would have something to say about it'. Of course Longbottom's intervention was a purely sectarian rather than feminist point, but it raised an important issue about the nature of political representation in the Catholic community of Liverpool. The powerful political bosses who ran the Catholic Caucus in the Labour Party were as much nominees of a Catholic hierarchy as representatives of a Catholic electorate, and they appeared to determine as much as reflect Catholic opinion. Steve Fielding has done much to explore the internal political and cultural life of Catholic Manchester in this period, but in Liverpool similar

---

[56]*Parliamentary Debates*, 272, 30 Nov 1932, 826-28.
[57]*Parliamentary Debates*, 304, 17 July 1935, 1136 - 40; 317, 12 Nov 1936, 1048.

studies are still awaited.[58] In the meanwhile one has to be cautious about generalizing about Catholic attitudes as a whole from the discourse of boss politics. Nevertheless this boss politics imposed a new context on women's activities in the Labour Party.

V

In this new context, women's influence in the Liverpool Labour Party was limited in the 1930s. The Women's Sections faded into insignificance. The only important arena was the Council Chamber, and only one woman was able to make a major impact there, namely Bessie Braddock. Elected to the Council in 1930, she put on almost a one-woman show there for a decade. Significantly she seems to have avoided working in the Women's Sections at all, and in fact fell out with them at times. Martin Pugh has described the women who came to predominate in the inter-war Labour Party as 'orthodox party loyalists ... who put party and class before sex'.[59] Bessie Braddock certainly put party and class before sex, but she was most emphatically not an orthodox party loyalist. In Parliament after 1945 she became a prominent figure on the right of the Party, but in the 1930s she was firmly on the left, and constantly involved in disputes with the Party leadership.

Not long after she had clashed with Luke Hogan over the Mothers' Welfare Clinic in April 1936, she was disciplined for publicly criticising a municipal candidate, Mrs Elliot, who was the chairperson of the Liverpool Labour Women's Central Council from its inception in 1922 right through to 1939. Mrs Elliot, she claimed, was a 'bad candidate', was 'not class-conscious', and had been unsympathetic to claimants on the local Public Assistance Committee. Braddock also criticised a Labour councillor as he 'had voted against the best interests of the working class mothers on the birth control issue' in the recent debate.[60] She was disciplined again in 1938 for speaking on a public platform with the NUWM.[61]

She would never have described herself as a feminist, but chaired the Maternity and Child Welfare Sub-Committee of the Council from its creation in 1934, and in that capacity did much work on behalf of women. In June 1936 her committee was responsible for the opening of a Maternity and Child Care Centre in Everton, claimed to be the only one of its kind in the country.[62] Only a few days later she organized a major national conference

---

[58]Fielding, thesis; *idem*, 'Irish Politics in Manchester, 1890 - 1914', *International Review of Social History*, xxxiii (1988).

[59]Pugh, 156 - 7.

[60]Labour Group Meeting, *Minutes*, 2 June 1936.

[61]Labour Group Meeting, *Minutes*, 11 Mar 1938.

[62]*Liverpool Daily Post*, 27 June 1936.

on Maternity and Child Welfare in Liverpool, working with many other non-party women's organizations. The conference called for birth control clinics to be established by all health authorities, and improved pre- and post-natal care, and received much publicity in the local press.[63]

It is difficult to place Bessie Braddock in the context of the feminist movement of the inter-war years. It has been claimed that a 'new feminism' placing a stress on the special attributes and needs of women began to predominate over the prewar 'equality feminism'. The implications of this new feminism are controversial. Some historians see it as failing to challenge, and in fact contributing to, 'a reconstruction of gender that circumscribed the roles, activities and possibilities of women'. Others have argued that it moved beyond 'a mere shedding of the fetters, beyond ... "me too feminism", beyond the sort of feminism which thinks only "in terms of men" and therefore betrays an inferiority complex'. Others again argue that stressing 'old' and 'new' feminism can give a 'somewhat facile division of feminists', disguising 'intricate patterns of thinking'.[64] However it is judged, Eleanor Rathbone was seen as the leading exponent of this new feminism. Her presidential address to NUSEC in 1925 expressed the shift of emphasis clearly. 'We can demand what we want for women, not because it is what men have got, but because it is what women need to fulfil the potentialities of their own natures and to adjust ourselves to the circumstances of their own lives'.[65] Protective legislation for women at work, family allowances, and the availability of birth control were the key demands of the new feminism. As we have seen, Bessie Braddock campaigned vigorously for birth control, but also strongly opposed family allowances. It is the case, perhaps, that she and Eleanor Rathbone represented two quite different discourses by the 1930s, with issues of class as well as gender contributing to the difference.

But of course Bessie Braddock was only one individual, and there were very few women to assist her in the Council. The number of women involved in municipal politics in Liverpool in this period was very small. Even before women had been enfranchised nationally, they had been involved in municipal

---

[63]National Conference on Maternity and Child Welfare, Liverpool, 1 - 3 July 1936, *Official Programme and Handbook.*

[64]Susan Kingsley Kent, 'Gender Reconstruction after the First World War' in Harold L. Smith (ed), *British Feminism in the Twentieth Century* (Aldershot, 1990), 80; Brian Harrison, *Prudent Revolutionaries: Portraits of British Feminists between the Wars* (Oxford, 1987), 104; Johanna Alberti, *Beyond Suffrage: Feminists in War and Peace, 1914 - 28* (1989), 165.

[65]Quoted in Susan Kingsley Kent, 'The Politics of Sexual Difference: World War I and the Demise of British Feminism', *Journal of British Studies,* 27 (1988), 240.

politics, as Patricia Hollis has recently shown.[66] In Liverpool the only party to select a woman candidate was the Liberal Party, for whom a Miss Johnson stood unsuccessfully in 1907 and again in 1910. The only other woman who stood for election before the first world war was Eleanor Rathbone, who was returned as an independent in 1910 and again in 1913. Labour's first woman candidate was Mary Bamber, winning in a by-election in 1919. But as Table 9.3 below shows, very few women were selected by any of the major parties.

Table 9.3: Women Candidates in Municipal Elections in Liverpool 1905 - 1938

	All Labour Candidates	All Labour Wins	Labour Women Candidates	Labour Women Wins
1905 – 9	18	3 (17%)	0	0
1910 – 14	52	14 (27%)	0	0
1919 – 23	108	16 (15%)	2 (2%)	1 (50%)
1924 – 28	166	51 (31%)	14 (8%)	1 (7%)
1929 – 33	191	75 (39%)	18 (9%)	10 (56%)
1934 – 38	192	73 (38%)	23 (12%)	6 (26%)
Total	727	232 (32%)	57 (8%)	18 (32%)

	All Tory Candidates	All Tory Wins	Tory Women Candidates	Tory Women Wins
1905 – 9	130	102 (79%)	0	0
1910 – 14	119	99 (83%)	0	0
1919 – 23	137	116 (85%)	2 (1%)	2 (100%)
1924 – 28	152	122 (80%)	8 (5%)	6 (75%)
1929 – 33	165	120 (73%)	10 (6%)	7 (70%)
1934 – 38	161	122 (76%)	7 (4%)	3 (43%)
Total	864	681 (79%)	27 (3%)	18 (67%)

---

[66]Patricia Hollis, *Ladies Elect: Women in English Local Government, 1865 - 1914* (Oxford, 1987).

	All Liberal Candidates	All Liberal Wins	Liberal Women Candidates	Liberal Women Wins
1905 – 9	102	61 (60%)	1 (1%)	0
1910 – 14	60	46 (77%)	1 (2%)	0
1919 – 23	59	29 (48%)	6 (10%)	5 (83%)
1924 – 28	43	16 (37%)	0	0
1929 – 33	33	16 (49%)	2 (6%)	2 (100%)
1934 – 38	25	16 (64%)	2 (8%)	2 (100%)
Total	322	183 (57%)	12 (4%)	9 (75%)

	All Other Candidates	All Other Wins	Other Women Candidates	Other Women Wins
1905 – 9	52	23 (44%)	0	0
1910 – 14	41	25 (61%)	2 (5%)	2 (100%)
1919 – 23	96	45 (47%)	7 (7%)	3 (43%)
1924 – 28	64	27 (42%)	5 (8%)	5 (100%)
1929 – 33	80	21 (26%)	10 (13%)	6 (60%)
1934 – 38	45	15 (33%)	11 (24%)	3 (27%)
Total	378	156 (41%)	35 (9%)	19 (54%)

	Total Candidates	Total Wins	Total Women Candidates	Total Women Wins
1905 – 9	302	189 (63%)	1 (0.3%)	0
1910 – 14	272	184 (68%)	3 (1%)	2 (67%)
1919 – 23	400	205 (51%)	17 (4%)	11 (65%)
1924 – 28	425	216 (51%)	27 (6%)	12 (44%)
1929 – 33	469	232 (50%)	40 (9%)	25 (63%)
1934 – 38	423	226 (53%)	43 (10%)	14 (33%)
Total	2291	1252 (55%)	131 (6%)	64 (49%)

Source: Municipal Election Results, Liverpool Official Red Books, 1906-1939.

The Labour Party did at least do better than the others, with 8 per cent of all their candidates between 1905 and 1937 being women, as opposed to 4 per cent and 3 per cent respectively for the Liberals and Tories. But in total on only 18 occasions were Labour women successfully elected on the council between the wars, and only 10 Labour women actually became councillors over the whole period (some of them were elected more than once). This compares very unfavourably with the experience in London recorded by Pat Thane. There 150 out of a total of 729 successful Labour candidates were women in the 1934 elections, a proportion of almost 20 per cent.[67] In Liverpool by contrast, only 6 out of 73 Labour winners between 1934 and 1938 were women, a proportion of less than 10 per cent.

Even when women were selected as candidates, they were often selected in wards where they had little chance of winning. To take one example, Sarah McArd, a leading local member of the ILP and the Women's Cooperative Guild and a stalwart of the Women's Sections, whose unswerving loyalty to Labour was demonstrated when the ILP was disaffiliated in 1932, was rewarded for her tireless work on behalf of the party with the following. In 1925 she was selected for St. Domingo ward, the stronghold of Harry Longbottom's Protestant Party, and lost. In 1926, 1927 and 1928, she unsuccessfully contested the safe Tory ward of Old Swan. In 1929 she was selected for a by-election in the fairly safe Labour ward of Edge Hill, and won, but in the 1931 elections she was swept away in the aftermath of the Catholic Cathedral controversy and the collapse of the Labour government. In 1934 she stood unsuccessfully in Wavertree West, another safe Tory seat. In 1936 she gamely contested St. Domingo again and lost, and finally in 1938 she lost again in the safe Tory seat of Fazakerley. Sarah McArd did eventually get a safe seat after the war in Bessie Braddock's ward of St. Anne's. Lesser persons than Sarah McArd must surely have given up early against this sort of odds, and it is no surprise that so few women joined Bessie Braddock on the Council.

As far as Parliamentary elections were concerned, no woman stood for Labour before the war. Bessie Braddock was selected for the Exchange Division, but war intervened before she could mount a challenge. Nationally the highest proportion of women candidates for Labour in a general election before the war was only 7 per cent in 1931.[68] It has been suggested that many women within the Labour Party positively chose not to stand for Parliament and preferred to stay close to their support in the local

---

[67]Thane, 140.
[68]Brian Harrison, *Separate Spheres: The Opposition to Women's Suffrage in Britain* (1978), 236 - 7.

community.[69] This was perhaps borne out in Liverpool when candidates were selected for the 1918 election. Mary Bamber was nominated, but withdrew, stating that 'she didn't think the time opportune for women Parliamentary candidates'.[70] Whatever the reason, Davie Logan never had a local woman to challenge him in Parliament before the war. Local feminists were represented indirectly in Parliament from 1929 when Eleanor Rathbone was elected as an independent for a Combined Universities seat. The political parties in Liverpool, however, retained an all-male approach to Parliamentary politics.

VI

One final way of attempting to assess women's impact on Labour is by linking it to local spending on those municipal services that might be seen as particularly relevant to women's welfare. This approach was used by Jane Mark-Lawson and her colleagues in their study of Preston, Lancaster and Nelson. The stronger women's influence was in a local Party, the more it might have been reflected in local municipal policies, and therefore in council spending. There are serious methodological problems in using this kind of financial data, as they point out in their work, but nevertheless it might be useful to compare similar figures for Liverpool. The results are shown in Table 9.4 below.

As can be seen, the figures for Lancaster, Preston and Nelson seem to bear out Jane Mark-Lawson's estimation of the relative impact of women on the Labour Party in each town. The figures for Liverpool are extremely interesting, if less clear cut in their implications. On education, Liverpool's expenditure seems similar to that of Preston. On maternity and child welfare, and parks, baths etc., Liverpool appears to rank alongside Nelson. Taken overall, Liverpool's provision in these areas is perhaps surprizingly generous. This may reflect the impact that women had on Labour policy in the 1920s, but also perhaps their impact on the other main parties. The importance of an extremely effective feminist like Eleanor Rathbone sitting as an Independent throughout the 1920s may also be reflected in the figures.

The continued or even increased generosity of provision in the 1930s is again intriguing. The increasing dependence of the Tories in Liverpool on a sectarian Protestant working class vote to maintain their hold on the Council in the 1930s may be relevant. Working class Tory voters' demands in terms of council provision had to be met if the sectarian alliance was to be maintained. It is also interesting that expenditure on maternity and child

---

[69]Margaret Stacey and Marion Price, *Women, Power and Politics* (1981), 91.
[70]Liverpool Labour Party, *Minutes*, 24 Nov 1918.

welfare was higher in Liverpool in the 1930s than in all the other areas. It seems likely that this reflects the key position of Bessie Braddock in chairing the Maternity Sub-Committee throughout this period and very forcefully and publicly campaigning for provision in this area.

Table 9.4: Approximate per capita Net Expenditure on Some Services in Financial Years 1924 - 5 and 1935 - 6

Service	Financial Year	Liverpool	Lancaster	Preston	Nelson
Education (per child under 15 years of age)	1924–5	£2 17s 0d	£2 13s 8d	£2 17s 7d	£4 1s 4d
	1935–6	£4 3s 5d	£3 8s 1d	£4 13s 10d	£5 1s 8d
Maternity and Child Welfare (per woman 15 - 44 years of age)	1924–5	3s 2d	7d	8d	5s 11d
	1935–6	9s 6d	4s 1d	5s 6d	8s 2d
Parks, Baths, Libraries and Recreation (per capita)	1924–5	5s 0d	8d	3s 4d	4s 11d
	1935–6	6s 4d	2s 9d	4s 7d	6s 8d

Source: Liverpool City Council, *Treasurer's Accounts*, 1924-5 and 1935-6; *Census of Population*, 1921 and 1931; Jane Mark-Lawson et al, 'Gender and Local Politics', 200.

The fact that we are comparing councils of such different size, and that Labour is never politically in power in Liverpool in the inter-war years, makes the link between Council expenditure and women's impact on the Labour Party difficult to assess conclusively. The evidence, though, does seem to suggest there was a connection between the two, even if other factors lying outside of the Party also have to be taken into account.

VII

To summarize, the relationship between the Labour Party and women in Liverpool was a complex one. It varied over time, with women's influence in the Party being stronger in the 1920s than the 1930s. It was influenced by the nature of gender relations in the local labour market, and also by the particular occupational groups that made up the early Labour Party. It was strongly affected by religious considerations from the late 1920s. It was also linked to national changes in the Labour Party in the late 1920s and early 1930s. Comparing the relationship with the few local studies from other parts of the country that we have, women seemed to have had less impact on Labour in Liverpool than they did in either London or Nelson, but more than in Lancaster. The nearest comparison seems to be with Preston, with greater influence in the 1920s declining in the 1930s, but for rather different reasons.

To put these conclusions in the context of the debate raised near the beginning of this essay on working class culture and politics, I would argue that class, religion and gender were all factors which influenced working class life and culture in Liverpool, and in turn affected the relationship between that culture and Labour politics. Neither an economic nor a cultural reductionism can do full justice to these complex historical relationships.

Appendix: Liverpool Chartists; Subscribers to the National Land Company, 1847-8

Alan Little

The 'Liverpool Chartists' discussed here are 171 Liverpool subscribers to the National Land Company. They are drawn from one of the most important and neglected sources on later Chartism - the comprehensive national list of subscribers from 1847-8, in the Board of Trade Papers.[1] This list with names, addresses and occupations is the largest single source of data on rank and file Chartist supporters, and has so far been subjected to very little serious analysis - probably because manually extracting names for a particular town or district is a very labour-intensive and tedious process.[2]

The list gives subscribers for the entire country, in (approximate) alphabetical order, as required for registration as a joint-stock company.[3] There is considerable duplication, but even taking this into account it contains the names, addresses and occupations of some twenty-five to thirty thousand Land Company subscribers.

The largest local sample yet extracted from this list is one of over 1,400 for Leicestershire.[4] This proved a useful exercise in giving quantitative support to the received opinion that hosiery workers were the backbone of Leicester Chartist support; and also revealed a hitherto unsuspected and very striking geographical concentration in the Saint Margaret's district of the town.

The same exercise has been carried out for Liverpool for comparison - a less important Chartist centre than Leicester, and so a more manageable sample to deal with by hand. This is a 'pilot' for a possible future project of

---

[1] Public Record Office, Kew - Board of Trade papers BT41/474 - 476.

[2] For previous uses of this material, see D. J. V. Jones, *Chartism and the Chartists* (1975), 134 - 7; D. Thompson, *The Chartists* (1984) pt 2; M. Chase, 'Chartism 1838 - 1858 - Responses in Two Teesside Towns', *Northern History* 24 (1988), 163.

[3] For an account of the compilation of the list, and the crippling legal obstacles to the registration of the Land Company as either a Joint Stock Company or a Friendly Society, see E. Yeo, 'Some Problems and Practices of Chartist Democracy' in J. Epstein and D. Thompson (eds), *The Chartist Experience* (1982), 368-372.

[4] A. Little, 'Chartism and Liberalism - Popular Politics in Leicestershire, 1842 - 1874' forthcoming PhD thesis, University of Manchester, ch 1.

making the list available on a computer database for statistical analysis. One hundred and ninety Liverpool names, addresses and occupations were found, with 19 obvious duplicates, giving a total of 171 individuals.

Entitling a discussion of subscribers to the Land Company 'Liverpool Chartists' is (deliberately) slightly debatable. One must question how far subscribing to the Land Company can be equated with Chartism. The Land plan was at its height at a time - 1846 to early 1848 - when the activities of the National Charter Association were at a low ebb. Only one of Liverpool's fifteen NCA committee members from 1841-2 appears on the Land Company list.[5] In the Leicester sample only approximately a quarter of known 1842 Chartists could be identified; the most prominent Chartist leaders of the later 1840s were absent, and a few prominent non-Chartists were present. We should not read too much into this, however - as Chase points out,[6] the Board of Trade list probably includes less than a third of the Land Company's subscribers. Chase also suggests that his sample of Teesside subscribers were younger and more likely to be lodgers than Chartists generally - but this is a tentative conclusion based on a small sample. But given the close association of the Land Company with the name of Feargus O'Connor, and the general prominence of the land in working class radical ideas, it seems reasonable to assume that subscribing would usually indicate at least some general sympathy with Chartist ideas. Land Company subscription may actually give a better picture of occupational and geographical foundations of Chartism as a mass movement, than figures for a minority of committed activists on the National Charter Association council lists. As John Belchem has pointed out, most large samples of 'Chartists' so far examined have been based on committee members of political organizations and/or those arrested during major crises - 'the evidence is restricted to the fully committed and/or unlucky'.[7] This applies to David Goodway's 1,152 London Chartists, to those arrested in 1839-40, and to Rob Sykes' discussion of the social composition of Chartism in the Greater Manchester region.[8] Despite all the qualifications

---

[5]*Northern Star*, 10 Apr 1841 and 30 Apr 1842.

[6]Chase, 163.

[7]J. Belchem, review of D. Thompson, *The Chartists* in *English Historical Review*, 100 (1985), 137.

[8]D. Goodway, *London Chartism* (Cambridge, 1982), 16-17, takes issue with I. J. Prothero, 'London Chartism and the Trades', *Economic History Review*, 2nd series, 24 (1971), 202-19, on the definition of un-politicized 'aristocratic' trades. Goodway's figures are compromised by being drawn from a variety of unconnected sources, particularly by the inclusion of the committee of the 1830s London Working Men's Association, in a discussion of rank and file Chartist support in the 1840s. C. Godfrey and J. Epstein, 'HO20/10; Interviews of 'Chartist Prisoners 1839-40', *International Review of Social History*, 24 (1979), 189-236. R. Sykes 'Popular Politics and Trade Unionism in South East Lancashire, 1829-42' unpublished PhD thesis, University of Manchester (1982), ch 12.

about how far the Land Company is representative of Chartism at large, its members form the largest sample of ordinary Chartist sympathisers we are ever likely to have.

On this basis, a local sample is of considerable value since it can be compared with Census figures for occupations of the population as a whole, to give a quantitative indication of which groups of workers were inclined to support Chartism. The technique of comparing percentages of various trades among known Chartists with the occupational structure of the whole population - as used by Goodway - has provided useful quantitative backing for his discussion of the London trades. Both he and Prothero have convincingly argued a connection between capitalist pressure on particular trades' 'craft' status and privilege, and the propensity of workers in those trades to support radical politics. The same type of analysis is applied in the table of occupations here, for occupations with five or more representatives. The occupational composition of the Land Company subscribers is compared to that of all males over 20 in Liverpool in the 1851 Census. (There are very few women in the sample, and it seems reasonable to assume that the vast majority of male subscribers would have been adults). The most striking features of the table of occupations are the overwhelming predominance of tailors and stonemasons, and the almost complete absence of dockers, warehousemen or seamen. This might tentatively suggest that Liverpool masons, like those of London and Manchester, were more 'politicized' than those in smaller provincial towns like Leicester, where masons were regarded as a politically apathetic 'aristocratic' trade.[9]

The geographical distribution of subscribers might also be fruitfully compared with the political and social geography of the town. Although the Liverpool subscribers were not as strikingly concentrated as their Leicester counterparts, there was a definite 'clump' around Hornby Street and Boundary Street in the Vauxhall Road area of north Liverpool, with a less dense scattering around the east and south sides - Cazneau Street and Soho Street, Copperas Hill and the streets between Bold Street and Duke Street. There were very few in the city centre.

---

[9]Little, ch 8

Table App.1: Occupations of Subscribers

Occupation	Number	% of Subscribers	% in Census	Index
Mason	33	19.64%	1.38%	14.23
Tailor	27	16.07%	2.85%	5.64
Labourer	20	11.90%	11.02%	1.08
Carpenter	9	5.36%	3.63%	1.48
Shoemaker	9	5.36%	3.75%	1.43
Blacksmith	5	2.98%	1.54%	1.94
Bookbinder	5	2.98%	0.12%	25.15
Engineer	5	2.98%	0.08%	37.20
Brassfounder	4	2.38%		
Cabinetmaker	4	2.38%		
Sawyer	4	2.38%		
Bricklayer	3	1.79%		
'Button Carder'	2	1.19%		
'No Trade'	2	1.19%		
Chandler	2	1.19%		
Combmaker	2	1.19%		
Cooper	2	1.19%		
Overlooker	2	1.19%		
Painter	2	1.19%		
Paper Maker	2	1.19%		
Spinner	2	1.19%		
'Operative'	2	1.19%		
Basketmaker	1	0.60%		
Brickmaker	1	0.60%		
Clerk	1	0.60%		
Coachsmith	1	0.60%		

Occupation	Number	% of Subscribers	% in Census	Index
Fringemaker	1	0.60%		
Gas Fitter	1	0.60%		
Glass Stainer	1	0.60%		
Housekeeper	1	0.60%		
Mariner	1	0.60%		
Moulder	1	0.60%		
Naturalist	1	0.60%		
Optician	1	0.60%		
Pipemaker	1	0.60%		
Plumber	1	0.60%		
Seamstress	1	0.60%		
Starchmaker	1	0.60%		
Stoker	1	0.60%		
Striker	1	0.60%		
Surgeon	1	0.60%		
Traveller	1	0.60%		
Weaver	1	0.60%		

INDEX

Albert Dock, 6
Ancient Order of Hibernians, 76, 208
Anglicans, 11, 12, 33, 35, 57, 109, 177, 189, 208
Anti-Monopoly Association (AMA), 65-6
Archdeacon, George, 72, 79
artisans, 3-5, 44-7, 50-2, 60-6, 104
Ashton, Nicholas, merchant, 26, 31

Balfe, J. D., informer, 83
Bamber, Mary, 234, 241, 244
Belfast, 74, 175, 195, 203
Berry, Henry, dock engineer, 24, 25
Birkenhead, 5, 28, 73, 87, 96, 115, 119, 140, 145, 154, 156, 170
birth control, 217, 233, 237-9
Blackburne, John, merchant, 26, 31
Bondfield, Margaret, 235
Booth, William, 160-1, 164-72
Boshell, Martin, 96-7
Braddock, Bessie, 217, 234, 236, 239-40, 243, 245
Brady, John, 74-5
Bramley-Moore, J. A., 189
Briggs, Richard, 196, 198, 208
Bristol, 2, 23, 74, 106
British Protestant Union, 189
Bullis, Mary, 167
Burke, Thomas, councillor, 180, 182, 195, 205
building trades, 3, 9, 44-6, 66, 107, 135-6, 140, 149, 152, 157, 232

Campbell, George, 31
canals, 25
carters, 6-7, 59-60, 63, 115, 136, 146, 153, 186, 201, 212
casual employment, 1, 5-8, 12, 15, 17, 18, 29, 43-4, 81, 136, 146, 203
Catholic Club, 74

Catholic Defence Association, 208
Catholic Defence League, 210
Catholic emancipation, 12, 34, 178-9
Catholic Young Men's Societies, 181, 201-2, 208
Catholics and Catholicism, 7, 10, 13-17, 20, 53, 55, 57, 60, 74, 76-8, 81, 88, 89, 109, 115-16, 119, 120, 160-72, 175-88, 190, 194-202, 206-15, 217, 236-9
Chartism, 3-5, 12, 13, 38-67, 68, 79-80, 82-6, 88, 91, 121, 138, 174, 247-51
Chester, 23, 87, 103
cholera, 108-9
Clarendon, 4th Earl, 82, 83, 92
clerical work, 16, 136, 156, 203, 231, 232, 250
Cobbett, William, 106
Communist Party, 235
Conservatives and the Conservative Party, 4-5, 9-12, 51-8, 60-6, 100, 110, 116-20, 122, 145, 189-90, 195, 204-06, 211, 217, 241, 243, 244
commerce, see trade
co-operative movement, 138, 142-4; see also Liverpool Co-operative Society; Women's Co-operative Guild
Cottle, Henry, 161, 165, 169
crime, 131-3, 168
Crosbie, William, mayor, 30
Cuddy, Joseph, 88, 91, 97
Cumella, Mary, 217
Currie, Dr. James, 32-3, 37
Curwen, Samuel, 21

Defoe, Daniel, 21
de-industrialization, 2, 28
Delamere, P. H., 73, 87, 95, 97
Denvir, John, 206
Derby, 17th Earl, 212-14